T0253183

Building Versatile Mobile Apps with Python and REST

RESTful Web Services with Django and React

Art Yudin

Apress®

Building Versatile Mobile Apps with Python and REST: RESTful Web Services with Django and React

Art Yudin
New York, NY, USA

ISBN-13 (pbk): 978-1-4842-6332-7 ISBN-13 (electronic): 978-1-4842-6333-4
https://doi.org/10.1007/978-1-4842-6333-4

Managing Director, Apress Media LLC: Welmoed Spahr
Acquisitions Editor: Aaron Black
Development Editor: James Markham
Coordinating Editor: Jessica Vakili

Distributed to the book trade worldwide by Springer Science+Business Media New York, 1 NY Plaza, New York, NY 10014. Phone 1-800-SPRINGER, fax (201) 348-4505, e-mail orders-ny@springer-sbm.com, or visit www.springeronline.com. Apress Media, LLC is a California LLC and the sole member (owner) is Springer Science + Business Media Finance Inc (SSBM Finance Inc). SSBM Finance Inc is a **Delaware** corporation.

For information on translations, please e-mail booktranslations@springernature.com; for reprint, paperback, or audio rights, please e-mail bookpermissions@springernature.com.

Apress titles may be purchased in bulk for academic, corporate, or promotional use. eBook versions and licenses are also available for most titles. For more information, reference our Print and eBook Bulk Sales web page at http://www.apress.com/bulk-sales.

Any source code or other supplementary material referenced by the author in this book is available to readers on GitHub via the book's product page, located at www.apress.com/978-1-4842-6332-7. For more detailed information, please visit http://www.apress.com/source-code.

Printed on acid-free paper

To those who keep trying and not giving up

Table of Contents

About the Author

Art Yudin is a FinTech enthusiast who has a great passion for coding and teaching. He earned a Master of Science in Banking and Finance from Adelphi University, Garden City, New York. He previously held asset management positions with international financial institutions. Art Yudin has founded a coding boot camp in New York City called Practical Programming | ProgramWithUs.com that helps aspiring programmers take first steps in coding. Currently, Art Yudin develops financial services software and leads classes and workshops in Python at Practical Programming in New York and Chicago.

About the Technical Reviewer

Vishwesh Ravi Shrimali graduated from BITS Pilani in 2018, where he studied mechanical engineering. Since then, he has worked with Big Vision LLC on deep learning and computer vision and was involved in creating official OpenCV AI courses. Currently, he is working at Mercedes-Benz Research and Development India Pvt. Ltd. He has a keen interest in programming and AI and has applied that interest in mechanical engineering projects. He has also written multiple blogs on OpenCV and deep learning on LearnOpenCV, a leading blog on computer vision. He has also coauthored *Machine learning for OpenCV 4* (2nd edition) by Packt. When he is not writing blogs or working on projects, he likes to go on long walks or play his acoustic guitar.

Acknowledgments

Thanks to my Wife for inspiring me every day. A very special thanks to my Mom and Dad for always supporting me.

Introduction

I enjoy watching travel videoblogs. Of particular interest are places in Africa and Asia. I have noticed that no matter how remote the place is or poverty-stricken the community, most natives have smartphones. As a matter of fact, in Africa, most web applications for microloans and livery services were initially designed and issued as mobile apps. Simply because potential users of those services do not have computers, but mobile devices have penetrated everywhere. Half of the world population has smartphones,[1] and the rate is still growing.

The smartphone is no longer a means of communication but rather a remote control to our lives. There is no task that cannot be done with a smartphone. We no longer go to the banks; there is an app for that. We order food, watch movies, chat with friends, and buy stuff online with mobile apps. So, if you have an idea to make a difference in the world, why not implement it as a mobile app?

This book will go through the process of building mobile applications for iOS and Android platforms. We will use Django – Python web framework – and React Native, JavaScript library. Some people might ask why you would not use Swift and Java. Well, the answer is we want to build a versatile mobile app. The Python Django framework would allow us to have one back-end solution for iOS and Android devices. Besides, you could use the same core to run a desktop version if you want.

You should regard this book as a practical guide to building versatile mobile apps. The main idea is to introduce Django and React Native and

---

[1]www.statista.com/statistics/330695/number-of-smartphone-users-worldwide/

show how they can be applied in mobile development. I will emphasize on the principal features of these modern technologies and explain how to use them. The goal of this book is to get you started constructing mobile web apps using Python. You can think of it as a trampoline to your future accomplishments in the field of web development. I hope this book will encourage you to practice and learn more about Django and React Native.

OK, what kind of mobile web app we would build in this book? I love pizza. Who doesn't love pizza? According to `http://thepizzajoint.com`, "Americans eat approximately 100 acres of pizza each day, or 350 slices per second."

Being a New Yorker, I think that here we have the best pizza in the world. However, recently, I have tried an amazing deep-dish pizza in Chicago, and it completely rocked my gastronomic experience. If you have never tried a deep-dish pizza at Uno, you should definitely put it on your bucket list. I understand that it might be difficult because you live somewhere far and probably also know an extremely good pizza spot you would recommend without any hesitation. There are more than 61,000 pizzerias[2] in this country, and each one of them has its own fans that would refer it as the best pizza in the universe. That is why we need a web app to share our favorite pizza places with other pizza lovers. We could call our mobile app pizzavspizza as a spot to compare and debate about pizza places. It would be cool to have all great pizza joints in one place. People could add their hometown pizzerias and find a good place to eat when they travel.

I am really excited to get started and go the whole way from the idea to building two mobile apps ready for the Apple App store and Google Play store. You can find updates and working back-end project at `pizzavspizza.com`. If you have any questions regarding our project you can always message me on Twitter or Instagram at artyudin_nyc. All code that we will use in this book is available at `https://github.com/programwithus`.

---

[2] `www.thepizzajoint.com/pizzafacts.html`

CHAPTER 1

Starting with Django

"You can create a mobile app with no Swift at all?" my client asked me surprisingly. We were sitting at a coffee shop, and I was pitching an idea to use Python and Django for his mobile app. "Yes, that's the idea," replied I.

I will not go through the whole confidential conversation between me and my client here. But I could tell you this, he was very excited to know that he could save some money not hiring two separate teams for iOS and Android apps. Also, as a bonus, I promised him a desktop version of a web app running on the same Django engine and sharing the same database.

In this book, I'll share with you the whole process of building truly versatile mobile apps with Django. For me, Python sounds like a natural choice for any task. Python is so much in demand these days due to its functionality and simplicity.

If you have never developed a web application before or may have used other solutions than Django, you would like to know all the main characteristics of a high-level Python web framework. That's why in this chapter, I want to explain what makes Django so popular and why it is superior compared to other web frameworks.

Along with that, we will build a solid foundation for understanding how web applications work. In order to do that, we will take a look at the Model-View-Controller pattern. This design pattern is widely used all over the world for all kinds of apps.

© Art Yudin 2020
A. Yudin, *Building Versatile Mobile Apps with Python and REST*,
https://doi.org/10.1007/978-1-4842-6333-4_1

The modern Internet cannot be imagined without HTTP protocol. To fully understand communications between back-end and front-end parts of web apps, we will discuss HTTP protocol and request methods.

I promise that by the end of the first chapter, you would have a running Django web app on your computer. Besides, you'll have a good understanding of how to get started with Django and the Django REST framework.

Django is the best choice for a web app

What is a common thing among Instagram with 400 million active users per day, Spotify with an annual revenue of over 4 billion, Dropbox, and Uber? The answer is Python. All these popular applications are powered by simple to learn and handle Python, the most popular programming language of 2020. If we want to be technically correct, we should probably mention Django, unequally advanced and versatile web framework written in Python.

What exactly is Django? Django is a collection of Python modules, what we call a web framework, designed for building web applications. It is a free, open source program available to anyone. I usually get this question asked, "how is a framework different from a software library or a package?". A software library is a collection of functions, but a framework is much more. For example, the Django framework maps URLs to functions and renders HTML pages, with activities such as handling cookies, sessions, and web security. Initially released to the public in 2005,[1] Django quickly gained popularity among web developers for its "batteries included" approach.

The convenience of Django is built-in ORM (object-relational mapping) that supports relational databases. Four fundamental tasks of any web application – create a record, read or retrieve a record, update a record, and

---

[1]`https://en.wikipedia.org/wiki/Django_(web_framework)`

delete a record – require a database. Compared to other web frameworks, Django comes with a built-in solution for an organized collection of data – SQLite. In spite of its name, SQLite is quite powerful. The first version of Facebook was running on SQLite. If you already have a database or want to use some other solution, Django can easily deal with PostgreSQL, MySQL, and Oracle. I heard some people even use the NoSQL database with Django, but to the best of my knowledge, Django does not support NoSQL.

In comparison to other web frameworks, Django provides essential tools like authentication and authorization, to name a few. Believe me, you don't want to spend time building your own authentication module, especially if you work alone or have limited resources. In Django, with just a few lines of code, you can authenticate users and assign role permissions. Also, Django provides features that are necessary for any web application: CSRF (Cross-Site Request Forgery) that prevents unwanted actions and XSS (Cross-Site Scripting) that guards against unauthorized code scripts on web pages and SQL injections (a code injection technique) and stops pirated SQL statements. Most of the other frameworks would use third-party solutions for security and authentication.

As you can see later in this chapter, Django is very easy to set up and use. Django is very scalable and can handle any project of any size; that is why it is so widely used in all industries by giants like Instagram, YouTube, Spotify, and others. No matter how big or small your team is, you can build professional looking modern web applications with Django.

There is a misconception that Django is difficult to understand and first you have to start with a smaller framework like Flask. In my opinion, it is not true at all, and I will show you, as we move along, how easy it is to start using Django.

MVC design pattern

Django uses MVC (Model-View-Controller) design pattern, a traditional way to organize your code. Figure 1-1 presents the typical MVC structure. MVC divides your code into three parts. Model is the core of your project; this is where data is coming from. View is the part where application communicates with a user, takes inputs, and displays data. Controller is the manager module handling user requests, manipulating data in the Model, and rendering templates in the View.

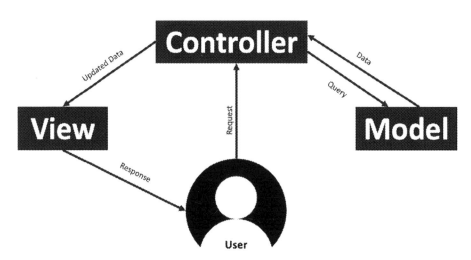

Figure 1-1. *Model-View-Controller pattern*

As we start designing Models and Views for our app in the next chapter, you'll see that in Django, Controller is called a View module. Some people find this confusing; that is why the official Django documentation has an explanation in the frequently asked questions: "Well, the standard names are debatable. In our interpretation of MVC, the 'view' describes the data that gets presented to the user. It's not necessarily how the data looks, but which data is presented. The view describes which data you see, not how you see it."[2]

It will not make much of a difference. If you are new to the MVC pattern or if you are an experienced developer, you will get used to this after you try Django and see how the framework manipulates and presents data.

How does Django exactly work? I want to start with the URL dispatcher. In Django, it's called the urls.py module where you configure all possible URL (Uniform Resource Locator) patterns and endpoints for your project. When a user enters a URL into a browser at the top of the screen, for example, `http://yourbestapp.com/nyc`, the browser sends a request over the Internet to a server where your app is deployed, and the server sends a response back to your browser. We will take a closer look at response later in this chapter.

But what happens when a server gets a request? The server would forward your URL to urls.py also known as the URL dispatcher and match yourbestapp.com/nyc to all URL patterns in the app. If there were no match, then it would return a 404 page not found error. However, if there were a perfect match, it would map it and invoke a particular View. A View could be designed as a function or a class. A View has to be defined in the view.py file, which in the MVC pattern plays the role of the Controller. The View would query data to the database, manipulate this data, and return it as a web response. The Model usually is defined in models.py as a class. Simply put, the Model represents the collection of data in a database. Each attribute of a Model class in models.py represents a database field. Consequently, the yourbestapp.com/nyc URL would trigger the View to

---

[2]`https://docs.djangoproject.com/en/2.2/faq/general/#django-appears-to-be-a-mvc-framework-but-you-call-the-controller-the-view-and-the-view-the-template-how-come-you-don-t-use-the-standard-names`

query the database, presumably containing restaurant information, and filter out the ones located in New York City. As a next step, this information would be sent as a web response.

HTTP protocol

In the preceding example, I have mentioned a request and a web response, the means by which computers communicate with each other. Usually, the requesting side is called a client, and the responding side is a server. A client could be a web browser, a web app, or a mobile device trying to get connected to a server. Communications between a client and a server are performed through messages. The client sends a message, and the server replies back with another message, called response.

This web messaging system, request-response, is achieved over the HTTP Protocol (Hypertext Transfer Protocol).[3] You have probably noticed that in your browser, all web addresses start with the http:// prefix.

All HTTP messages specify an action they intend to do; these actions are called methods or sometimes verbs. There are eight of them, but the most commonly used are GET and POST. Table 1-1 shows the list of HTTP request methods.

---

[3]There are other protocols, such as FTP, Gopher, and SOAP; however, HTTP is the most popular and widely used.

Table 1-1. *HTTP request methods[4]*

Method	Description
GET	The GET method is used to retrieve information from the given server using a given URI. Requests using GET should only retrieve data and should have no other effect on the data.
HEAD	Same as GET but transfers the status line and header section only.
POST	A POST request is used to send data to the server, e.g., customer information, file upload, etc., using HTML forms.
PUT	Replaces all current representations of the target resource with the uploaded content.
DELETE	Removes all current representations of the target resource given by a URI.
CONNECT	Establishes a tunnel to the server identified by a given URI.
OPTIONS	Describes the communication options for the target resource.
TRACE	Performs a message loop-back test along the path to the target resource.

GET is used when a client sends a request to read or retrieve information from a server, and POST is used when a client sends information to a server. For example, filling in and posting a form or creating a post on a social network would require a POST method. A response message on the other hand sends a status code, indicating whether the request was successful or not, and the resource data. The most known status code is 404 page not found, which means the content was moved or deleted based on your request. The 403 code means that the user does not have permissions to access the information, and the 201 code indicates that everything is OK. You do not need to know all status codes to build a web app. However, it would be beneficial to understand major groups. Table 1-2 shows the list of HTTP status codes.

---

[4]www.tutorialspoint.com/http/http_methods.htm

Table 1-2. *List of HTTP status codes*[5]

Codes	Status
1xx	Information response
2xx	Success
3xx	Redirection
4xx	Client errors
5xx	Server errors

As I have mentioned earlier, a response message also includes requested data which could come in different formats. Most commonly used formats would be HTML or JSON (JavaScript Object Notation).

Recently, I was shopping for a new refrigerator and was surprised to know that these days you could get a fridge that would place an online order for a food. This type of client, fridge, sending request to online stores does not need HTML with colors and images. Plain JSON text format would be enough for a fridge or any other device connected to Wi-Fi. On the other hand, I as a client would use a browser to look at data coming in HTML format with descriptive photos.

Django is a server-side web framework that means it generates an HTML template on a server and sends it via HTTP response to a client. HTML templates would work for a web browser just fine, but we are building a mobile app and our front-end would require web-browsable APIs (application programming interfaces). We humans need to see information in the form of text or images in a browser; however, devices and web applications use APIs to interact with each other. As browsers, applications also send data messages via the HTTP protocol. There are several methods on how devices can send data over the WWW (World Wide Web); the most popular and the one we will be using for our app is REST (Representational State Transfer).

---

[5]https://en.wikipedia.org/wiki/List_of_HTTP_status_codes

RESTful APIs

What is REST? If you google it, you will find a bunch of articles referring to Roy Fielding and his doctoral dissertation where he introduced the term REST and explained it as a software architectural structure. I'll do my best and try to explain this concept with plain words.

The communication process between a client and a server via the HTTP protocol could be more efficient and flexible if web applications are designed according to certain rules – called architectural style. To build a true RESTful API, you must follow the architectural style and take into account a couple of constrains.[6] The major one is the uniform interface which implies that an application should be structured in a clear manner, and each URI (Uniform Resource Identifier) should be specific and define a resource. In other words, each request action should serve its own purpose.

For example, if a client wants to write a new post, then the social media application should provide an endpoint with a POST method which would create a new resource. Identically, when a client sends a GET request, the API would return the state of that resource, including the title, the date it was created on, the actual post, and anything else related to that object in JSON format.

JSON is the most popular format for API communication these days, adapted by all Internet users and used in the majority of APIs. JSON is a lightweight format in some way similar to Python's built-in dictionary data structure. If you are not familiar with the dictionary data structure, I would definitely recommend you to learn it.

The REST architecture is stateless. Stateless simply means that HTTP messages between the client and the server are not dependent on each other and treated independently. The server is not saving a client state and treats every request separately from the previous one; this makes the whole architecture simpler.

---

[6]https://restfulapi.net/rest-architectural-constraints/

The REST architecture and callable APIs would make our Django back-end engine versatile and adaptive to all UIs (user interfaces). If, later, you need to add a desktop version, you could easily achieve this using the same code we are about to create in the next chapters.

To build a RESTful structure on top of Django, we will use a powerful and easy-to-use Django REST framework. Django REST will handle the essential part of the API process – serialization or converting our data to JSON format. Besides that, Django REST takes care of authorization and routing. In other words, Django REST is specifically designed to build RESTful web applications. That is exactly what we need for a mobile app.

Enough with a theory. We have reached the point where we install Django and the Django REST framework.

Note   The installation process described here should work for Mac and Windows. Keep in mind that commands mentioned here are specific for Unix and Linux platforms. Windows command prompt might not accept them. I'll do my best and duplicate commands for Windows. I guess if you are a Windows user, you know them better than me. Also, later, we would need to test our React Native mobile app on an iOS simulator or Android emulator. If you are planning to develop iOS apps, you would need to use Xcode. To the best of my knowledge, it is impossible to install Xcode on Windows. You can run a virtual machine on your PC, but then you will still be using macOS.

Django installation

First of all, we need to launch a virtual environment on your machine. You are probably familiar with the medical term clean room; in TV series, like the ER, they would always set up a clean room, a control environment, before the operation. Following the same logic, we need to isolate a directory where we install all our packages. The benefit of a virtual environment is to prevent conflicts between dependencies of different libraries. For example, you can run multiple projects using different versions of Django and/or other packages. Additionally, for each project, you should create a requirements.txt file which would hold a list of all installed packages and their exact versions. This would ease setting up the process of deploying your project to a server and will help other collaborators to install the same packages on their machines.

Without further ado, let's create a new folder for our project. Open a terminal window, and using Linux command mkdir (make directory) or Windows CMD command md, create a folder named pizzavspizza as follows:

```
mkdir pizzavspizza
```

Then, using command cd (change directory), switch to pizzavspizza directory:

```
cd pizzavspizza
```

Within our newly created directory, let's set up a virtual environment.

Note   For our project, we will be using Python 3. If you don't have Python 3, install it on your Mac or Windows. Go to www.python.org, choose Downloads from the menu bar, and download the latest version. The process is quite simple for a Mac. For Windows, I would recommend to select the "Add to PATH" option to have the ability to run Python everywhere on your computer.

Before we start installing packages, I want to take a step back and say a couple of words about the Python version we will be using for our project.

Apple used to ship Macs with preinstalled Python 2.7; try the python command in your terminal:

```
python
```

If you use an older version of Mac, this command should launch Python 2.7. If you recently bought a Mac and installed Python yourself, then the `python` command launched Python 3.x.

In our project, we will be using Python 3. We are building an application from a fresh start, so it would be better to use the latest version of Python. The last version of Django that still supports Python 2.7 is 1.11 which is way too old for us.

Note   As I write this book, Apple has issued a new version of OS Catalina where the Python 2 default version of Python was deprecated. If you recently bought a Mac with macOS Catalina, then the command python would launch a newer version of Python that you downloaded from `www.python.org` or would return an error message if you have not installed Python yet. In case you have two different versions of Python installed on your computer, Python 2.7 and Python 3.x, then you would need to use the python3 command going forward. The same would be true for PIP. PIP3 command would be used to install packages.

All package installations in the Python environment are handled by PIP, package installer or package manager. Do not install Python packages without PIP. Downloading libraries from questionable sources might result in getting a virus installed along. PIP knows where to find the latest version of a package and how to install it. PIP comes with Python by default, and you can find a list of all available PIP commands if you run the pip command, like this:

```
pip
```

Although PIP comes with Python, sometimes you might get an error like

```
pip command not found
```

In that case, you would need to launch it with the following command for Mac:

```
sudo apt-get install python3-pip
```

The sudo command gives you administrative privileges to install packages on Mac and prompts to enter a password.

Note   sudo apt-get would not work on Windows. To launch PIP on Windows, you need to download the get-pip.py file at `https://pip.pypa.io/en/stable/installing/#do-i-need-to-install-pip` and execute get-pip.py with the python command: `python get-pip.py`. After that, relaunch the Command Prompt.

The next step is to install a virtual environment with the PIP command that should work for Mac and Windows:

```
pip install virtualenv
```

After we installed a virtual environment, we can launch it with the command

```
virtualenv venv
```

venv is the name of the folder where all dependencies and virtual environment files will be installed; you can call it anything. However, venv is considered to be best practice for a name where you hold your virtual environment files.

If for some reason you skip a directory name after the virtualenv command, all files would be installed into the current directory. The reason we encapsulate all virtualenv files in one folder is that we do not want to take any of these files to a remote repository later in production, when we deploy our project to a server.

In the production, we will set up a new virtual environment on a server and install all packages from our requirements.txt file.

As a next step, we would need to activate our virtual environment with the following command for Mac:

```
source venv/bin/activate
```

For Windows, use

```
venv\Scripts\activate
```

If you see (venv) before your home directory name, you are in an activated virtual environment and ready to install and run Django.

If you want to check the Python version in your virtual environment, you can run the command

```
python --version
```

I am using Python 3.8.0. Do not worry if you have a different Python version than 3.8; all Python 3 versions are more or less similar and can be used interchangeably. Later in production on a live server, where we would be deploying our application, we might use a different Python 3.x version. It is not a problem as long as you are using any Python 3.x version. I guess everything I said here would be true for newer versions of Python in the future.

Now we are ready to install Django. At the moment when I write this, the latest official version is Django 3.1. Please keep in mind that any other version might be working differently. Before you install Django, I would definitely recommend referring to a supported versions page: `www.djangoproject.com/download/`. There, you can find a current version as well as release dates and support periods. In any way, it is quite simple to switch from one version to another if you understand the main principles of Django. The Django project is run by a team of volunteers, and they are doing a great job keeping the documentation up to date at `www.djangoproject.com`.

So, if you want to install the version I am using in this book, you can specify the Django version 3.1 and use this command:

```
pip install django==3.1
```

Otherwise, install a current version of Django with PIP:

```
pip install django
```

There is an option to see all versions of Django available for installation; run PIP and leave a version argument blank, like this:

```
pip install django==
```

Figure 1-2. *List of all available Django versions*

This command will give you an error since we have not specified a version and will list all available versions for installation as you see in Figure 1-2.

To make sure Django is installed and to save it to requirements.txt, run the following command:

```
pip freeze
```

The freeze command will show you all packages currently installed in your virtual environment; you can see them in Figure 1-3.

```
(venv) (base) programwithus:pizzavspizza programwithus$ pip freeze
asgiref==3.2.10
Django==3.1
pytz==2020.1
sqlparse==0.3.1
```

Figure 1-3. *List of all packages installed*

Do not worry if you get some other packages installed besides Django; based on your environment and Django version, you might get additional libraries like pytz, the library for accurate and cross-platform timezone calculations, and sqlparse, a SQL parser module. Asgiref is the latest addition to smooth async functions. We will talk about async functions later. Just keep in mind that the pip install django command might add other dependencies based on the Django version.

Now with the command

```
pip freeze > requirements.txt
```

create a new file requirements.txt and write the names of all installed packages into that file.

The next big step would be to launch our back-end project. The word project in Django means a collection of modules and apps. The Django project is what would be our web application engine.

Using the following command, let's create our pizza project and name it pizzaproject:

```
django-admin startproject pizzaproject
```

The command startproject forms a Django project directory structure for pizzaproject. Let's take a closer look at the files that were created along in this directory (Figure 1-4).

```
— pizzaproject
   ├— manage.py
   └— pizzaproject
        ├— __init__.py
        ├— asgi.py
        ├— settings.py
        ├— urls.py
        └— wsgi.py
   ├— requirements.txt
   └— venv
```

Figure 1-4. *Directory created by the startproject command, listing all default files in the Django project*

Main modules in Django project

The most confusing part for beginners is another pizzaproject folder within a pizzaproject directory. Let me remind you that the command startproject creates a collection of elements for our future web app, and the directory pizzaproject inherits the name and operates as a core of our Django project. Let's glance at all the files we have in our pizzaproject directory.

__init__ module

First of all, __init__.py is a standard file for all Python directories. If accidentally you remove this file from the directory, Python would not regard this folder as a part of the Python package.

Settings module

Settings.py is the main control tower in our project; this is where you configure your application. The settings file contains all available apps. OK, this might be confusing at the beginning. I have used the word "app" to describe our initiative here. However, Django comes with a bunch

17

of built-in features called apps. In Django, an app is a specific part that encapsulates code based on its purpose. I know at first it sounds too complicated since we regard our whole project as an application, but in Django, an app is just a part, and a project can have many apps responsible for different tasks. In the settings.py file (Figure 1-5), we can find a list of all installed apps by default. By the way, you could always add more apps as needed. Later, we will install the django-cors-headers package and would add it to the INSTALLED_APPS list. Django considers stand-alone packages as apps. Let's briefly go over the apps we already have in the list. Later, we will create an app and add it to INSTALLED_APPS too.

```
INSTALLED_APPS = [
    'django.contrib.admin',
    'django.contrib.auth',
    'django.contrib.contenttypes',
    'django.contrib.sessions',
    'django.contrib.messages',
    'django.contrib.staticfiles',
]
```

Figure 1-5. *List of installed apps in the settings.py file*

Admin app

The Admin app is responsible for the admin interface; we will see it in action later when we define our first Model.

Auth app

The Auth app handles user authentication and authorization, one of those perks that makes Django very popular.

Contenttypes app

The Contenttypes app can be regarded as a framework itself.[7] It is a very powerful database management system that manages generic relations, foreign key instances, among all models in the Django project. I'll give you an example to illustrate how generic relations work.

Suppose we have a Pizzeria Model in a project that keeps all data about pizzerias and a separate Model for Chinese places. To store comments and reviews, we would need a Comment Model. What would be the best way to connect them all to retrieve data efficiently based on different queries? One approach would be to duplicate the Comment Model and connect each copy to the Pizzeria Model and the Chinese places Model separately. So the Pizzeria Model would have its own Comment Model just for Pizzerias. Another option would be to create a new app specifically designed for comments and reviews. We would have one Comment Model in that app. We could keep all comments and reviews in one place and associate them with instances of Pizzerias and Chinese places. This solution would be preferable. We would be able to filter comments and reviews by any instance of a Pizzeria or a Chinese place or maybe by a user who left a review. Besides, we could retrieve comments for all restaurants and sort them by best reviews.[8] This would be possible with the Contenttypes app. The Contenttypes app quietly gathers information about all models used in the Django project. This Django feature makes models more reusable.

Sessions app

The Sessions app is handling communications between a client and a server via the HTTP protocol. It identifies each client and administrates cookies, information sent by a server, and saves it in a client's browser.

---

[7]https://docs.djangoproject.com/en/2.2/ref/contrib/contenttypes/
[8]https://docs.djangoproject.com/en/2.2/ref/contrib/contenttypes/

Messages app

As the name implies, the messages app is responsible for communication with a user by displaying notification messages. It mostly used Django HTML templates to enhance the user experience by sending SUCCESS or ERROR messages. We are not planning to use Django templates for our app so we could leave it at that.

Staticfiles app

The Staticfiles app is used to deal with all kinds of static files, like images, JavaScript files, and CSS files. It is used in a production mode and acts as a server for static files. In the last chapter of this book, when we deploy our back-end project to a server, we will talk more about static files.

We are done with INSTALLED_APPS for now and can get back to other key elements in the settings.py file.

Secret key

By default, Django creates a secret key to access the project. It is defined in the settings file as a long string. The best practice would be to keep this key along with all other sensitive information in a separate file and import it in settings.

Allowed hosts

Allowed hosts is a list to hold all permissible hosts of our project. By default, it is empty, and we can leave it empty while we work on our project and run the Django project in a development mode. However, after deployment to a server, we would need to specify an IP address or a domain name for our website. Sometimes, people would use "*" in the Allowed hosts list, meaning that all hosts are allowed. That might be OK for the development process, but I would definitely recommend replacing it with your exact IP address as soon as you get one for your project.

```
ALLOWED_HOSTS = ['*']
```

Middleware

Middleware is a collection of code components, compiled as classes, to modify the HTTP request and response between a client and a web application. The Django documentation says that Middleware is a framework of hooks into Django's request/response processing.[9] Middleware processes request/response data through security, sessions, CSRF, authentication, and messaging classes, and each piece of code performs its task. For example, the Sessions app that we have discussed before is implemented through middleware. When a user sends POST request to our web application, CSRF class is called through middleware. All components in Middleware are customizable, and you can modify the Session management or encryption according to your needs.

WSGI application

WSGI stands for Web Server Gateway Interface and is pronounced as "Whisky."[10] In a nutshell, it is a liaison between a server and a web application, our Django project. I will show how to use WSGI during the deployment phase.

Databases

Here, you connect the Django project to a database. We have not initialized one yet. To create a database, we would run the command migrate, and

---

[9]https://docs.djangoproject.com/en/2.2/topics/http/middleware/
[10]https://en.m.wikipedia.org/wiki/Web_Server_Gateway_Interface

our database will be created under the default name db.sqlite3. By default, Django uses the SQLite3 database; as I've mentioned before, despite its name lite, it is quite powerful. If you want to use a PostgreSQL or an Oracle database, this would be the place to declare them in a Django project.

Auth Password Validators

Auth Password Validators is a list where you keep your password validators. As I have mentioned before, Django comes with a pretty strong authentication and authorization features. The built-in Auth app has a default User model which would require a user to create a password at registration. This registration feature is not a toy; it won't allow to pick something elementary like 12345 as a password. You will have a chance to test it when we will be creating a superuser, an administrator of our Django project. Although default validators are doing a good job, Django is highly customizable, and you can always create and add your own validators. You might want users to have at least one special character and a number in a password.

Static

A static section is where you define your static files' paths. In the development mode, all static files are stored in the static directory on your computer. As you deploy your project, you would have to provide the full path to your static files on a server. This is where the Staticfiles app would find all your static files in the deployment. Again, we will get back to static files in Chapter 8.

Other settings

Besides everything we have discussed so far, the file settings.py hosts language and time settings. These are not essential to our project. If your future projects require anything else, payment acceptance, third-party authentication, or any other general settings for the whole project, you should define them in settings.py.

URL module

The next file in our project directory is urls.py. This is the main URL dispatch system, which contains all URL patterns. We have discussed it briefly before; when a user enters a URL into a browser and sends an HTTP request, Django is looking for a match among the defined URL patterns in the urls.py, and if an analogue is found, the corresponding View would be invoked.

WSGI and ASGI modules

We have touched briefly WSGI when we were discussing middleware. WSGI stands for Web Server Gateway Interface. It is an interface between a server and your application. The main task of WSGI is to pass a client request to your application, a gateway to the World Wide Web.

The command startdjangoproject has created a default interface for our application, which is supposed to be quite sufficient for most cases; however, like everything in Django, WSGI can be customized based on your hosting server requirements.

Latest versions of Django come with a new ASGI module. An ASGI module supports asynchronous event-based architectures. While deploying to production, you point the server to either the WSGI.py or ASGI.py module. We will get back to these modules in Chapter 8.

Manage module

Manage.py, as other modules we have seen so far, is automatically created within any Django project. It is a service file running administrative tasks. Every time you need to start a task, you need to run it with this file.

Make sure you are in the directory, pizzaproject, where manage.py is located. You can see the list of all available commands (Figure 1-6) if you run the following command:

```
python manage.py
```

Figure 1-6. *List of commands you call with the manage.py file*

We will use and discuss most of these commands in the process of working on our project. I just want to note that you can create your own tasks. This is possible with the help of the BaseCommand class; any file saved in a special management directory would be added as a custom command to the list of commands and could be called through manage.py.

I always get this question asked: how can you automate tasks in Django? Well, we can create a special task that would be run by Django. Also, we can set time when this task should be called. For example, if we want to send emails to all our subscribers with a list of all new pizza places recently added, we can create a task for that. In a specially created directory commands, we will compile a module that would fetch all new records from the Model and email them. The name of this module in the commands directory would become a new command.

OK, we have covered a lot of theory, and we are ready to take some practical actions. First and foremost, we need to initialize a database where we would hold all data for our web application. As we discussed earlier, the default name of our database, unless you want to change it in settings.py, would be db.sqlite3. Our initial SQLite database would use the default schema for built-in apps: Admin, Auth, and Contenttypes. Any other tables we would need for our project should be designed in models. py as a Model. In the meantime, we can initialize a new database with essential models like User and Permission by running migrate task from the administrative list. Make sure you are in the right directory where the manage.py file is.

```
python manage.py migrate
```

The migrate command would create a new file db.sqlite3. Usually, you run the makemigrations command before migrate. I'll explain makemigrations in the next chapter. Initially, when you are just initializing a database for the first time, there are default blueprints for essential Models; that is why we can skip the makemigrations command for now.

You can see the results after we ran the migrate command; the database models were created for the following default apps: Admin, Auth, Contenttypes, and Sessions (Figure 1-7).

```
Operations to perform:
  Apply all migrations: admin, auth, contenttypes, sessions
Running migrations:
  Applying contenttypes.0001_initial... OK
  Applying auth.0001_initial... OK
  Applying admin.0001_initial... OK
  Applying admin.0002_logentry_remove_auto_add... OK
  Applying admin.0003_logentry_add_action_flag_choices... OK
  Applying contenttypes.0002_remove_content_type_name... OK
  Applying auth.0002_alter_permission_name_max_length... OK
  Applying auth.0003_alter_user_email_max_length... OK
  Applying auth.0004_alter_user_username_opts... OK
  Applying auth.0005_alter_user_last_login_null... OK
  Applying auth.0006_require_contenttypes_0002... OK
  Applying auth.0007_alter_validators_add_error_messages... OK
  Applying auth.0008_alter_user_username_max_length... OK
  Applying auth.0009_alter_user_last_name_max_length... OK
  Applying auth.0010_alter_group_name_max_length... OK
  Applying auth.0011_update_proxy_permissions... OK
  Applying sessions.0001_initial... OK
```

Figure 1-7. *By applying migration, we created a database and tables from default apps Admin, Auth, Contenttypes, and Sessions*

If you run the command ls (stands for list) in your Mac terminal or dir command for Windows

```
ls
```

or dir command for Windows

you will see all files in the current directory and a new addition, db.sqlite3, that would hold all our data.

After we have initialized our database, we can sign up the first user with administrative rights. Using the command createsuperuser, let's create an administrator for our application.

```
python manage.py createsuperuser
```

The createsuperuser command prompts you to enter a username, email, and password. Auth Password Validators will make sure we won't use 12345 as a password; Django takes security and authorization very seriously, and you have to provide a strong password. If your password is strong and you entered it correctly twice, you will see "Superuser created successfully" (Figure 1-8).

```
Username (leave blank to use 'programwithus'): Art
Email address: class@programwithus.com
Password:
Password (again):
Superuser created successfully.
```

Figure 1-8. *The createsuperuser command prompts you to create a username and password*

At this point, we can launch our application using a developer server and go through administrative functions of Django. To launch our application, we need to run our project on a server, and Django provides a built-in server for the development mode.

Using the command runserver, we will launch the internal server:

```
python manage.py runserver
```

Now, you should see a running server at http://127.0.0.1:8000/ (Figure 1-9).

```
Django version 3.1, using settings 'pizzaproject.settings'
Starting development server at http://127.0.0.1:8000/
Quit the server with CONTROL-C.
```

Figure 1-9. *The runserver command will start the Django internal server*

You can copy the http://127.0.0.1:8000/ IP address and pass it into the browser. This will redirect us to the Django landing page (Figure 1-10).

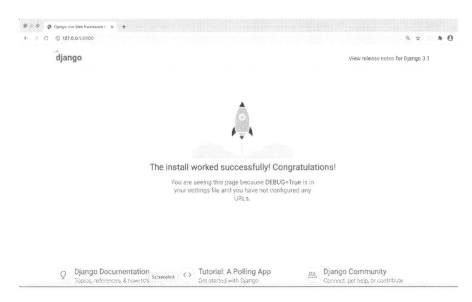

Figure 1-10. *Django landing page*

If you see this web page in the browser, then you have your Django project running successfully. Now, Django is running in the development mode locally on your computer. Later, to make changes to our project, we would need to exit the server mode by pressing keys Control and C on your keyboard.

```
control c
```

While our server is running, let's take a closer look at the Django admin page and examine the User model. In your browser, where you have the lending page running, add a sub-URL /admin to your http://127.0.0.1:8000/ address.

```
http://127.0.0.1:8000/admin/
```

This should take you to the admin login page where you can enter your username, the one you have created before, and the password (Figure 1-11).

Figure 1-11. *Django admin login*

Afterward, we should be redirected to the Django Admin Index page (Figure 1-12).

Figure 1-12. *Django Admin Index page*

Built-in Admin works like a backdoor to your web application. You can save some time building admin HTML templates and Views and start using Admin features that are already there. Usually, I would recommend creating your own custom HTML templates and Views for administrative functions if you have more than 50 administrators entering and altering data. Otherwise, the Admin built-in solution is totally fine. The Admin Index page is highly customizable. You can customize the HTML template and admin any way you like.

Presently, on the Admin page, we see two database models Groups and Users; they were created by the migrate command and came from the Auth app. Click Users and you'll see your record (Figure 1-13). You do not have to add users in the command prompt any more. You can add them in the Admin menu with the ADD USER button. In the next chapter, we will create our own custom Model and will include it in the Django administration.

Figure 1-13. *Django Admin Index page, Users table*

Django REST framework installation

We have our Django back-end set up successfully, and it is time to add the Django REST framework to our project. Adding Django REST is no different than installing any other Python package. For all libraries, we would use the pip install command (Figure 1-14). Make sure your development server is not running. You can stop it with the Ctrl+C command.

pip install djangorestframework

The Django REST framework is easy to use, and we will cover all the major components in the course of this book.

```
^C(venv) (base) programwithus:pizzaproject programwithus$ pip install djangorestfrawork
Collecting djangorestframework
  Downloading djangorestframework-3.11.1-py3-none-any.whl (911 kB)
     |████████████████████████████████| 911 kB 2.4 MB/s
Requirement already satisfied: django>=1.11 in /Users/programwithus/pizzavspizza/venv/li
b/python3.8/site-packages (from djangorestframework) (3.1)
Requirement already satisfied: asgiref~=3.2.10 in /Users/programwithus/pizzavspizza/venv
/lib/python3.8/site-packages (from django>=1.11->djangorestframework) (3.2.10)
Requirement already satisfied: sqlparse>=0.2.2 in /Users/programwithus/pizzavspizza/venv
/lib/python3.8/site-packages (from django>=1.11->djangorestframework) (0.3.1)
Requirement already satisfied: pytz in /Users/programwithus/pizzavspizza/venv/lib/python
3.8/site-packages (from django>=1.11->djangorestframework) (2020.1)
Installing collected packages: djangorestframework
Successfully installed djangorestframework-3.11.1
```

Figure 1-14. *Django REST framework installation process*

Do not forget to add djangorestframework to requirements.txt because later when we go into production, we would need to install the version we used in the development mode.

pip freeze > requirements.txt

As a Django extension, Django REST has to be added to the INSTALLED_APPS list, rest_framework, in the settings.py file (Figure 1-15).

```
# Application definition

INSTALLED_APPS = [
    'django.contrib.admin',
    'django.contrib.auth',
    'django.contrib.contenttypes',
    'django.contrib.sessions',
    'django.contrib.messages',
    'django.contrib.staticfiles',
    'rest_framework',
]
```

Figure 1-15. *Adding the Django REST framework to Installed Apps in the settings.py file*

When I add something to the INSTALLED_APPS list, I usually leave a trailing comma, for apps that might be added in the future. Do not forget to save your settings.py after the alteration.

In this chapter, we have covered all steps of setting up a back-end project. I hope by now you have an understanding of how to launch a Django project. We will start building our pizza vs. pizza application in the next chapter. With the back-end platform in place, we will construct the essential components of MVC. Also, we will continue working with the Django REST framework and building a solid foundation for our mobile app.

CHAPTER 2

Let's build our back-end web app

In this chapter, using Django and RESTful APIs, we will design the back-end of our web application. We will build the back-end part of our pizzavspizza web application. Also, we will discuss all the main aspects of the Django web app and implement CRUD operations. By the time you finish this chapter, you would have a working Django web application.

Design your Django app

From the previous chapter, you should remember that the Django project can hold multiple apps, smaller parts of the whole project. Some of them come as default built-ins of Django, and others could be created and added by developers. All CRUD operations related to one object should be encapsulated within a separate app. As a rule of thumb, your code is separated into apps based on data and the purpose.

First things first, let's create a new internal Django app by using the command startapp. The purpose of this app would be to collect, store, and manipulate data about pizza places. We will name this app Stores. Before you execute the following command, make sure your internal server is not running and you are in the folder where the manage.py file is. All Django commands are executed through the manage.py file, like this:

```
python manage.py startapp stores
```

© Art Yudin 2020

A. Yudin, *Building Versatile Mobile Apps with Python and REST*,
https://doi.org/10.1007/978-1-4842-6333-4_2

After running the startapp command, you should get the folder titled Stores in your home project directory. The Stores folder is a directory where we will place all code associated with our internal pizzerias app. Inside the Stores app, Django has created essential files that would help us in implementing the MVC design. Before we take a closer look at these files, we would need to append the Stores app to the INSTALLED_APPS list in the settings.py file. Rookie mistake, developers often forget to add the app they have created to the INSTALLED_APPS list in the settings.py file (Figure 2-1). If by mistake you skipped this step, Django would not be able to see any code in that app. This would be a really frustrating experience especially for a Django newbie.

```python
# Application definition

INSTALLED_APPS = [
    'django.contrib.admin',
    'django.contrib.auth',
    'django.contrib.contenttypes',
    'django.contrib.sessions',
    'django.contrib.messages',
    'django.contrib.staticfiles',
    'rest_framework',
    'stores',
]
```

Figure 2-1. *The Stores app has been added to INSTALLED_APPS list in the settings.py file*

As you can see in Figure 2-2, our Stores app folder contains six files and the migrations folder. I'll explain their purpose as we move through our project. We will need these files to hold snippets of our code. However, there are two major components of the MVC design that we would want to start with right away. As you have probably guessed, I am talking about models.py and views.py.

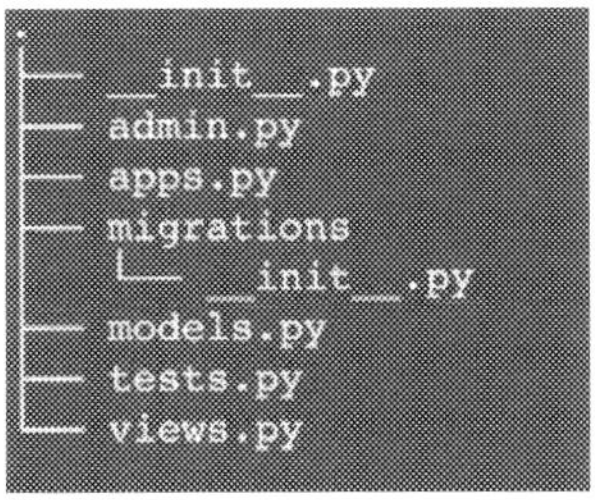

```
├── __init__.py
├── admin.py
├── apps.py
├── migrations
│   └── __init__.py
├── models.py
├── tests.py
└── views.py
```

Figure 2-2. *Files created by default within the Stores app directory*

Models.py is the file where you define your Models, tables containing related data. The best practice is not to overload your app and define no more than four or five Models in the models.py file within one app. Remember each app is supposed to deal with one key aspect of the whole project. For example, the Auth app manages all Models and methods related to the User, user authentication, and permissions. In our case, the Stores app should hold all data related to each pizzeria and methods to manipulate this data.

Views.py handles a controller function of MVC. This is the place where you want to manipulate data. Everything related to retrieving and writing data to the database should be done here in the form of functions or classes. We will implement Create, Retrieve, Write, and Delete methods as built-in generic classes. As a golden rule, nothing works more efficiently than a built-in solution. As we move along, we will add more functionality by customizing base classes using the Django REST framework. Generic Views cover all the main operations you would need to get started with your web application.

Although Django did a pretty good job initializing our Store directory with essential files to hold our code, in my opinion, there is one main piece that is missing. I am hinting on the local URL schema. In order to keep all things related to our Stores app in one place, we would need to have a local URL dispatcher. This approach would be considered the best practice since an app itself can be regarded as a separate Python package and might be used in multiple Django projects. To define local URL patterns, we would need another file in the Stores directory named urls.py. I know we already have urls.py in our main project folder; however, it would be a good idea to keep local URLs separately. Make sure you are in the Stores folder, and using the Linux touch command for Mac or the echo command for Windows or through your text editor, create the urls.py file.

```
touch urls.py
```

Now your Store directory should have the urls.py file and look like Figure 2-3.

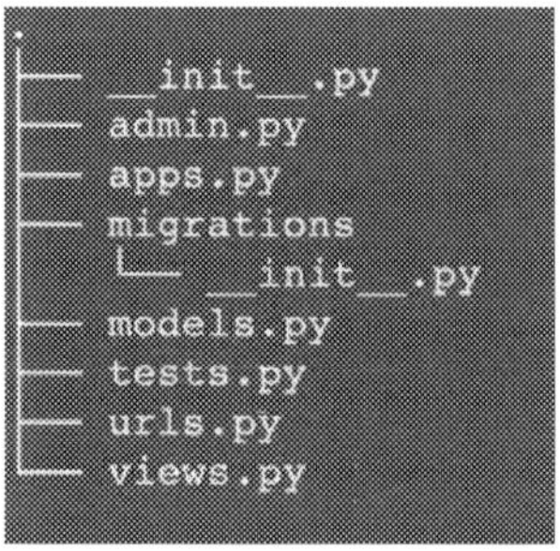

Figure 2-3. *Stores app directory after we added the urls.py file*

Please make no mistake, although two urls files are named the same, they would hold different URL patterns. The general or main file is stored in the pizzaproject directory and serves as a URL dispatcher for the whole Django project; the other one is a local URL schema placed into the Stores app. Later, we will connect them. The client's request would hit global urls.py in pizzaproject first and then would be redirected to the app's URL file.

Define Models

The cornerstone of any app is a Model. A Model is a collection of data. In a Model, you define all attributes of the object as fields, similar to a SQL table schema. Needless to say, before you start coding, you have got to have a clear blueprint of your Model. All little details have to be thought through ahead of time to avoid bumps down the road.

All technicalities such as how many characters you should allow for a place name field should be thought through before defining a Model. For example, would a web application accept US address format only or should we allow all international formats? If US clients only, then we would need to have a list of all 50 states. But what if someone lives in Canada and wants to register with us too? Should we have a list of Canadian provinces and territories or just leave this field blank and allow a user to write anything in the state field? What about international users? It would be really frustrating when a web application requires a state to get registered, and you simply don't have states in your country. I have seen that before. This would be a terrible example of user experience.

It would be possible to alter your Model later; however, it would be better to take into account all little things on the stage of design to avoid explaining your mishaps later with a well-known phrase "it is not a bug, it is a feature."

The Django Model is designed as a class with fields related to the database. You can regard it as a table. This is very convenient; no matter what database is attached, you always use Django fields and do not have to worry about the SQL syntax.

Let's start with a pseudocode first and compose a blueprint for the main model where we would store the pizzeria name, address, contact details, and a photo of the place itself.

As I have mentioned before, each model is defined as a class in the models. py module, and all fields are attributes of that class. Shortly, each pizzeria is an object with a number of characteristics, such as a city where it is located.

37

In our Stores app, we would need to create a class called Pizzeria and add the following fields:

> Name of the pizzeria: The name should not be longer than 200 characters. The field cannot be left blank. The name does not have to be unique.
>
> Street: Up to 400 characters or can be left blank.
>
> City: Up to 200 characters and cannot be left blank.
>
> State: For now, let's concentrate on US pizzerias only and add a list of all states.
>
> Zip code: It should be five digits, and we can leave it blank with a default value of 0.
>
> Website: It should be a URL or can be left blank.
>
> Phone number: Format should be ten digits, no parentheses or dashes.
>
> Description of a pizzeria: It should be plain text or can be left blank.
>
> Pizzeria image or logo: Attached png or jpg file, stored in a special folder – pizzeriaImages – and could be left blank. We will place there a default image.
>
> Email: This field could be left blank or be up to 200 characters.

Also, I usually add an active field, as a Boolean value, to filter later by current records. If the pizzeria goes out of the business, we would mark it as inactive.

After we have a solid plan, we can convert it into a code. As our guide, we can use the Django Model field reference.[1] Django documentation

---

[1]https://docs.djangoproject.com/en/2.2/ref/models/fields/

provides the list of all possible options and field types. Each field is designed as a Class where you can specify the number of characters, whether it can be left blank or not, and a bunch of other stuff based on a field type. Going field by field, we can write code in our models.py file, as you can see in Figure 2-4.

```python
class Pizzeria(models.Model):
        pizzeria_name = models.CharField(max_length=200,
                blank=False)
        street = models.CharField(max_length=400, blank=True)
        city = models.CharField(max_length=400, blank=True)
        state = models.CharField(max_length=2, null=True,
                blank=True)
        zip_code = models.IntegerField(blank=True, default=0)
        website = models.URLField(max_length=420, blank=True)
        phone_number = models.CharField(
                validators=[RegexValidator(regex=r'^\1?\d{9,10}$')],
                max_length=10,
                blank=True
                )
        description = models.TextField(blank=True)
        logo_image = models.ImageField(
                upload_to='pizzariaImages',
                blank=True,
                default="pizzariaImages/pizzalogo.png"
                )
        email = models.EmailField(max_length=245, blank=True)
        active = models.BooleanField(default=True)
```

```
from django.db import models
from django.core.validators import RegexValidator

# Create your models here.

class Pizzeria(models.Model):
    pizzeria_name = models.CharField(max_length=200, blank=False)
    street = models.CharField(max_length=400, blank=True)
    city = models.CharField(max_length=400, blank=True)
    state = models.CharField(max_length=2, null=True, blank=True)
    zip_code = models.IntegerField(blank=True, default=0)
    website = models.URLField(max_length=420, blank=True)
    phone_number = models.CharField(validators=[RegexValidator(regex=r'^\1?\d{9,10}$')], max_length=10, blank=True)
    description = models.TextField(blank=True)
    logo_image = models.ImageField(upload_to='pizzeriaimages', blank=True)
    email = models.EmailField(max_length=256, blank=True)
    active = models.BooleanField(default=True)
```

Figure 2-4. *Model Pizzeria in the models.py file*

For the phone number, I used a RegexValidator to validate the input of phone numbers. It is a good idea to have all phone numbers stored in the same format. Later, you might want to add a call button to your application; people could dial with a touch of a button, and it would be helpful to have a phone number stored as ten digits without dashes or round brackets.

A RegexValidator is a built-in feature based on simple regex, regular expression matching operations, which helps you to validate data before you write it into a database. All you have to do is to import it from django. core.validators[2] and create a matching regex expression. In our case, our validator would make sure that we get exactly ten digits.

Our logo_image field uses the Django ImageField class which by default requires the Pillow library. Pillow is a Python library to process images.

We would need to add the Pillow library to our project with a familiar pip command:

```
pip install Pillow
```

After you install Pillow, do not forget to add it to requirements.txt as we always do with newly added packages.

```
pip freeze > requirements.txt
```

---

[2]https://docs.djangoproject.com/en/3.0/ref/validators

As a rule of thumb, every time you design a new Model in models.py or make changes to an existing Model, you have to execute two commands: makemigrations and then migrate.

```
python manage.py makemigrations
```

If that went successfully and you did not misspell anything in your models.py, you should see a Migrations message like the one in Figure 2-5.

Figure 2-5. *Successful message after running the makemigrations command*

The makemigrations command creates a blueprint for our table in the database and keeps the history of our migrations in our app in the migrations folder. Make no mistake, our Model is not in the database yet; makemigrations is an intermediate step. In the migrations folder, you will see the 0001_initial.py file with a blueprint for our Model. If later you want to see the history of all your migrations, you can find them stored as a separate file in the migrations directory. If you take a closer look inside this file, you will see that Django automatically added an id field. This is a primary key, a unique identifier; later, we will use it to fetch all information on a particular record in our Model (Figure 2-6).

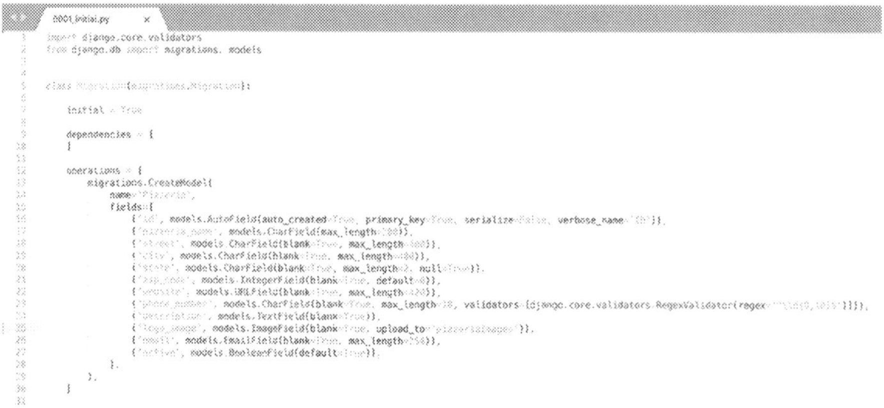

Figure 2-6. *Initial migrations for the Model Pizzeria in the newly generated 0001_initial.py*

After we have created a blueprint for our Model, we need to actually initiate a table in our database db.sqlite3 with a familiar command migrate.

```
python manage.py migrate
```

After running the migrate command, you should see a message (Figure 2-7) that Django applied our migrations. Now our database is ready, and we can write data in it.

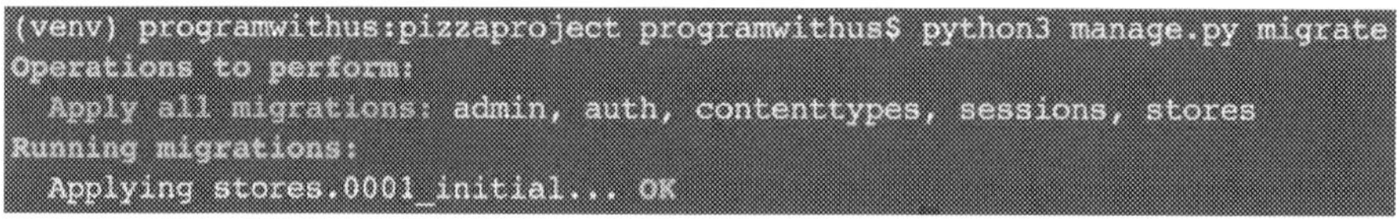

Figure 2-7. *All migrations were successfully applied, and the Model was created in the database*

In Chapter 1, we have already worked with the Django admin interface; now we can register our Model in the admin.py file to have access to our database. This would be handy before we add a front-end solution. Admin built-in templates would help us to add and update information in the database.

Go to the file admin.py and import our Model Pizzeria on the top of the file.

```
from .models import Pizzeria
```

The dot before models in our import statement is referring to the app folder. Please keep in mind that if we want to import our Pizzeria model somewhere else, like in a different app or in any file outside its native Stores app, we would need to provide the full path like this:

```
from stores.models import Pizzeria
```

The admin.site.register command will create a form for a Model in the admin interface. Now register the Pizzeria model with the admin interface (Figure 2-8).

```
admin.site.register(Pizzeria)
```

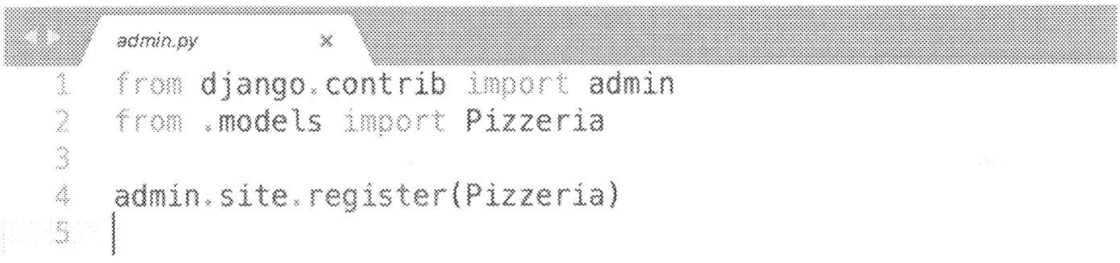

Figure 2-8. *Registering the Pizzeria Model in admin.py*

After we registered our Pizzeria Model in admin.py, we can launch our internal server with a routine runserver command.

```
python manage.py runserver
```

In your browser, navigate to

```
http://127.0.0.1:8000/admin
```

If the admin asks you for your credentials, enter your username and password; if not, then it would take you directly to the main admin interface (Figure 2-9).

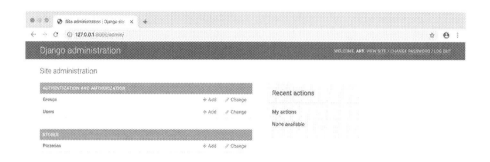

Figure 2-9. *Admin interface with the Pizzeria Model*

Under our app Stores, we will find Model Pizzeria. By pressing the Add button, we can write a couple of pizza places into the database. We would need them for later. To build retrieve methods, we would need some data to fetch from the database.

I have added three pizzerias to my database; however, my admin interface shows them as a Pizzeria object (Figure 2-10). To see the name of the place and city, we would need to convert some fields of our Pizzeria model into strings. In the models.py file under our Pizzeria Model, add the method __str__(). This method using Python string's method format() will convert pizzeria_name and city fields into strings (Figure 2-11).

```
def __str__(self):
return "{}, {}".format(self.pizzeria_name, self.city)
```

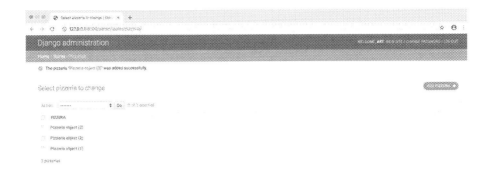

Figure 2-10. *Admin interface after we added three new pizza places*

```
models.py
1   from django.db import models
2   from django.core.validators import RegexValidator
3
4   # Create your models here.
5
6
7   class Pizzeria(models.Model):
8       pizzeria_name = models.CharField(max_length=100, blank=False)
9       street = models.CharField(max_length=400, blank=True)
10      city = models.CharField(max_length=400, blank=True)
11      state = models.CharField(max_length=2, null=True, blank=True)
12      zip_code = models.IntegerField(blank=True, default=0)
13      website = models.URLField(max_length=420, blank=True)
14      phone_number = models.CharField(validators=[RegexValidator(regex=r'^\d{10}$')], max_length=10, blank=True)
15      description = models.TextField(blank=True)
16      logo_image = models.ImageField(upload_to='pizzeriaImages', blank=True)
17      email = models.EmailField(max_length=254, blank=True)
18      active = models.BooleanField(default=True)
19
20      def __str__(self):
21
22          return "{}, {}".format(self.pizzeria_name, self.city)
23
24
```

Figure 2-11. *Define a new __str__() method of the Pizzeria Model*

After you refresh the admin web page in the browser, you should see the name of each pizzeria and city (Figure 2-12).

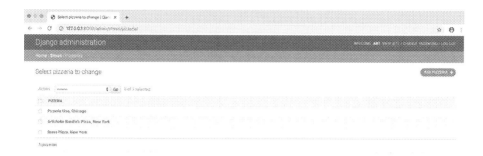

Figure 2-12. *After we added the __str__() method to the Pizzeria Model, pizzeria_name and city attributes have been converted to strings*

Writing CRUD Views

Now that we have a couple of records in our database, we can start writing Views for our CRUD pattern. Our Retrieve functionality will be presented with two Views: List View, rendering all pizzerias in the database, and Detail View to get all details of the object. In our case, these would be street address, contact information, description, and so on. We will start with the List View.

The process of adding a View to the app will be pretty much the same every time we do that. To compose a new View, follow these three steps.

The first step would be to design a Serializer in serializers.py. The second step is to code the View itself in views.py. The third step is to add a new URL pattern to the URL dispatcher in local urls.py.

The List View would fetch all records from our Pizzeria Model and render them in JSON format. For serializing our objects into JSON, we would need Django REST's help. The Django REST framework comes with built-in serializers to convert Django objects into JSON.[3] Serializers are easy to use, and usually they are defined as a form, with an option to use all fields from your Model or add custom fields. We will proceed with a simple option – ModelSerializer – which would resemble our Pizzeria Model. It is always a

---

[3]`www.django-rest-framework.org/api-guide/serializers/`

good practice to keep your code clean and neat; thus, we need to create a separate file for our serializers. In our Stores directory, create the file called serializers.py using the Linux command touch or through your text editor.

```
touch serializers.py
```

In the newly created serializers.py file, import the class serializers from Django REST, and from models.py, import the Pizzeria Model.

Subsequently, define a new class PizzeriaListSerializer (Figure 2-13). Our new serializer would inherit ModelSerializer and would include pizzeria name, city, and zip code fields from our Pizzeria Model as a list. We will use PizzeriaListSerializer to render all pizza places in our database in a List View. A List View usually contains a limited number of details, I would say the most important ones, like name, city, and some other major attributes. It also includes the id field.

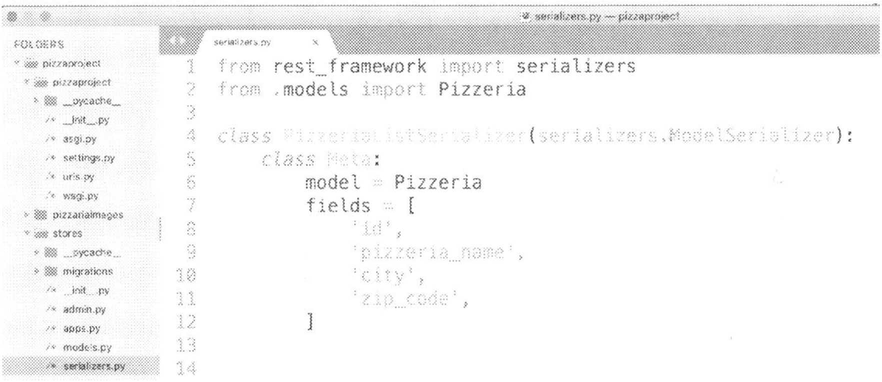

Figure 2-13. *PizzeriaListSerializer in the serializers.py file*

Within our PizzeriaListSerializer, we define the inner metadata class called Meta. The Meta class will transfer all information from our Model to Django REST. You can think of it as a function or a decorator. In class Meta, you can define any other specific details related to a model, like ordering and other constraints.

```
class PizzeriaListSerializer(serializers.ModelSerializer):
    class Meta:
        model = Pizzeria
        fields = [
            'id',
            'logo_image',
            'pizzeria_name',
            'city',
            'zip_code',
            'absolute_url'
        ]
```

The next step would be to define a List View in views.py. Before we get to custom Views, we can start with generic Views which are perfect for CRUD methods. Import generics from Django REST.[4]

After that, import the Pizzeria Model and define PizzeriaListAPIView. The best practice would be to combine a model name and a View that we inherit from as a name of the class. This naming convention would come in handy when you have multiple models and a bunch of views for each model. In our PizzeriaListAPIView, we need to at least define a Queryset and Serializer class. If needed, the queryset could contain filters or look for a specific object from a Model; it is very similar to SQL queries. In our List View, we leave the Queryset as all(), meaning that we want to get all objects from the Pizzeria Model. The Serializer class requires a Serializer related to the List View; in our case, it would be PizzeriaListSerializer. You can use the same serializer in multiple views; however, it would be cleaner to define a specific serializer for each view. Do not forget to import your PizzeriaListSerializer from serializers.py (Figure 2-14).

---

[4]www.django-rest-framework.org/api-guide/generic-views/

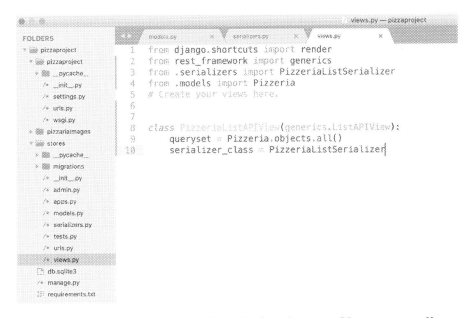

Figure 2-14. *PizzeriaListAPIView in the views.py file presents all objects from the Pizzeria Model in the Stores app*

How to design URLs for an application

The only step left is to set up the URL pattern in our URL dispatcher. All patterns affiliated to Views in our Stores app will be kept in our local urls. py file in the Stores directory.

In urls.py located in the Stores directory, add the following code:

```
from django.urls import path
```

The path function holds a URL pattern and invokes the corresponding View. We can import each View one by one or all of them at once. Usually, I import the whole Views module, not to worry about the views I might add in the future.

```
from . import views
```

All patterns will be held in the urlpatterns list:

```
urlpatterns = [ path('', views.PizzeriaListAPIView.as_view(),
name="pizzeria_list"), ]
```

Empty path ' ' means that PizzeriaListAPIView will be invoked, with
the help of the as_view() method, if a user enters nothing else but a
domain name or, in the case of the development server, the local address
http://127.0.0.1:8000/. In other words, a list of pizzerias will be
rendered on our landing page. We also need to add the argument "name"
which is just a label we could use later to reference our URL (Figure 2-15).

Figure 2-15. *Adding a URL schema to urls.py in the Stores app*

Our local urls.py has to be connected to the global URL dispatcher,
urls.py in the pizzaproject directory. To connect them, we need to import
the include function to our Stores app URLs to the main urls.py file. Add
the include function to the django.urls import path like this:

```
from django.urls import path, include
```

After that, add a root path for the Stores app urls.py to the urlpatterns list (Figure 2-16):

```
path('', include('stores.urls')),
```

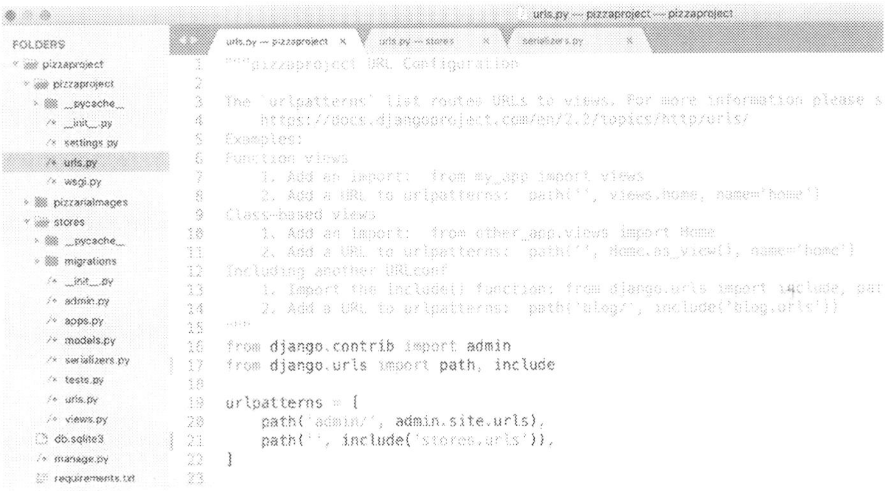

Figure 2-16. *Include Stores app URLs into global urls.py in the pizzaproject directory*

The path with an empty schema would handle a request and redirect it to the urls.py file in the Stores app, following the argument 'stores.url' in the include function. This is pretty much it for our List View. Every time we will be adding a View to our views.py file, we would need to follow these steps: code a View and add a URL pattern to a local urls.py file within the app.

We need to connect the global URL dispatcher with local/app urls.py only once, for each new app that you might add to your Django project.

At this point, we can put our code to test and restart the development server with the runserver command.

```
python manage.py runserver
```

If you get error messages, inspect your code carefully; most of the time, it is a matter of misspelling or missing stuff.

The Django REST framework has its own built-in HTML templates. When we open `http://127.0.0.1:8000/` in the browser, we can see a list of all pizzerias we have so far in our database (Figure 2-17). Built-in HTML templates are a very useful feature; we can test our code before we create our own front-end solution. All information from our database is coming in JSON format. The List View we just created can be used as an API endpoint. Upon a GET request, our server can send this data to our mobile application.

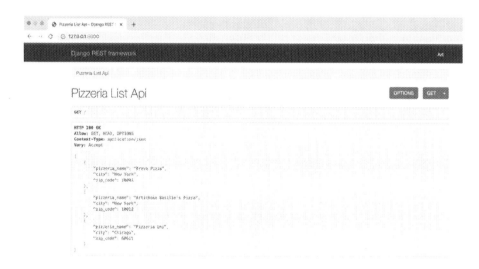

Figure 2-17. *The Pizzeria API List View renders all data from the Pizzeria Model in JSON format*

Detail View

A Detail or Retrieve View is similar to a List View; the only difference is that we would need to pass a unique identifier into the URL to query our database and fetch the object with all details. In our case, we would use the id field; however, if you build a blog or a social media platform, a slug can be used. For an internal company app, people might use an employee id to query a corporate database.

Similar to a previous example, we start with a Serializer for our Detail View. We can call it PizzeriaDetailSerializer. In comparison to our List Serializer, PizzeriaDetailSerializer would have all the fields from the Pizzeria Model included (Figure 2-18).

Figure 2-18. *Design of PizzeriaDetailSerializer in the serializers.py file in the Stores app*

Do not forget to import your PizzeriaDetailSerializer into views.py. For a Detail View, we would use a RetrieveAPIView class that comes from the generic collection.

Our class PizzeriaRetrieveAPIView name would have the name of the class we are inheriting from and the name of the Model (Figure 2-19). For a unique identifier, we would need to add a lookup_field attribute to specify the field to query our Model with.

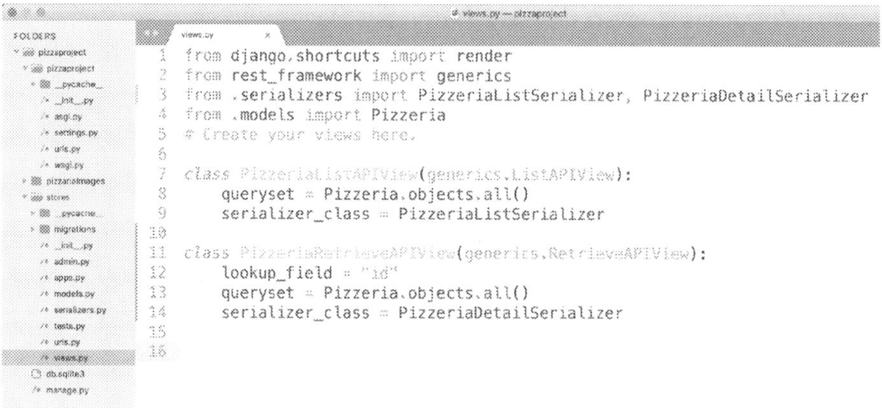

Figure 2-19. *PizzeriaRetrieveAPIView in the Stores app views.py*

We would use the id field to query our database and would need to assign it as "id" to lookup_field. If you try to look up the id field in models. py, you will not see it. A primary key or id field is always created for any Model by default, and you do not have to add it manually. If you took a closer look at our first migration in the migrations folder, you would see that the id field was the first one in our Model schema.

Queryset and Model attributes would be the same as in the previous List View.

As a last step for setting up a Detail View, we need to add a path to our urlpatterns schema list in the Stores app urls.py file (Figure 2-20).

```
path('<int:id>/', views.PizzeriaRetrieveAPIView.as_view(),
name="pizzeria_detail"),
```

```
urls.py                    ×
1    from django.urls import path
2    from . import views
3
4
5    urlpatterns = [
6        path('', views.PizzeriaListAPIView.as_view(), name='pizzeria_list'),
7        path('<int:id>/', views.PizzeriaRetrieveAPIView.as_view(), name='pizzeria_detail'),
8
9    ]
```

Figure 2-20. *URL pattern for PizzeriaRetrieveAPIView in the Stores app urls.py file*

'<int:id>/' is a pattern for an integer and the name of the field we would need to pass after our domain name or IP address to fetch details on a particular object. We would need to add the View we want to invoke, PizzeriaRetrieveAPIView, and come up with a label name for this view. Usually, the name will reflect the purpose of the view, and "pizzeria_detail" sounds good enough to me. For your future projects, you can find more URL pattern examples in the URL dispatcher[5] portion of the Django documentation.

Make sure your development server is running, and test this view in the browser. Since I have just three pizzerias in my database, I would open http://127.0.0.1:8000/3/ with ID 3 for the third record in my database (Figure 2-21).

---

[5]https://docs.djangoproject.com/en/3.0/topics/http/urls/

Figure 2-21.

Create View

The logic behind all other Views would be the same, design a View and add a corresponding URL pattern. Also, do not forget about Serializers.

As we discussed before, serializers could be reused in different Views.

I guess that every new pizzeria we would want to add to our database would have the same attributes. PizzeriaDetailSerializer, the one we already have, would be a perfect fit for the Create View. We would need all Pizzeria Model fields to create a new profile.

The main difference between Retrieve Views and Create Views would be the different HTTP methods. Before, we were getting the data from a server. Our List and Detail Views used the GET method. Now, we would be posting data, and the method would be POST. This is what I had meant when we were talking about the RESTful architecture. Each endpoint correlates to a specific method or action. Without further ado, using the generic view CreateAPIView, create a new class in views.py under the name PizzeriaCreateAPIView. We would still use the same Model – Pizzeria – and PizzeriaDetailSerializer as you can see in Figure 2-22.

```
     views.py — pizzavspizza
  urls.py          ×     views.py          ×
1   from django.shortcuts import render
2   from rest_framework import generics
3   from .serializers import PizzeriaListSerializer, PizzeriaDetailSerializer
4   from .models import Pizzeria
5   # Create your views here.
6
7
8   class PizzeriaListAPIView(generics.ListAPIView):
9       queryset = Pizzeria.objects.all()
10      serializer_class = PizzeriaListSerializer
11
12  class PizzeriaRetrieveAPIView(generics.RetrieveAPIView):
13      lookup_field = "id"
14      queryset = Pizzeria.objects.all()
15      serializer_class = PizzeriaDetailSerializer
16
17  class PizzeriaCreateAPIView(generics.CreateAPIView):
18      queryset = Pizzeria.objects.all()
19      serializer_class = PizzeriaDetailSerializer
```

Figure 2-22. *PizzeriaCreateAPIView in the Stores app views.py file*

Consequently, we would add a correlating URL pattern to our URL dispatcher in the Stores urls.py file (Figure 2-23). Considering that we would be adding a new record to our database, we would not need an id field. Django by default creates a new id for every object that we write into our database. A unique URL pattern to invoke the Create View would contain the word "create". Again, "create" is not a magic word, and you can pick anything else for the URL pattern. In my opinion, "create" is up to the task.

```
path('create/', views.PizzeriaCreateAPIView.as_view(),
name="pizzeria_create")
```

```
     urls.py — pizzavspizza
  urls.py          ×     views.py          ×
1   from django.urls import path
2   from . import views
3
4
5   urlpatterns = [
6       path('', views.PizzeriaListAPIView.as_view(), name='pizzeria_list'),
7       path('<int:id>/', views.PizzeriaRetrieveAPIView.as_view(), name='pizzeria_detail'),
8       path('create/', views.PizzeriaCreateAPIView.as_view(), name='pizzeria_create'),
9
10  ]
11
```

Figure 2-23. *URL pattern for PizzeriaCreateAPIView in the Stores app urls.py file*

As always, run your code with the runserver command to launch the development server.

Invoke the newly built Create View with the http://127.0.0.1:8000/create/ URL (Figure 2-24).

```
python manage.py runserver
```

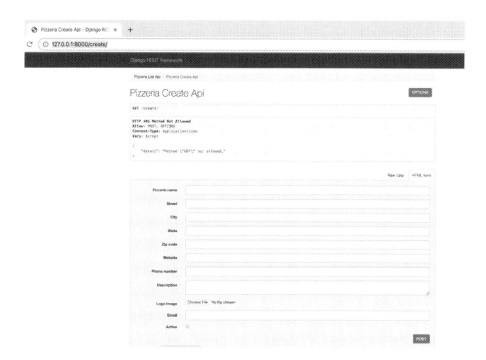

Figure 2-24. *Launching PizzeriaCreateAPIView with the URL pattern http://127.0.0.1:8000/create/*

Our Create View is running, and we can add a new pizza place to our database. Please note the warning message in the header "Method \ 'GET\' not allowed." and the "POST" button under the form. It means that PizzeriaCreateAPIView would accept a POST action only, due to the nature of generic CreateAPIView we have inherited from.

To give our View a test run, fill out this form and upload an image of your pizza place. When you are done, you should see that your record was successfully created (Figure 2-25), and then you can see it in the list view fetched with other places if you invoke your List View, as we did before.

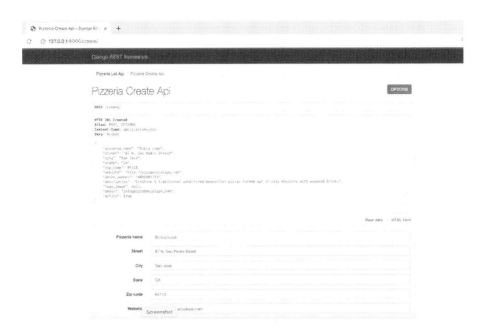

Figure 2-25. *A new pizza place was successfully created*

Update View

At this point, you probably have looked up the Django REST framework documentation or guessed that there has to be a generic UpdateAPIView, and you are right, there is one. However, UpdateAPIView is not quite user-friendly in my opinion. If we think about the process of updating a record in a database, there are two operations: first, you need to retrieve an object by id, and then update the information. Generic UpdateAPIView does the second operation; it provides a form to update the object. It would be helpful to see the information you are updating, not just empty fields. That is why we would go with RetrieveUpdateAPIView. The main difference is characterized in the name itself. RetrieveUpdateAPIView first pulls out the object; you can examine all details and then update them. The code we are about to write is really similar to our Detail View.

In the views.py. file, define a new class under the name PizzeriaRetrieveUpdateAPIView (Figure 2-26). We would need to define a lookup_field to find a single object in the database before we make any changes. Other attributes of PizzeriaRetrieveUpdateAPIView are the same as before, and we can use the Pizzeria Model and PizzeriaDetailSerializer again.

```
 1  from django.shortcuts import render
 2  from rest_framework import generics
 3  from .serializers import PizzeriaListSerializer, PizzeriaDetailSerializer
 4  from .models import Pizzeria
 5  # Create your views here.
 6
 7
 8  class PizzeriaListAPIView(generics.ListAPIView):
 9      queryset = Pizzeria.objects.all()
10      serializer_class = PizzeriaListSerializer
11
12  class PizzeriaRetrieveAPIView(generics.RetrieveAPIView):
13      lookup_field = "id"
14      queryset = Pizzeria.objects.all()
15      serializer_class = PizzeriaDetailSerializer
16
17  class PizzeriaCreateAPIView(generics.CreateAPIView):
18      queryset = Pizzeria.objects.all()
19      serializer_class = PizzeriaDetailSerializer
20
21  class PizzeriaRetrieveUpdateAPIView(generics.RetrieveUpdateAPIView):
22      lookup_field = "id"
23      queryset = Pizzeria.objects.all()
24      serializer_class = PizzeriaDetailSerializer
```

Figure 2-26. *PizzeriaRetrieveUpdateAPIView in the Stores app views.py file*

Conventionally, we have to construct a new URL pattern that would retrieve an object by id. In our Stores urls.py file (Figure 2-27), we already have a URL with id; to differentiate between the pizzeria_detail URL and the one that would invoke PizzeriaRetrieveUpdateAPIView, we would need to add a sub-URL prefix like this:

```
path('update/<int:id>/', views.PizzeriaRetrieveUpdateAPIView.
as_view(), name="pizzeria_update"),
```

```
     urls.py          ×      views.py          ×
 1   from django.urls import path
 2   from . import views
 3
 4
 5   urlpatterns = [
 6       path('', views.PizzeriaListAPIView.as_view(), name='pizzeria_list'),
 7       path('<int:id>/', views.PizzeriaRetrieveAPIView.as_view(), name='pizzeria_detail'),
 8       path('create/', views.PizzeriaCreateAPIView.as_view(), name='pizzeria_create'),
 9       path('update/<int:id>/', views.PizzeriaRetrieveUpdateAPIView.as_view(), name='pizzeria_update'),
10
11   ]
```

Figure 2-27. *URL pattern for PizzeriaRetrieveUpdateAPIView in the Stores app urls.py file*

After that, we can switch to development server mode and try to update one of our objects with the following URL in the browser: http://127.0.0.1:8000/update/3/ (Figure 2-28). Just make sure you are using an existing object id; otherwise, you would get an error.

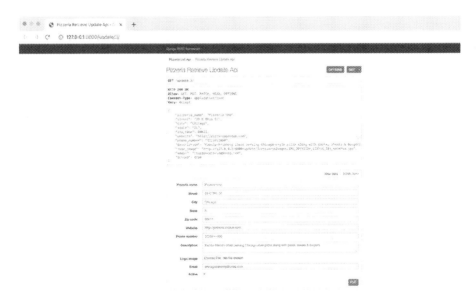

Figure 2-28. *Updating pizzeria with id 3*

In our header, we see all methods that we allowed to use with PizzeriaRetrieveUpdateAPIView, GET, PUT, and PATCH. The built-in Django REST HTML template uses the method PUT, as you can see the blue button on the bottom of the page. The method PUT usually refers to an existing object in comparison to a POST which would send any data to a server.

You could give it a try and change something. If your request was successful, you immediately would see the updated information in JSON format at the top of this page.

Delete View

The last but definitely not the least is the Delete View. In Django REST, this feature is implemented with the generic DestroyAPIView. People use delete and destroy interchangeably, and it would be a tough question to say which convention is preferable. I would vote for the "delete" terminology due to the name of the HTTP method delete. DestroyAPIView allows you to send a DELETE request only.

In our views.py, let's create a PizzeriaDestroyAPIView class which would inherit from the generic DestroyAPIView. We do not need to include a Serializer as an attribute of this class, just a lookup_field and Queryset (Figure 2-29).

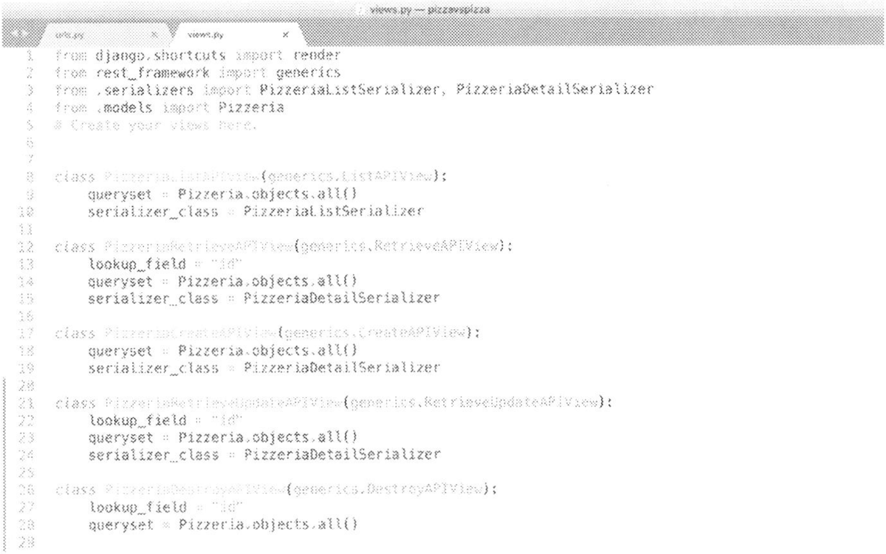

Figure 2-29. *PizzeriaDestroyAPIView in the Stores app views.py file*

Our URL pattern would include the keyword "delete" and id of the object we are trying to get rid of (Figure 2-30).

```
path('delete/<int:id>/', views.PizzeriaDestroyAPIView.as_view(),
name="pizzeria_delete")
```

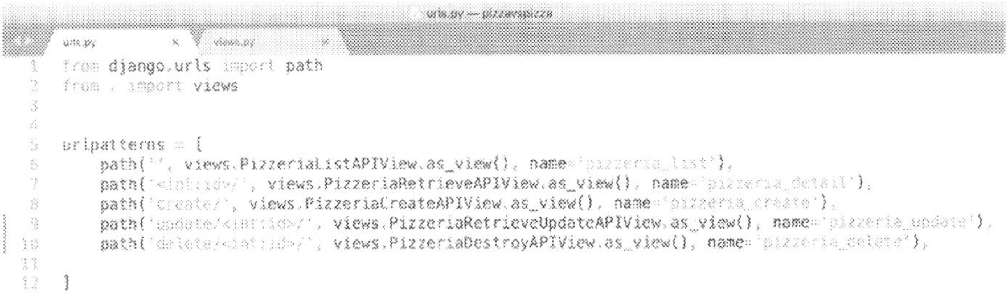

Figure 2-30. *URL pattern for PizzeriaDestroyAPIView in the Stores app urls.py file*

When you run this URL in your browser (`http://127.0.0.1:8000/delete/3`), you should see a message that the GET method is not allowed because PizzeriaDestroyAPIView accepts only a DELETE method. The only way to send this type of request from the built-in HTML page would be to click the red button delete in the right corner. Subsequently, you should get a warning message that you are about to delete an object in your database. This is a standard feature in Django so you would not delete something important by accident. If you no longer need the object with id 3, you may proceed, and PizzeriaDestroyAPIView would delete this object from your database. After you have deleted an object, you won't be able to see it on the list if you refresh the `http://127.0.0.1:8000/` page.

In this chapter, we have built a simple Django back-end app. This web app performs all CRUD operations and provides API endpoints that we would use in the next chapters of this book. The Django REST framework helped us with the RESTful architecture.

Although we have a fully functional app, we are not done with it. As we go through this book, we would add different features to our core app such as authentication.

CHAPTER 3

Getting started with React

In this chapter, I'll explain our choice for a front-end, and we will go over all the pros of using React. We will talk about the difference between React and React Native, and I will show how to get started with React and the main modules in React. If you are new to JavaScript and React, I would strongly recommend you to go over the next two chapters. In Chapters 3 and 4, I will demonstrate the main components of React that we will be using in React Native. We will learn all the aspects of React by assembling an intermediate version of a front-end app. If you are eager to start with a mobile app version right away, you can skip to Chapter 5.

In this chapter, we will start working with React – our choice for the front-end part of our pizzavspizza mobile web application. React is a JavaScript library and would be a perfect fit for our MVC structure. We will use it as a View, and React would be responsible for user interactions. Since React is written in JavaScript, I would strongly advise you to take a short JavaScript tutorial if you have never used it before. In some sense, JavaScript is similar to Python. Please do not throw stones at me if you think differently. There are some similarities. Python and JavaScript are both high-level programming languages and share many common concepts in programming. If your first programming language was Python, believe me, you will pick up the JavaScript logic and syntax in a matter of days, although it is quite different than the Python syntax.

© Art Yudin 2020
A. Yudin, *Building Versatile Mobile Apps with Python and REST*,
https://doi.org/10.1007/978-1-4842-6333-4_3

A widespread perception is that JavaScript is a client-side scripting language to make static HTML (Hypertext Markup Language) more fun. That is true. However, lately, with the rise of Node.js, a platform that allows you to run JavaScript both on the client and the server side, people build amazing stuff and even, as I've heard, perform machine learning tasks.

With the popularity of the RESTful architecture, web developers have tried many front-end solutions to make their applications more versatile and dynamic. I personally tried different technologies from a web template system Mustache and trendy jQuery to complex AngularJS. We can discuss the pros and cons of all these solutions, and frankly, if I was writing this book 4–5 years ago, I would probably add AngularJS to the title of this book; nonetheless, today the winner is clearly React.

Why React

React was developed by Jordan Walke, a Facebook software engineer for building dynamic single-page web applications.[1] The need for single-page applications came along with social giants like Facebook, Twitter, and others. It is costly to generate web pages on a server and then send them to a client. Pass a client HTML frame and let JavaScript do all the work on a client side. For example, when a web page greets you with "Good Morning!" or "Good Evening!", it has a JavaScript function that reads time from your browser and renders an appropriate message. This process eliminates excessive traffic and pricy server usage as well as shifts all the heavy lifting to your browser. React is a perfect tool for that since the concept behind this JS library is to use the same fragment of code over and over again. This fragment of code is called a component, and we will talk more in detail about components later in the chapter.

---

[1]https://en.wikipedia.org/wiki/React_(web_framework)

React is a clear choice for us to design a robust front-end part of our app. The back-end written in Django will serve APIs, and React will handle all user inputs and manipulate views as a single-page application. Besides, the combination of HTML and JavaScript would add a swell look to our application and spotlight it. In the endless sea of web applications, user experience and design play a great deal. Do not get me wrong; the functionality of the product is important; nonetheless, speed and convenience of the web application are paramount.

React and React Native

With the growing popularity of mobile platforms and the evolution of iPhone and Android phones in 2015, Facebook issued another flavor of React – React Native. React Native was specifically created to match the content with Android and iOS libraries.

Switching from traditional platforms, Facebook went after customers with mobile devices around the globe.

React Native is a game changer; you do not need to develop two different applications as before, one for Android and the other one for iPhone. You write code once, and it is paired with the native mobile software. React Native is a huge saver of time and money especially for developer teams without resources of tech giants.

The main advantage of React Native is that it uses the actual native components of iOS or Android, rather than simply converting JavaScript code to Swift or Java for Android. There is no need to learn Swift or Java to use native mobile components; believe me, that saves a lot of time.

Using our back-end written in Python and adding React Native as a front-end, we will create a versatile mobile web application. In this chapter, we will start with React since React Native is derived from it. In order to better understand React Native, it would be canny to start with the origin.

Starting with a generic introduction to React, we will gradually connect our back-end with our front-end application. After that, we will add React Native features to set up a mobile solution for iPhone and Android platforms.

How to get started with React

First of all, you would need to install Node.js on your computer. Node.js is an environment that runs JavaScript on a server. Node.js has gained enormous popularity due to a wide use of single-page applications and React. The easiest way to install Node.js is to download the "recommended for most users"[2] LTS version from `www.nodejs.org`. Go to `www.nodejs.org` and download node. The installation process is pretty straightforward; just follow the setup steps. After you are done with the installation process, run the following command in your terminal:

```
node -v
```

You should get the version installed on your computer; in my case, at the moment I am writing this book, it is 13.11.0.

Node.js comes with npm, Node Package Manager. Similar to pip, npm helps to locate and install JavaScript libraries. Let's check what version of npm you have on your computer:

```
npm -v
```

I am currently using 6.13.7.

If the node and npm commands worked fine then you are ready to start building the front-end part of our web application. I will explain all major modules as we go through a launch process.

---

[2]`www.nodejs.org`

To launch a React application, we need to run the create-react-app command

```
npx create-react-app front_pizzavspizza
```

npx is the command to run node module scripts; if you want to see all available options for this command, you can run npx in your terminal. create-react-app is the command to launch a new React project, and front_pizzavspizza is the name of our frond-end project. I specifically used the prefix front in front_pizzavspizza to be sure that some dependencies would not clash with our back-end Django application in the pizzavspizza folder. You can see that npx has created a brand-new folder with all modules and dependencies named as our application – front_pizzavspizza – and we have all major application commands listed.

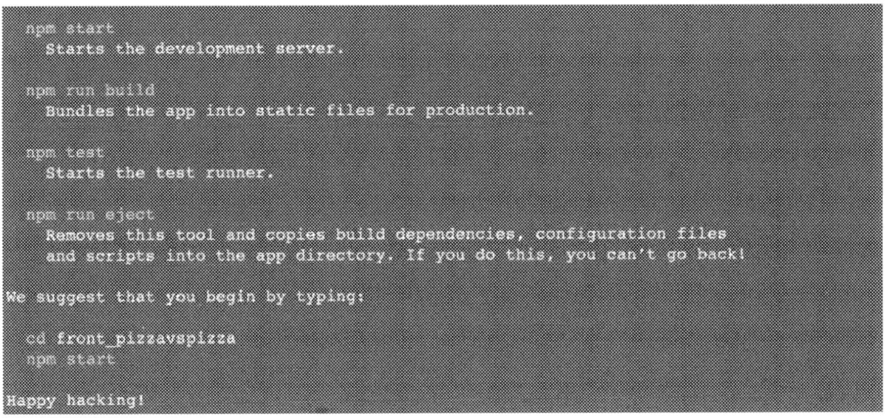

Figure 3-1. *npm commands to run the React application*

React built-in commands

All commands that you see in Figure 3-1 are defined in the dictionary in the package.json file under the scripts name. Command names are used as keys to launch related react-scripts. The actual code for these scripts is stored in node_modules, and you can go straight to the source on the GitHub page: `https://github.com/facebook/create-react-app/`. This would probably be a good idea if you want to get a deeper understanding; here, I would briefly go over all major commands.

npm start

npm start is a command that would start a development server, kind of similar to what we've seen in Django – runserver command. If you want to see how your application would look on a server, you can test it locally on your machine by running this command.

npm run build

Usually, you would run the npm run build command before you go into production mode and are ready to deploy your project to a server. The main purpose of this command is to make your code run faster. The principle behind the react-script build is to compile all files from the src directory into a few files. It creates a production version of your app and stores it into a build folder. You will find the build directory after you run the build command. It is a good idea to run this command as you make changes to your application.

npm test

npm test, as you might have guessed, is a testing command, I would say a lighter version of the run command. The setting for this command can be found in the package.json file. With this command, you can test the whole application or one specific file.

npm run eject

npm run eject is a command for the more experienced users to give them a full control of dependencies. npm run eject will copy or eject all modules and dependencies directly from your project. Usually, you would want to do something like that when new modules you're adding to your project would not interfere with existing modules. We will get to this command when we will be talking about React Native CLIs.

Finally, it's showtime. Launch your first React application on the developer server. Make sure that you are still inside of your project folder front_pizzavspizza and run your React developer server by using this command:

```
npm start
```

The npm start command will run the app on the local server in a browser of your choice. If it will not start automatically, navigate to http://localhost:3000 in the browser. Upon a successful app launch you should see a spinning React sign in your browser now (Figure 3-2).

Figure 3-2. *Successfully launched the React app running on localhost:3000*

First look at built-in files in the React app

In our project directory, we have three folders: node_modules, public, and src. The node_modules folder contains a gazillion of different files we need for the Node.js platform and dependencies for our React project. We do not need to touch it. This folder with all the files can be easily recreated based on dependencies listed in package.json and package-lock.json files, as you can see in Figure 3-3. If you work with a team of developers, everyone can download all these files independently, and there is no need to take node_modules to a remote git repository and share it with others. That is why any React project comes with a built-in .gitignore file to make sure you would not accidently drag node_modules files with your application to a remote directory. In Chapter 8 we will take a closer look at .gitignore.

```
package.json                    ✕

{
    "name": "front_pizzavspizza",
    "version": "0.1.0",
    "private": true,
    "dependencies": {
        "@testing-library/jest-dom": "^4.2.4",
        "@testing-library/react": "^9.5.0",
        "@testing-library/user-event": "^7.2.1",
        "react": "^16.13.1",
        "react-dom": "^16.13.1",
        "react-scripts": "3.4.1"
    },
```

Figure 3-3. *All dependencies listed in the package.json file*

public and src folders represent the main interest for us as React developers. Let's zoom in into the public folder. The public folder is a directory for static files like HTML, CSS, and images. By default, React has created an index.html file – a lending page of our application. If you open the index.html file, you would see a standard HTML structure, with head and body tags. To see how it works, you can change the text in <title> tags to

```
<title>My Pizza vs Pizza App</title>
```

After reloading the running app in the browser you can see the new page title, My Pizza vs Pizza App (Figure 3-4).

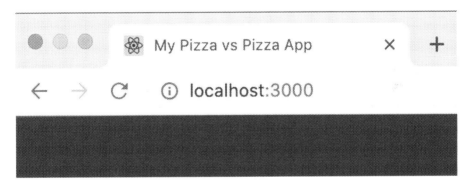

Figure 3-4. *Updated page title*

In the index.html file, you can see a standard div[3] tag with id "root". Id is a unique attribute in JavaScript, and it is used to manipulate the content of a div container. Let's locate the code for this id="root". All JavaScript code is stored in the src directory. The central front-end file in the src folder is the index.js file. This file is referencing 'root' wrapped in the ReactDom element (Figure 3-5).

---

[3]The <div> tag is used in HTML to define a section or a container for other HTML elements. Using CSS, you can determine the position of this section on a web page and other style attributes like color and size.

```
1  import React from 'react';
2  import ReactDOM from 'react-dom';
3  import './index.css';
4  import App from './App';
5  import * as serviceWorker from './serviceWorker';
6
7  ReactDOM.render(
8    <React.StrictMode>
9      <App />
10   </React.StrictMode>,
11   document.getElementById('root')
12 );
13
14 // If you want your app to work offline and load faster, you can change
15 // unregister() to register() below. Note this comes with some pitfalls.
16 // Learn more about service workers: https://bit.ly/CRA-PWA
17 serviceWorker.unregister();
18
```

Figure 3-5.   *ReactDom element in the index.js file*

At this point, I want to step back and explain how React exactly makes changes to a web page.

The virtual DOM

You probably know that any HTML web page uses the DOM (Document Object Model) as a skeleton. The DOM is a collection of elements formed as a tree structure. Although the HTML DOM is static, it can be manipulated with the help of JavaScript. Based on the JavaScript code and some incoming data, the browser would generate a DOM and render the content. Declarative programming in React allows to create UI components and render them faster by updating small parts of the HTML DOM.

Before React, the browser would rebuild the HTML DOM every time there was a change in the incoming data. That would be a relatively slow process. To speed up this process, React has its own DOM; it is called the virtual DOM. The virtual DOM is a vital part of React. The virtual tree structure consists of methods that simulate elements of a "real" HTML DOM. React will create a copy of the virtual DOM every time there is a new data coming. Since the virtual DOM is stored in RAM, this operation would be faster and more efficient. React reconciles the virtual DOM with the "real" DOM using the Diffing Algorithm and updates smallest elements in the user interface.

Responsible for this process is the ReactDOM package. You can see ReactDOM in action at the top of our project in the index.js file. The ReactDOM method render() passes the main component <App /> to the div container with id "root" in index.html (Figure 3-6).

```
index.js              ×
1   import React from 'react';
2   import ReactDOM from 'react-dom';
3   import './index.css';
4   import App from './App';
5   import * as serviceWorker from './serviceWorker';
6
7   ReactDOM.render(
8     <React.StrictMode>
9       <App />
10    </React.StrictMode>,
11    document.getElementById('root')
12  );
13
14  // If you want your app to work offline and load faster, you can change
15  // unregister() to register() below. Note this comes with some pitfalls.
16  // Learn more about service workers: https://bit.ly/CRA-PWA
17  serviceWorker.unregister();
18
```

Figure 3-6. *index.js file*

This component App is kept in the App.js file. App.js holds the JavaScript code that manipulates and renders information in index.html through index.js.

What is a component in React

Let's take a closer look at what is inside of App.js. After all imports of React itself, logo, and CSS, we can spot the function App(). This function definitely looks like JavaScript, but in the body we see a bunch of tags – something that looks like <div className="App"> and could remind you of HTML. Make no mistake, this is not HTML, but JSX (JavaScript XML). Although they kind of have similar syntax, JSX is JavaScript with some roots of Extensible Markup Language. Its main role is to design a blueprint of a component. It's about time to give the definition of a component. A React component is a small, reusable piece of code that returns a React element to be rendered on a web page.[4] When I heard it for the first time, I immediately thought of a function. A React component acts as a function that takes arguments – we call them props (stands for properties). This component manipulates data and renders the result. Like a function, you can use it over and over again. Very convenient. Large components contain smaller components, and smaller components might contain the smallest components – reminds me of the Russian folk doll, matryoshka (Figure 3-7).

Figure 3-7. *Matryoshka, Russian folk dolls*

With that being said, the function App() is a component written with JSX. JSX uses the same structure as HTML, yet many tags as you probably noticed are different. For example, in React, instead of class, you have to use className. Since "class" is taken and used in JavaScript and HTML. Similar to the class in HTML, className specifies an attribute of the div container. In my opinion, if you are a little bit familiar with HTML, you would be able to catch the main idea behind JSX easily.

The best way to understand how React component works is to move a couple of things around in App.js. You can see the <img> tag holding the React logo and the <a> link tag wrapped around "Learn React". We can

---

[4]https://reactjs.org/docs/glossary.html#components

change "Learn React" to "Pizza vs Pizza" and replace <a> tags with <h1> tags. An <h1> tag is wildly used in HTML and stands for heading and one means font size. I don't think it would be a good idea to go too deep in XML and HTML here and compare all HTML tags to JSX. You can google them or go right to the JSX source: `https://reactjs.org/docs/introducing-jsx.html`. In the <img> tag, we can replace {logo} with our own image: `https://bit.ly/book-pizza`. I have uploaded a pizza image to save you some time looking for one. In the future, you can use any image of your choice. All you have to do is to provide a valid path as src in the img tag. Finally, the text in <p></p> tags can be replaced with the description of our project – "Web App for Pizza Lovers". You can see all these changes in Figure 3-8.

```
import React from 'react';
import logo from './logo.svg';
import './App.css';

function App() {
  return (
    <div className="App">
      <header className="App-header">
        <img src="https://bit.ly/book-pizza" className="App-logo" alt="logo" />
        <p>
          Web App for Pizza Lovers
        </p>
        <h1>
          Pizza vs Pizza
        </h1>
      </header>
    </div>
  );
}

export default App;
```

Figure 3-8. *Changes in App.js*

Do not forget to save the changes and make sure your internal development server is running on `http://localhost:3000/` in the browser. Now our landing page should look like Figure 3-9.

Figure 3-9. *React project after changes in App.js*

One little thing is bothering me and probably you, the inconsistent highlighting of our code in App.js. It is difficult to separate tags from text based on the color scheme. Most of the text editors would require a plugin to correctly highlight JavaScript ES6. Babel is a tool that could be easily added to any popular text editor. You can find a step-by-step instruction on how to add Babel to the text editor of your choice here: `https://babeljs. io/docs/en/editors`. After you install Babel, your code should be properly highlighted.

Babel

The Babel tool is essential for the latest version of JavaScript. The latest features of JavaScript cannot be rendered in outdated browsers, so Babel will convert the code you write to ES5. You can see it in action on their website: `https://babeljs.io/repl`. Run your JavaScript code and see how it is being converted to an earlier version (Figure 3-10).

```
1 var word = () => console.log("Hello World!");
```

```
1 var word = function () {
2   return console.log("Hello World!");
3 };
```

Figure 3-10. *Babel transpiles the latest version of JavaScript down to ES5*

Anatomy of a React Component

Let's gather all pieces together and see how we can use React to render JSON data, similar to what our Django app serves. We will build a component from scratch. In our code directory src, we create a new folder for all our components and name it pizzerias. Inside that folder, we create a new component saved as a file pizzeriaslist.js like in Figure 3-11.

Figure 3-11. *Creating the new folder pizzerias and a file for the new React component – pizzeriaslist.js*

Before we start with the component itself, we need some dummy data to test our component. As you recall, our back-end solution would be serving the API in JSON format. To mimic API data, we need to create another file in our pizzerias folder, dummydata.json. The Dummydata file would hold similar information to our List View API. I just created three dummy objects with "id", "pizzeria", and "city" keys. Feel free to use your own data and pizzerias names (Figure 3-12).

```
1   [
2       {
3           "id":1,
4           "pizzeria": "The Empire pizza",
5           "city": "New York"
6       },
7       {
8           "id":2,
9           "pizzeria": "Urbs in horto pizza",
10          "city": "Chicago"
11      },
12      {
13          "id":3,
14          "pizzeria": "Hollywood pizza",
15          "city": "Los Angeles"
16      }
17  ]
18
```

Figure 3-12. *Dummy data for our list component*

In our component pizzeriaslist.js file, we need to import React itself.

```
import React from 'react';
```

As I have mentioned before, a component could be done as a class or a function. I would like to start with the class, and later I would show you a different approach. To define a component as a class, we need to extend the built-in component by importing it as a module. Please amend the first line in pizzeriaslist.js to

```
import React, { Component } from 'react';
```

Along with that, we would need to import our dummy data from dummydata.json.

```
import DummyData from './dummydata.json';
```

After the Component is imported into the namespace, we can reference it and create our own component, as a class, PizzaList, like this:

```
class PizzaList extends Component {
                    //Code

}
```

All React components must have a render() method responsible for the seeable result. The render() method would always be called in a component. Other methods' execution would be up to us. To rephrase it, a React component designed as a class must have at least a render() method. A render method returns a React element wrapped as JSX. We will need to add return() to the render() method of our component. To see the component and render() method in action, we would return the "pizza name goes here" phrase.

```
class PizzaList extends Component{
        render(){
                return(
                    <h6>Pizza Name Goes Here</h6>
                )
            }
        }
```

The PizzaList component should be exported out of the file to be accessible.

```
export default PizzaList;
```

At the end our pizzeriaslist.js file should look like Figure 3-13.

```
pizzeriaslist.js        ×
 1   import React, { Component } from 'react';
 2   import DummyData from './dummydata.json';
 3   |
 4   class PizzaList extends Component{
 5       render(){
 6           return(
 7                       <h6>Pizza Name Goes Here</h6>
 8                   )
 9       }
10   }
11   export default PizzaList;
```

Figure 3-13. *Simple React component saved as pizzeriaslist.js*

Our custom component PizzaList needs to be imported into the main App component. The Import statement inside of the App.js file should be wrapped as JSX within tags.

```
import PizzaList from'./pizzerias/pizzeriaslist'
```

```
<PizzaList/>
```

You have probably noticed that JSX compared to HTML does not need both opening and closing tags. Most of the time, JSX combines opening and closing tags as one with a forward slash as you can see in Figure 3-14.

```
     App.js            ×
 1   import React from 'react';
 2   import logo from './logo.svg';
 3   import PizzaList from './pizzerias/pizzeriaslist'
 4   import './App.css';
 5
 6   function App() {
 7     return (
 8       <div className="App">
 9         <header className="App-header">
10           <img src="https://bit.ly/book-pizza" className="App-logo" alt="logo" />
11           <p>
12             Web App for Pizza Lovers
13           </p>
14           <h1>
15             Pizza vs Pizza
16           </h1>
17           <PizzaList/>
18         </header>
19       </div>
20     );
21   }
22
23   export default App;
24   |
```

Figure 3-14. *Import the PizzaList component to the App.js file and return it as JSX*

Make sure everything is saved and your local server is running. Your updated app should look like the one in Figure 3-15 if you open the localhost:3000 URL in the browser. If you get an error message that you think is incorrect, try to reboot the app in the terminal. With Ctrl+C, exit the server mode and restart the app with the command npm start.

Figure 3-15. *"Pizza Name Goes Here" message is rendered on our app landing page*

If we want to render our made-up pizzeria names from the dummydata.json file, we would need to iterate through an array containing key/value pairs.

For iteration, we would need to use the JavaScript function map(). A function map implemented in many programming languages, for example, map(), is one of the built-in functions in Python, and works like a definite loop. If you are not familiar with this function or need to refresh the syntax, you can find more information and examples here: `https://developer.mozilla.org/en-US/docs/Web/JavaScript/Reference/Global_Objects/Array/map`.

We can replace "Pizza Name Goes Here" with "pizzeria" and "city" – the values from our DummyData in the PizzaList component. One thing you have to keep in mind is that the return() method in the component is able to return only one object. If you need to return many elements, then you would need to wrap them in <div> </div> tags as one container.

Note   The return() method in a component can render only one element. If you need a component to render many elements, wrap them in a single div container.

Our loop would look like this:

```
{DummyData.map( p =>
<h4>{p.pizzeria} - {p.city}</h4>
)}
```

Dummy data comes from the dummydata.json file in the form of an array. We iterate through this sequential structure, grabbing each object value by keys – pizzeria and city. The object itself is being represented with a variable name p (Figure 3-16).

```
pizzeriaslist.js          ×
1    import React, { Component } from 'react';
2    import DummyData from './dummydata.json';
3
4    class PizzaList extends Component{
5        render(){
6            return(
7                <div>
8                    {DummyData.map( p =>
9                        <h4>{p.pizzeria} - {p.city}</h4>
10                       )
11                   }
12               </div>
13           )
14       }
15   }
16   export default PizzaList;
```

Figure 3-16. *Using map() to iterate through the DummyData array to fetch values from each object*

Consequently, fetched values, pizzeria and city, should be rendered on our lending page (Figure 3-17).

Figure 3-17. *Rendering data from JSON into our app*

Props

Props are an essential part of React. With the help of Props, you can pass inputs into components. Props stands for properties and can contain a single value or a set of values.

In the PizzaList component, we render a set of values. We can break that set down into smaller elements. Breaking your components into smallest ones would be considered to be the best practice.

In our pizzerias folder, let's create a new file for a detail component. Let's name it pizzeriadetail.js (Figure 3-18).

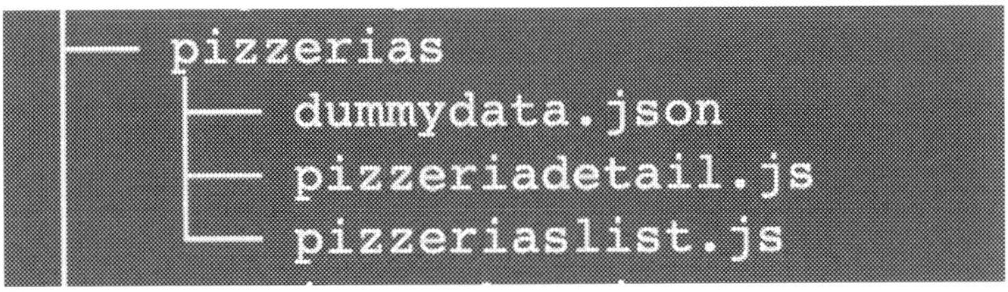

```
├── pizzerias
│       ├── dummydata.json
│       ├── pizzeriadetail.js
│       └── pizzeriaslist.js
```

Figure 3-18. *Create a new file, pizzeriadetail.js, to hold the detail component*

The idea is to pass information into the component PizzaDetail. The PizzaDetail component would be a close copy of the PizzaList component with a few changes and would render details of each object from DummyData. At the beginning of pizzeriadetail.js, import React and Component. On the bottom of the same file, export the PizzaDetail component. PizzaDetail would extend the React Component (Figure 3-19).

Don't forget to package all details that you want to be rendered by the PizzaDetail component as one <div> container. Again, return() of the render method can return one element only. My PizzaDetail will return the same details as before. However, this time, I'll add an "id" (Figure 3-19).

```
<div>
    <h4>{p.id}</h4>
    <h4>{p.pizzeria}</h4>
    <h4>{p.city}</h4>
</div>
```

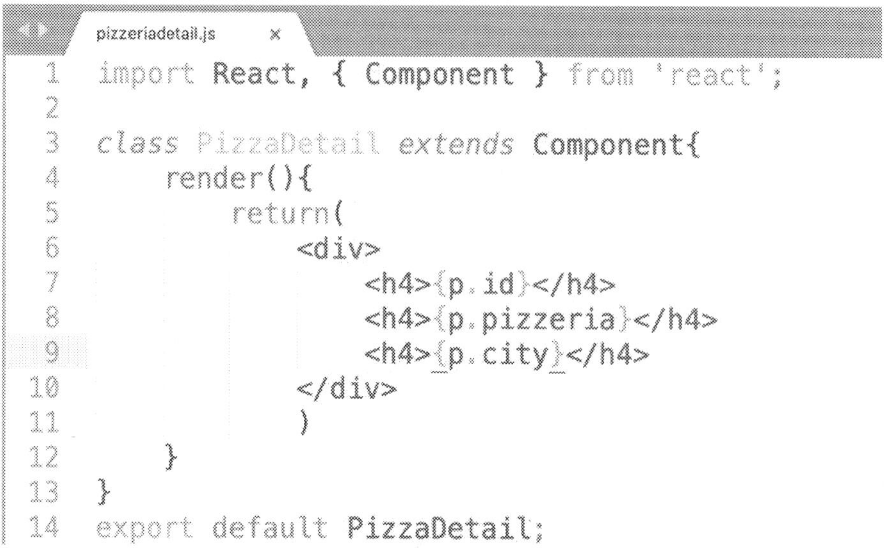

```
     pizzeriadetail.js    ×
1    import React, { Component } from 'react';
2
3    class PizzaDetail extends Component{
4        render(){
5            return(
6                <div>
7                    <h4>{p.id}</h4>
8                    <h4>{p.pizzeria}</h4>
9                    <h4>{p.city}</h4>
10               </div>
11               )
12       }
13   }
14   export default PizzaDetail;
```

Figure 3-19. *New PizzaDetail component*

You might ask me where all data would be coming from. This is where Props would come into play. We will pass the data as Props into the PizzaDetail component. As always, we would need to start with imports and bring the subcomponent into pizzeriaslist.js.

```
import PizzaDetail from './pizzeriadetail';
```

While we are working on the pizzeriaslist.js file, let's make some changes to our return() method. We need the map() function to return the PizzaDetail component and pass values in it. To keep our code clear and not to make too many changes to our PizzaDetail component, we would replace our variable name p with item. We would use p as a keyword argument to pass each item as props (Figure 3-20).

```
<div>
    {DummyData.map( item => {
    return <PizzaDetail p ={item} />
       })
    }
</div>
```

```
pizzeriaslist.js        ×
1   import React, { Component } from 'react';
2   import DummyData from './dummydata.json';
3   import PizzaDetail from './pizzeriadetail';
4
5   class PizzaList extends Component{
6       render(){
7           return(
8               <div>
9                   {DummyData.map( item => {
10                  return <PizzaDetail p = {item}/>
11
12                      })
13                  }
14              </div> |
15              )
16          }
17      }
18  export default PizzaList;
```

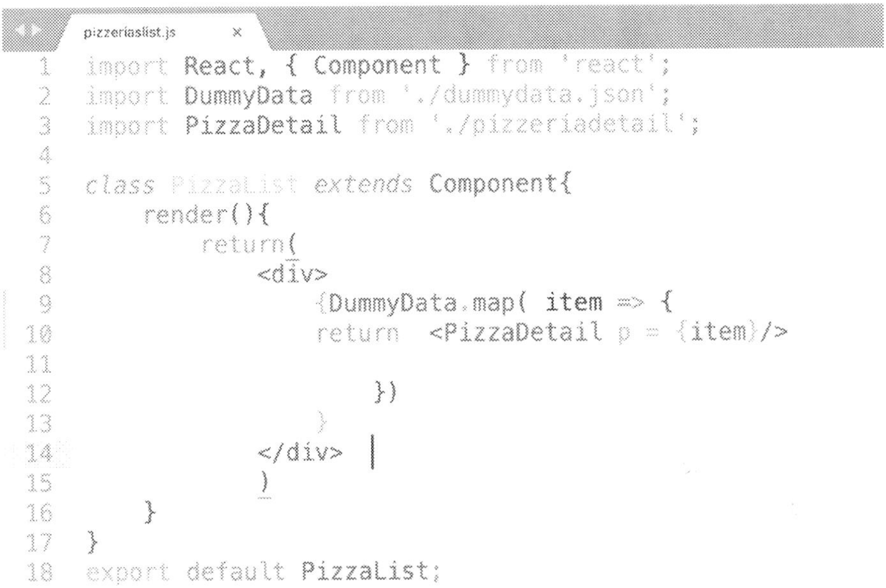

Figure 3-20. *The final version of the PizzaList component after we amended the function map with the PizzaDetail component and Props*

Finally, add props to our PizzaDetail component. Within the component itself, define the constant variable p as props (Figure 3-21).

```
const p = this.props.p
```

```
1  import React, { Component } from 'react';
2
3  class PizzaDetail extends Component{
4      render(){
5      const p = this.props.p
6          return(
7              <div>
8                  <h4>{p.id}</h4>
9                  <h4>{p.pizzeria}</h4>
10                 <h4>{p.city}</h4>
11             </div>
12             )
13      }
14  }
15  export default PizzaDetail;
```

Figure 3-21. *The final version of the PizzaDetail component receiving Props from PizzaList*

You can test the code we just wrote by reloading our lending page in the browser. The rendered information has not really changed except this time we have an id for each item (Figure 3-22). Later, we will use the id of each element as a key.

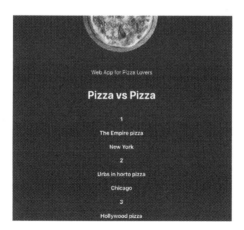

Figure 3-22. *Our lending page after we used Props to pass values from the PizzaList to PizzaDetail component*

State

If at some point of your life you would be interviewing for a junior React developer position, be prepared to answer the question "What's the difference between state and props in React?" Believe me, this question always pops up during the technical job interview.

In a nutshell, props and State are variables; the main difference is that State is initialized and managed by a component itself. I would compare State to an __init__ method in a Python object, where you define the main attributes of the object.

Props on the other hand are like arguments that we pass from one component to the other one. For example, we pass props from a parent component to a child component, pretty much how we did it in the previous example. Compared to State, props should never be modified in the child component. If you need to change something within a component, you should do it through State. There will be many examples of that in the coming chapters.

In the next chapter, we will connect our front-end intermediate React app with the back-end portion of our Pizza vs. Pizza project. I'll show you how to replace a dummy JSON with the actual data from the database. We will learn how to make API calls from a front-end React app.

CHAPTER 4

Assembling pieces of our app

In previous chapters, we have started the Django project and React project, representing back-end and front-end parts of our mobile application. In this chapter, I will explain how to attach a user interface to our engine and structure our MVC model. React will help us to gather all pieces together and make our CRUD more versatile and user-friendly. The purpose of this chapter is not to build a desktop version of our app but rather to show you React in action and prepare you for React Native. We are not going to spend a lot of time on styling bells and whistles because our ultimate goal is a mobile app. Nonetheless, if you decide to continue with a desktop version, this chapter would provide you with a solid foundation for many additional React features.

Cross-origin resource sharing

After we have launched the React project and run it on localhost:3000 and the Django project runs on the 8000 server, you are probably asking yourself a question of how we would connect these two together. The general idea is to call APIs and to render data from the back-end with React. However, Django would not accept an outside request from an unknown source. Usually, when you deploy your projects to a production

© Art Yudin 2020
A. Yudin, *Building Versatile Mobile Apps with Python and REST*,
https://doi.org/10.1007/978-1-4842-6333-4_4

server, you would replace temporary developer server URLs with domain names. Any website by default restricts access to its resources from other domains. To allow our React application to fetch URLs from the Django project, we would need to install and enable CORS (cross-origin resource sharing). There is a Django extension, django-cors-headers, that adds CORS headers to responses[1] with very flexible settings. We will go through the whole process right now. If you would like to learn more about this package and see other available options, go right to the source: `https://pypi.org/project/django-cors-headers/`.

Anytime you would want to add a library to your Django project, make sure your virtual environment is engaged. Also, do not forget to append the package name and version to the requirements.txt file. In your pizzavspizza directory, if you use Mac, run the `source` command to engage the virtual environment.

`source venv/bin/activate`

For Windows, activate virtualenv in the Scripts directory, like this:

`\pizzavspizza\venv\Scripts\activate`

If your virtual environment is on, you can move to the installation of django-cors-headers with the pip command.

`pip install django-cors-headers`

django-cors-headers is an app, and we need to add 'corsheaders' to INSTALLED_APPS in the Django settings.py file (Figure 4-1).

---

[1]`https://pypi.org/project/django-cors-headers/`

```
32
33   INSTALLED_APPS = [
34       'django.contrib.admin',
35       'django.contrib.auth',
36       'django.contrib.contenttypes',
37       'django.contrib.sessions',
38       'django.contrib.messages',
39       'django.contrib.staticfiles',
40       'corsheaders',
41       'rest_framework',
42       'stores',
43   ]
44
```

Figure 4-1. *Add 'corsheaders' to the INSTALLED_APPS list in the settings.py file*

Also, we need to add 'corsheaders.middleware.CorsMiddleware' and 'django.middleware.common.CommonMiddleware' to the MIDDLEWARE list in the same settings.py file. Try to place them at the beginning of the list (Figure 4-2).

```
45   MIDDLEWARE = [
46       'corsheaders.middleware.CorsMiddleware',
47       'django.middleware.common.CommonMiddleware',
48       'django.middleware.security.SecurityMiddleware',
49       'django.contrib.sessions.middleware.SessionMiddleware',
50       'django.middleware.csrf.CsrfViewMiddleware',
51       'django.contrib.auth.middleware.AuthenticationMiddleware',
52       'django.contrib.messages.middleware.MessageMiddleware',
53       'django.middleware.clickjacking.XFrameOptionsMiddleware',
54   ]
55
```

Figure 4-2. *Put corsheaders.middleware.CorsMiddleware on top of the MIDDLEWARE list in the settings.py file*

The last step in the process of setting up and configuring CORS for our Django project would be to add the CORS_ORIGIN_ALLOW_ALL or CORS_ORIGIN_WHITELIST option. CORS_ORIGIN_ALLOW_ALL when set to True would allow all sites to access our APIs. This is totally normal when you are in the development mode. If you want to be specific and indicate all domains that would have the permission to grab data from your site, then you would need to assign them as a list to CORS_ORIGIN_WHITELIST. The latter option would be preferable for the production mode. For simplicity, we will set CORS_ORIGIN_ALLOW_ALL = True (Figure 4-3).

```
33  INSTALLED_APPS = [
34      'django.contrib.admin',
35      'django.contrib.auth',
36      'django.contrib.contenttypes',
37      'django.contrib.sessions',
38      'django.contrib.messages',
39      'django.contrib.staticfiles',
40      'corsheaders',
41      'rest_framework',
42      'stores',
43  ]
44
45  MIDDLEWARE = [
46      'corsheaders.middleware.CorsMiddleware',
47      'django.middleware.common.CommonMiddleware',
48      'django.middleware.security.SecurityMiddleware',
49      'django.contrib.sessions.middleware.SessionMiddleware',
50      'django.middleware.csrf.CsrfViewMiddleware',
51      'django.contrib.auth.middleware.AuthenticationMiddleware',
52      'django.contrib.messages.middleware.MessageMiddleware',
53      'django.middleware.clickjacking.XFrameOptionsMiddleware',
54  ]
55
56  CORS_ORIGIN_ALLOW_ALL = True
57
```

Figure 4-3. *CORS configurations in settings.py*

Fetch API with Axios

As you remember in the previous chapter, we went over a React component structure and coded a PizzaList component that would read dummy JSON. It is time to replace dummy data with actual records from our database.

Make sure both of your projects are running on local servers. Just to remind you, start Django with the command runserver, and you should see it in the browser at http://127.0.0.1:8000. Sometimes, for simplicity's sake, developers would replace the 127.0.0.1 part with a localhost, and the final IP would look like localhost:8000.

```
python manage.py runserver
```

React starts with the command npm start, and it will be running in another browser window if you navigate to localhost:3000.

```
npm start
```

At the moment, our PizzaList component has just one method render() and loops through DummyData imported from a file. We need to replace DummyData with the actual data. The best place to call an API in the React component would be the componentDidMount() method. Before we add this method to our component, let me briefly explain how it works.

Lifecycle of a component

At the moment, our PizzaList component has just one method render(). As I have mentioned before, render() is essential to a component. When you are rendering a component, React is inserting, or the right word would be mounting, this element into the DOM. Later, this component might be updated with new data or completely unmounted from the DOM, or simply saying, deleted. This process is called the lifecycle of a component (Figure 4-4). You can draw an analogy with an actor on the stage. An actor comes on the stage and performs, like a component becomes a part of the DOM and renders something. If the audience liked the performance, an actor could present another gig, pretty much like the same component being updated with new data. Finally, when the show is over, an actor leaves the stage, and we unmount a component for the time being.

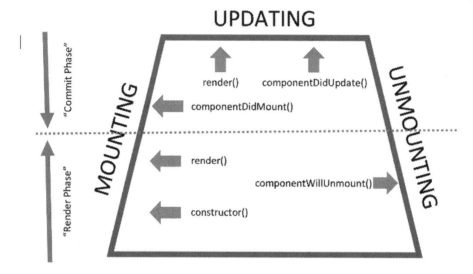

Figure 4-4. *Lifecycle of a component*

If we split the mounting process into steps, we would see that first the constructor() method comes into play, then render(), and lastly componentDidMount(). So far, we have mostly used the render() method. In the next chapter, we will see a practical application of constructor() and componentDidMount() methods. The constructor method is used for two things, initializing an object and handling events. All attributes of an object should be in place before the render() method adds a component to the DOM. Consequently, componentDidMount() fired after a component was added to the DOM. The main idea behind componentDidMount() is to add supplementary statements to a component. This method would be ideal to make an API call within a component.

Although technically the componentDidMount() method is called after the component has been rendered, it would be a good idea to place it above the render method. That is exactly where we will define it in the PizzaList component. Inside componentDidMount(), we will call our API with the help of the JavaScript library Axios. There are two options on how you can call an API in React: Axios or method fetch. Both of them do the same thing – send a request to a server. I encourage you to try both options and see what would work for you. Fetch is a JavaScript method, and you do not have to install it. I have an example of the fetch method in footnotes in case you would want to give it a try.[2] Here, I will use Axios. The Axios syntax is simpler, besides we would need it for the React Native part.

To start with Axios, we would need to install it with the npm command.

```
npm install axios
```

After Axios is installed, we can import it in our pizzeriaslist.js file.

```
import axios from 'axios'
```

The next step is to implement our first API call in componentDidMount. To send a GET request and fetch data from our database, we would use the axios.get method. The syntax is pretty simple, and you can find all available options for all HTTP requests here: www.npmjs.com/package/axios. The method axios.get would return a response, and for now we just print this data with console.log().

```
componentDidMount(){
    axios.get("http://127.0.0.1:8000/")
    .then((response) => {
    console.log(response)
    })
```

---

[2]The documentation for JavaScript fetch() can be found at the source US/docs/Web/API/Fetch_API/Using_Fetch. This is an example of how to call an API with Fetch():

```
fetch("http://127.0.0.1:8000/")

.then(response => response.json())

.then(data => console.log(data));
```

```
.catch(function (error) {
    console.log(error);
 })
}
```

You can find incoming data from the API in the browser. Make sure your local server is running on the localhost:3000 port. Right click of your mouse should get the developer tools menu with the inspect option (I am using Chrome browser). Choose inspect option and make sure the Console menu is chosen to see the JavaScript code in action. There might be a few warnings. Disregard them for now, and look for Array (3). You'll find Array (3) next to the pizzeriaslist.js:8 line of code. Click this little arrow to expand the Array. The Array holds all data that came from our Django project (Figure 4-5) and structurally looks like JSON.

```
                                          pizzeriaslist.js:8
▼Array(3)
  ▶ 0: {id: 1, pizzeria_name: "Bravo Pizza", city: "New York", zip_code: 10…
  ▶ 1: {id: 2, pizzeria_name: "Artichoke Basille's Pizza", city: "New York"…
  ▶ 2: {id: 3, pizzeria_name: "Pizzeria Uno", city: "Chicago", zip_code: 60…
    length: 3
  ▶ __proto__: Array(0)
```

Figure 4-5. *Data printed by console.log()*

OK, the API call went through just fine, and we can set up incoming data as property value of the PizzaList component by adding it to State.

In the PizzaList component, initialize State and define pizzeriasData as an empty array like this:

```
state = {
    pizzeriasData:[]
    }
```

After State is defined, we need to pass our data into it. Replace console.log command with the setState method.

```
this.setState({pizzeriasData: response.data})
```

The attribute data will get us JSON from the response. The last but not least change should be done to the render method in the PizzaList component. We need to replace DummyData in our render method with the actual data.

```
this.state.pizzeriasData
```

Replace the dummy data with pizzeriasData from state:

```
render(){
 return(
  <div>
    {this.state.pizzeriasData.map( item => {
        return <h3>{item.pizzeria_name},{item.city}</h3>
        })
    }
  </div>
)}
```

Item in this case is a variable name. pizzeria_name and city are field names from our database. Do not forget to remove DummyData import from your file. Ultimately, your pizzeriaslist.js file should look like the one in Figure 4-6.

```
pizzeriaslist.js        ×
1   import React, { Component } from 'react';
2   import PizzaDetail from './pizzeriadetail';
3   import axios from 'axios'
4
5   class PizzaList extends Component{
6
7       state = {
8           pizzeriasData:[],
9       }
10
11
12      componentDidMount(){
13          axios.get("http://127.0.0.1:8000/")
14          .then((response) => {
15              this.setState({pizzeriasData: response.data})
16          })
17          .catch(function (error) {
18              console.log(error);
19          })
20      }
21
22      render(){
23          return(
24              <div>
25                  {this.state.pizzeriasData.map( item => {
26                  return  <h3>{item.pizzeria_name}, {item.city}</h3>
27                  })}
28
29              </div>
30              )
31      }
32  }
33  export default PizzaList;
```

Figure 4-6. *PizzaList component in pizzeriaslist.js after we have
replaced dummy data with the API*

Before we get to our PizzaDetail component, let's briefly take a look at
warnings we got while inspecting our data in the browser. Yellow ones are
just warnings that could be easily fixed. The warning " 'logo' is defined but
never used" could be fixed if you remove the line

```
import logo from './logo.svg';
```

from the App.js file. We are not using the default image anyway. Red
warnings are more weighty than yellow ones. The error message

"Download error or resource isn't a valid image" means that the old React image can't be found anymore. We can delete this link, since we are not using it anymore.

```
<link rel="manifest" href="%PUBLIC_URL%/manifest.json"/>
```

The warning "Each child in a list should have a unique "key" prop." is worth mentioning here because keys are very important in React (Figure 4-7).

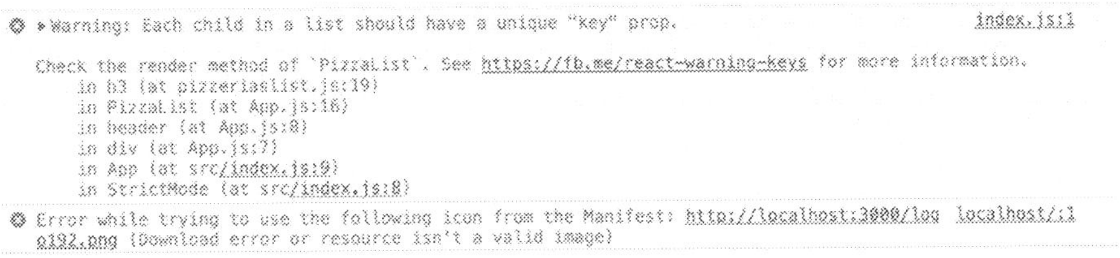

Figure 4-7. *Warning messages from the browser console*

React compares virtual DOM with "actual" HTML DOM and updates changes. It would be faster to update one small element if information has changed than the whole div container holding the whole set of data. In our case, React would update each pizzeria separately, based on the key, rather than all of them. Helping React with the right object to update, we would need to add a unique and static id from our database directly to the <h3> tag. If you take a closer look at each object we are receiving from the API in Figure 4-5, every pizzeria starts with "id". If you can't find one, make sure you have added the "id" field to serializers in the Django project. This "id" could be used as a key in the React app. Precisely, we should add the key to line 26 (Figure 4-6) in the pizerriaslist.js file as the warning message is suggesting.

```
render(){
  return(
    <div>
        {this.state.pizzeriasData.map(item => {
```

```
        return <h3 key={item.id} >{item.pizzeria_name},
        {item.city}</h3>
})}
    </div>
)}
```

Afterward, the key warning should be gone, and each pizzeria record should be assigned a key with an original id. You still might see a yellow warning that PizzaDetail is defined but never used. That is OK for now.

Detail view

Now is the time to call the detail API and set the detail view of our app. Before we get to the front-end part, we need to review `PizzeriaListSerializer` in the serializers.py file in our Django project.

Django REST offers a neat solution to build custom methods and bind them to API data as an extra field in a serializer. This mechanism allows you to perform any manipulation on an object and return the result as an attribute of the object. We will start with a simple example and create a method to return an absolute URL of the detail view for our Pizzeria model. The URL for a `PizzeriaRetrieveAPIView` has two parts, a root URL and an id of an object. Despite the fact that you can just concatenate the object's id to a root URL, an absolute URL would be a preferred solution. An absolute URL comes as an attribute from the object itself; there would never be any mismatch.

The composition of the SerializerMethodField requires two things: you need to declare the name of the field and define a method with a prefix get_ to the field name.

In the present case, we need to declare an absolute URL field within PizzeriaListSerializer like this:

```
absolute_url = serializers.SerializerMethodField()
```

Do not forget to include absolute_url in the serializer itself as a field, line 16 (Figure 4-8). Then define and compose a get_absolute_url method:

```
def get_absolute_url(self, obj):
    return reverse('pizzeria_detail', args=(obj.pk,))
```

Our custom method would take the obj argument referring to the Pizzeria instance itself and return the `PizzeriaRetrieveAPIView` URL pattern. This would be possible with the help of reverse calling URL with a `'pizzeria_detail'` label defined in the URL dispatcher urls.py file.

Lastly, we would need to import reverse from the Django REST framework.

```
from rest_framework.reverse import reverse
```

The updated `PizzeriaListSerializer` would look like the one in Figure 4-8.

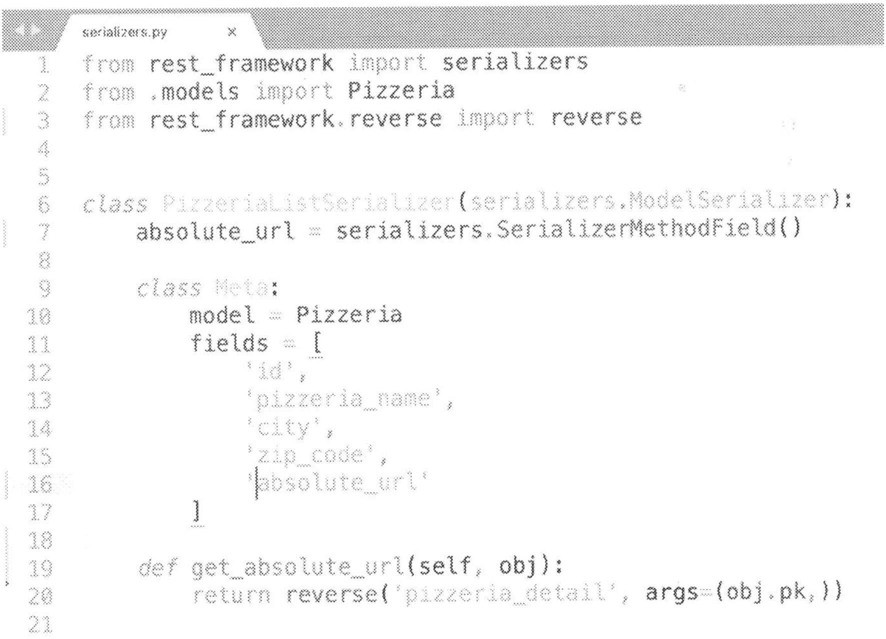

Figure 4-8. Method get_absolute_url in PizzeriaListSerializer

After we have added a custom field to our `PizzeriaListSerializer`, we would be able to see `absolute_url` in our JSON data. Our ultimate goal here is to call the `absolute_url` API by clicking the Pizzeria name from our list view. Then we will pass Pizzeria details to the PizzaDetail component. To render PizzaDetail on a click and call the absolute_url, we would need to compose two new methods in the pizzeriaslist.js file. You might ask why we would need two separate methods for a simple job. By all means, you can squeeze everything into one method, but it would be a better practice to make each method responsible for one single task, like fetching an API.

Our API call method would be named getPizzaDetail and would accept a Pizzeria instance as an argument. Using the Axios get method, we would fetch information and set that data as a PizzaList component attribute.

```
getPizzaDetail(item){
axios.get("http://127.0.0.1:8000".concat(item.absolute_url))
        .then((response) => {
            this.setState({pizzeria: response.data})
        })
        .catch(function (error) {
            console.log(error);
        });
}
```

I hope everything in the getPizzaDetail method makes sense to you by now. We pass the Pizzeria instance into the getPizzaDetail method. Item represents the instance, and we can access its attribute absolute_url. To fetch all the details of pizerria, we call the axios.get method. If the API call is successful, then we can store the received response as "pizzeria" in State.

The next method, showPizzeriaDetails, would invoke the getPizzaDetail method and change the special attribute showComponent to true at the moment a user clicks a particular Pizzeria. In our State, we would initially define it as false. That would ensure the PizzaDetail component would not be revealed ahead of time.

```
showPizzeriaDetails(item){
    this.getPizzaDetail(item);
    this.setState({ showComponent: true });
  }
```

As our State is getting more laborious, we need to use the constructor method. The constructor method initializes State and binds methods. The constructor method would be called before the component is mounted.

```
constructor(props) {
    super(props);
    this.state = {
      pizzeriasData: [],
      pizzeria: " ",
      showComponent: false,
    };
    this.getPizzaDetail=this.getPizzaDetail.bind(this);
    this.showPizzeriaDetails=this.showPizzeriaDetails.
    bind(this);
  }
```

Finally, we would need to invoke the showPizzeriaDetails method with the event handler onClick in the render() method and pass the clicked object as an argument. We place the PizzaDetail component into the render() method and pass pizzeria details as props. The conditional operator "?" would make sure that PizzaDetail is called only if the showComponent value was changed to true.

```
render() {
    return (
      <div>
        {this.state.pizzeriasData.map((item) => {
          return (
            <h3 key={item.id} onClick={() => this.
            showPizzeriaDetails(item)}>
              {item.pizzeria_name}, {item.city}
            </h3>
          );
        })}

        {this.state.showComponent ? (
          <PizzaDetail pizzariaDetail={this.state.pizzeria} />
        ) : null}
      </div>
    );
  }
```

Ahead of moving to the PizzaDetail component, you could compare your code to the PizzaList component (Figure 4-9).

```
pizzeriaslist.js          ×
1   import React, { Component } from "react";
2   import PizzaDetail from "./pizzeriadetail";
3   import axios from "axios";
4
5   class PizzaList extends Component {
6     constructor(props) {
7       super(props);
8       this.state = {
9         pizzeriasData: [],
10        pizzeria: " ",
11        showComponent: false,
12      };
13      this.getPizzaDetail = this.getPizzaDetail.bind(this);
14      this.showPizzeriaDetails = this.showPizzeriaDetails.bind(this);
15    }
16
17    getPizzaDetail(item) {
18      axios
19        .get("http://127.0.0.1:8080".concat(item.absolute_url))
20        .then((response) => {
21          this.setState({ pizzeria: response.data });
22        })
23        .catch(function (error) {
24          console.log(error);
25        });
26    }
27
28    showPizzeriaDetails(item){
29      this.getPizzaDetail(item);
30      this.setState({ showComponent: true });
31    }
32
33    componentDidMount() {
34      axios
35        .get("http://127.0.0.1:8080/")
36        .then((response) => {
37          this.setState({ pizzeriasData: response.data });
38        })
39        .catch(function (error) {
40          console.log(error);
41        });
42    }
43
44    render() {
45      return (
46        <div>
47          {this.state.pizzeriasData.map((item) => {
48            return (
49              <h3 key={item.id} onClick={() => this.showPizzeriaDetails(item)}>
50                {item.pizzeria_name}, {item.city}
51              </h3>
52            );
53          })}
54
55          {this.state.showComponent ? (
56            <PizzaDetail pizzeriaDetail={this.state.pizzeria} />
57          ) : null}
58        </div>
59      );
60    }
61  }
62  export de
```

Figure 4-9. *PizzaList component with an option to invoke the showPizzeriaDetails method on click*

109

Earlier, in the previous chapter, we have created the pizzeriadetail.js file. It is the time to alter the PizzaDetail component and render all attributes of a pizzeria coming through the fields of PizzeriaDetailSerializer.

Keep in mind that at the moment, I will not be styling the appearance of our app. Again, in this chapter we are learning the React principles. We will take care of the appearance when we start building our mobile app. Now I want to concentrate on barebones of CRUD. The only style I'll add would be to differentiate PizzaDetail from the PizzaList component.

At the beginning we need to assign our props coming from PizzaList component to a variable obj in the render() method. As a matter of fact, we will be replacing old dummy props with the actual data.

```
const obj = this.props.pizzariaDetail;
```

Using a minimum of style, I will add yellow border and change the color of the text to yellow in our <div> container.

```
<div style={{ color: "yellow", border: "1px solid yellow" }}>
```

With the help of a few <h4>, <h5>, and <h6> tags, I will arrange detail information from obj in the following order as you can see in Figure 4-10. The old variable p would be replaced with obj. Also, replace the old names with the actual attributes coming from our model (Figure 4-10).

```
pizzeriadetail.js    ×
1   import React, { Component } from "react";
2
3   class PizzaDetail extends Component {
4     render() {
5       const obj = this.props.pizzariaDetail;
6       return (
7         <div style={{ color: "yellow", border: "1px solid yellow" }}>
8           <h4>{obj.pizzeria_name}</h4>
9           <h5>
10            Address: {obj.street} {obj.city} {obj.state} {obj.zip_code}
11          </h5>
12          <h6>Phone: {obj.phone_number}</h6>
13          <p>{obj.description}</p>
14        </div>
15      );
16    }
17  }
18  export default PizzaDetail;
19
```

Figure 4-10. *PizzaDetail component, data from PizzeriaDetailSerializer comes from obj and structured with JSX*

If all your local servers are running, you can open our front-end part in the browser and test the detail component by clicking the pizzeria name from the list. As a result, you should see a box with yellow text rendering detail information (Figure 4-11).

111

Figure 4-11. Front-end view of our app rendering detail information

Create view

The create part of CRUD in my opinion is the most exciting one. We can implement it with the JSX React form and Axios post method.

We will define the component PizzaForm in a new file pizzeriaform.js in our folder pizzerias. The same directory where all our components are kept. Create the pizzeriaform.js file (Figure 4-12). The steps to compose the form component would be the following: in the render method of the form component, define inputs for all fields we want the user to fill in, bundle incoming data with handle method, and set State. Then call PizzeriaCreateAPIView with axios.get method and send data.

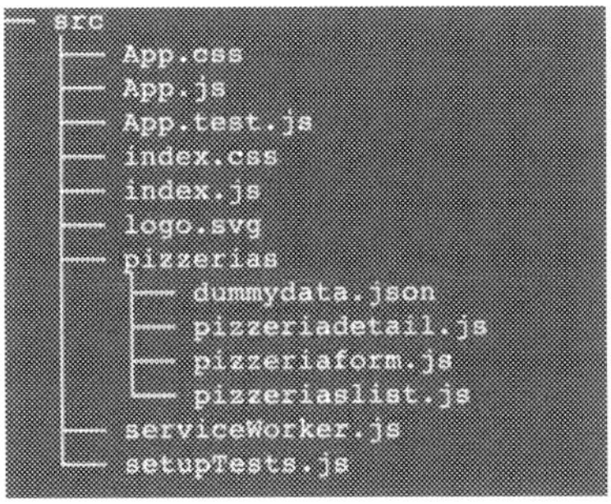

Figure 4-12. Newly created pizzeriaform.js for the PizzaForm component

In pizzeriaform.js, import React and Axios.

```
import React, { Component } from "react";
import axios from "axios";
```

We need to define the PizzaForm component.

```
class PizzaForm extends React.Component {
    //Code
}
export default PizzaForm;
```

Before we get to the coding part, I would like to go over the structure we need to put in place in the PizzaForm component. As you remember, any component would require a render() method; this is where we would place the JSX <Form> with all input fields. Most of the web forms use a submit button. Our case would not be an exception, and we would bind one to our form.

Besides the submit button and input fields, we would need to set up two event handler methods. The handleSubmit method would be triggered on submit and the handleChange method on input. I'll start with handleChange() that would be triggered on incoming data and take event as an argument. Moreover, handleChange method would set entered data as State. The second method, handleSubmit(), would call axios.post() and send the data. This method would be triggered by the built-in onSubmit handler in the form. Adding "handle" designation to a method name is conventional in React.

```
handleChange(event) {
    //Code
  }
  handleSubmit(event) {
    event.preventDefault();
  }
  render() {
    const { pizzeria_name } = this.state;
    return (
      <form onSubmit={this.handleSubmit}>
        <div>
          <input
            type="text"
            name="pizzeria_name"
            value={pizzeria_name}
            onChange={this.handleChange}
          />
        </div>

        <input type="submit" value="Submit" />
      </form>
    );
  }
```

We need to define pizzeria_name in the render() method and would use it as "name" key and value equivalent. The built-in onChange event handler would be bind to the handleChange method. Best practice would be to include event.preventDefault() into handleSubmit method to prevent accidental clicks.

Inside the constructor method, we would define the attributes. Make sure the name of an attribute in State would match the value of the "name" key in the input. Also, we would need to bind our custom methods to the component in the constructor.

```
constructor(props) {
    super(props);
    this.state = {
      pizzeria_name: " ",
    };
    this.handleChange = this.handleChange.bind(this);
    this.handleSubmit = this.handleSubmit.bind(this);
  }
```

Immediately upon rendering form in the browser, pizzeria_name is an empty string. That's what we have set as a default value in the constructor. As soon as we receive a value from the user, we would command setState to reassign pizzeria_name to incoming text in the handleChange method.

```
handleChange(event) {
this.setState({[event.target.name]:event.target.value});
  }
```

This setup would help us to grab values and assign them to the right attributes with the help of "name" and value keys from input form.[3] event. target.name gives us the option to bundle multiple inputs from our form. The PizzaForm component should be imported into pizzeriaslist.js and

---

[3]https://reactjs.org/docs/forms.html

added to the PizzaList component. Make sure <PizzaForm/> would go into the main <div> container the render() method returns.

```
<div>
<PizzaForm/>
</div>
```

To test our solution, place `console.log(this.state.pizzeria_name)` in handleSubmit method and enter any text into the prompt and hit submit button. With the help of inspect tool, you could see the same text in the browser console (Figure 4-13).

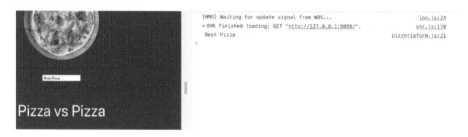

Figure 4-13. *In the browser console, you can see the same text you entered into the prompt on the web page*

The final step is to call axios.post() method and send our inputted pizzeria name. I will replace console.log() with an API call like this:

```
handleSubmit(event) {
    event.preventDefault();
    console.log(this.state.pizzeria_name);
    axios
      .post("http://127.0.0.1:8000/create/", {
        pizzeria_name: this.state.pizzeria_name
      })
```

```
    .then((response) =>{
      console.log(response);
    })
    .catch(function (error) {
      console.log(error);
    });
  }
```

Please remember that the pizzeria_name key in the method .post()
has to match the field name in PizzeriaDetailSerializer. Make sure your
Django project is up and running. I will enter "My Hometown Pizza" into
the prompt and click submit button. If you do the same and reload the web
page in the browser, you should see "My Hometown Pizza" in our list of
Pizzerias (Figure 4-14).

Figure 4-14. *"My Hometown Pizza" has been successfully written*
into our database and then rendered in List View

Additionally, you can inspect the response we received and printed in the console. Status is 201 and the "Created" message proves that we have successfully entered a new pizzeria brand into our database (Figure 4-15).

```
                                              pizzeriaform.js:27
  {data: {…}, status: 201, statusText: "Created", headers: {…}, config: {…}, …}

  ▶ config: {url: "http://127.0.0.1:8000/create/", method: "post", data: "{"pizz…
  ▶ data: {id: 18, pizzeria_name: "My Hometown Pizza", street: "", city: "", sta…
  ▶ headers: {content-length: "184", content-type: "application/json"}
  ▶ request: XMLHttpRequest {readyState: 4, timeout: 0, withCredentials: false, …
    status: 201
    statusText: "Created"
  ▶ __proto__: Object
```

Figure 4-15. *Status 201 proves the successful execution of the post method and the creation of new object*

I hope you got the idea behind React forms. With the same logic we could add the rest of the PizzeriaDetailSerializer fields to our render method. We will not accept the id field, since it would be assigned automatically. Also, active field would be set as True by default. We will not attach any images to the form in this example. Sending images requires more explanation. We will cover the process of attaching and sending photos in detail in Chapter 7. For now, we just omit this field.

```
render() {
  const {
    pizzeria_name,
    street,
    city,
    state,
    zip_code,
    website,
    phone_number,
    description,
    email,
```

```
} = this.state;
return (
  <form onSubmit={this.handleSubmit}>
    <div>
    Pizzeria
      <input
        type="text"
        name="pizzeria_name"
        value={pizzeria_name}
        onChange={this.handleChange}
      />
    </div>
    <div>
    Address
      <input
        type="text"
        name="street"
        value={street}
        onChange={this.handleChange}
      />
    </div>
    <div>
    City
      <input
        type="text"
        name="city"
        value={city}
        onChange={this.handleChange}
      />
    </div>
```

```
<div>
Zip
  <input
    type="text"
    name="zip_code"
    value={zip_code}
    onChange={this.handleChange}
  />
</div>
<div>
Website
  <input
    type="text"
    name="website"
    value={website}
    onChange={this.handleChange}
  />
</div>
<div>
Phone
  <input
    type="text"
    name="phone_number"
    value={phone_number}
    onChange={this.handleChange}
  />
</div>
<div>
Description
  <input
    type="text"
```

```
          name="description"
          value={description}
          onChange={this.handleChange}
        />
      </div>
      <div>
      Email
        <input
          type="text"
          name="email"
          value={email}
          onChange={this.handleChange}
        />
      </div>

      <input style={{backgroundColor:'white'}} type="submit"
      value="Submit" />
    </form>
  );
}
```

Aside from input "name" and value keys, I have wrapped each <input> into <div></div> tags to give our form a little bit of structure. Define all input "name" keys as consts above the form. For style, I added white color to submit button for visibility. I know that styling is far from perfect at the moment, and we will add styling later when we start building a mobile front-end. After the render() method, we need to add the same "name" key inputs to the constructor and define them as empty strings.

```
constructor(props) {
    super(props);
    this.state = {
      pizzeria_name: " ",
```

```
      street: " ",
      city: " ",
      state: " ",
      zip_code: " ",
      website: " ",
      phone_number: " ",
      description: " ",
      email: " ",
   };
   this.handleChange = this.handleChange.bind(this);
   this.handleSubmit = this.handleSubmit.bind(this);
 }
```

Finally, we would need to pass all values into axios.post() method as a dictionary.

```
handleSubmit(event) {
    event.preventDefault();
    axios
      .post("http://127.0.0.1:8000/create/", {
        pizzeria_name: this.state.pizzeria_name,
        street: this.state.street,
        city: this.state.city,
        state: this.state.state,
        zip_code: this.state.zip_code,
        website: this.state.website,
        phone_number: this.state.phone_number,
        description: this.state.description,
        email: this.state.email,
      })
      .then((response) => {
        console.log(response);
      })
```

```
  .catch(function (error) {
    console.log(error);
  });
}
```

Note   Before you enter values into form fields, make sure they are entered in the correct format and would match our validation fields in Django Model. For example, a website value should start with "http://" and a phone number would be exactly ten digits. We will add validation to input fields in Chapter 7.

Make sure both of your local servers are up and running. As a test, I will enter my favorite pizzeria place name near our office in Chicago, Pizano's (Figure 4-16).

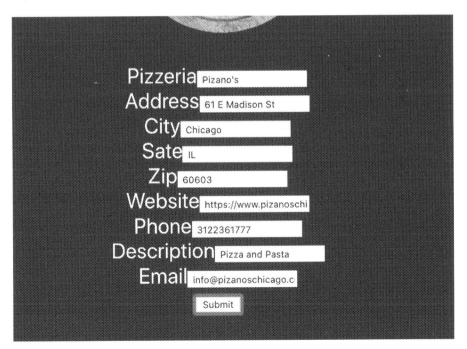

Figure 4-16. *Entering information in the form*

If all information was entered correctly and you had no errors in pizzeriaform.js, you would need to refresh the browser and click the newly created Pizano's record, and the web app would render all details for that joint (Figure 4-17).

Figure 4-17. *Component PizzaDetail renders details for clicked record*

Update view

In general, update is quite similar to create method and done with PATCH request. You might ask, why won't we use the method PUT? The answer is PUT replaces the whole object, and the PATCH applies partial changes. Following the REST architectural style, we will add a custom serializer field update to PizzeriaDetailSerializer in serializers.py in our Django project and define it as SerializerMethodField(). The logic is very simple; we will use SerializerMethodField() every time we need to add a method to our pizzeria instance. We went through the steps of creating a method field in the detail view previously in this chapter. This time, I'll just show you PizzeriaDetailSerializer with update field in it (Figure 4-18).

```
24
25    class PizzeriaDetailSerializer(serializers.ModelSerializer):
26        update = serializers.SerializerMethodField()
27
28        class Meta:
29            model = Pizzeria
30            fields = [
31                'id',
32                'pizzeria_name',
33                'street',
34                'city',
35                'state',
36                'zip_code',
37                'website',
38                'phone_number',
39                'description',
40                'logo_image',
41                'email',
42                'active',
43                'update',
44            ]
45
46        def get_update(self, obj):
47            return reverse('pizzeria_update', args=(obj.pk,))
48
```

Figure 4-18. *PizzeriaDetailSerializer with a SerializerMethodField update*

As you can see in Figure 4-18, the logic is straightforward; we define the field, include the field "update" into fields list, and create the method with an unchangeable prefix get before the name of the field. Only this time, we include "pizza_update" label from urls.py file. Reverse method would get us the URL pattern for update view by this label.

In the front-end portion, we need to add "update" button to PizzaDetail component in the pizzeriadetail.js file. Clicking that button would reveal another component PizzaUpdate, which we have not created yet.

```
<button
style={{ backgroundColor: "white" }}
onClick={()=> this.updatePizzeriaDetails()}>
    Update
</button>
```

To render PizzaUpdate component, we will add the event handler "onClick" and create "updatePizzeriaDetails" method.

```
updatePizzeriaDetails() {
    this.setState({ showComponent: true });
  }
```

"updatePizzeriaDetails" is a simple method that would toggle showComponent from False to True on a click. Also, we would need to add PizzaUpdate component to the render method in PizzaDetail.

```
{this.state.showComponent ? <PizzaUpdate pizzariaUpdate={obj}
/> : null}
```

Please note that we are passing an object as props to PizzaUpdate component. Our PizzaUpdate component would take the pizzeria instance that has to be updated.

The last part in PizzaDetail component is the constructor method. We will define showComponent in State and bind the updatePizzeriaDetails method.

```
constructor(props) {
    super(props);
    this.state = {
```

```
    showComponent: false,
  };
  this.updatePizzeriaDetails = this.updatePizzeriaDetails.
  bind(this);
}
```

Finally, our PizzaDetail component should look like the one in Figure 4-19.

```
 4
 5    class PizzaDetail extends Component {
 6      constructor(props) {
 7        super(props);
 8        this.state = {
 9          showComponent: false,
10        };
11        this.updatePizzeriaDetails = this.updatePizzeriaDetails.bind(this);
12      }
13      updatePizzeriaDetails() {
14        this.setState({ showComponent: true });
15      }
16
17      render() {
18        const obj = this.props.pizzariaDetail;
19        return (
20          <div style={{ color: "yellow", border: "1px solid yellow" }}>
21            <h4>{obj.pizzeria_name}</h4>
22            <h5>
23              Address: {obj.street} {obj.city} {obj.state} {obj.zip_code}
24            </h5>
25            <h6>Phone: {obj.phone_number}</h6>
26            <p>{obj.description}</p>
27            <button
28              style={{ backgroundColor: "white" }}
29              onClick={() => this.updatePizzeriaDetails()}
30            >
31              Update
32            </button>
33            {this.state.showComponent ? <PizzaUpdate pizzariaUpdate={obj} /> : null}
34          </div>
35        );
36      }
37    }
38    export default PizzaDetail;
39
```

Figure 4-19. *Component PizzaDetail will show the PizzaUpdate component on click*

Finally, it is time to create pizzeriaupdate.js file and construct PizzaUpdate component. After you create pizzeriaupdate.js and declare the PizzaUpdate component, import them to the pizzeriadetail.js file on top. PizzaUpdate for the most part would look like PizzaForm component. Since the logic would be the same and I do not want to waste your time, we will go over the "description" field only. The description field would be used to be an updatable field as an example here. If you want to make all fields of your serializer updatable, just follow the same steps we are about to do for "description" field. In general, the process would be to have an input for each field and send the incoming data with axios.patch() method – exactly what we will do right now with "description" field.

I will copy PizzaForm component to my pizzaupdate.js and modify it a bit. For starters, I will set obj to be changed in State as obj_to_update and will assign props that were passed from PizzaDetail as a value. Keep in mind that React State is immutable and would not be changed if props were changed. Initializing State from props in the constructor is tricky. If you are planning to change your props later, you should not initialize them in state. However, there are exceptions. We are not planning to change our props at any time in PizzaUpdate component; thus, we could set them in State. Also, I'll initialize "value" as a key for the actual data we are about to update. At first, it would render the old data in the description field, and the user could amend it with new information.

```
constructor(props) {
    super(props);
    this.state = {
      obj_to_update: this.props.pizzariaUpdate,
      value: this.props.pizzariaUpdate.description,
    };
    this.handleChange = this.handleChange.bind(this);
    this.handleSubmit = this.handleSubmit.bind(this);
  }
```

As you can see in constructor, we are binding the same handleChange and handleSubmit methods we used to submit the form in PizzaForm component. I'll slightly adjust the handleChange method to one value being extracted from <input> tag, since in this example, we use the description field only.

```
handleChange(event) {
    this.setState({ value: event.target.value });
  }
```

Our handleSubmit will call the axios.patch() method. PATCH method is similar to POST and requires a URL and data we are sending. We would concatenate our URL for updating to the domain name or IP and send the data as value from State. In the following example, the "description" is a Model field we are trying to update, and this.state.value represents the information we captured from a user.

```
handleSubmit(event) {
    event.preventDefault();
axios .patch("http://127.0.0.1:8000".concat(this.state.obj_to_
update.update), {
        description: this.state.value,
      })
      .then((response) => {
        console.log(response);
      })
      .catch(function (error) {
        console.log(error);
      });
  }
```

The render() method is quite similar to what we did in PizzaForm component; we have removed all fields except "description". Also, we do not need "name" key since there is only "description" value. I have added a minimum of style, red color for text and border, to make this element visible on the page.

```
render() {
    const { value } = this.state;
    return (
        <div style={{ color: "red", border: "1px solid red" }}>
            <form onSubmit={this.handleSubmit}>
                <div>
                    <h6>Updating</h6>
                    <input type="text" value={value} onChange={this.
                    handleChange} />
                </div>
                <input
                    style={{ backgroundColor: "white" }}
                    type="submit"
                    value="Submit"
                />
            </form>
        </div>
    );
}
```

The finished puzzle of PizzaUpdate component should look like the one in Figure 4-22. We can test it and see PATCH request in action. Make sure both of your servers are up and running. I am going to choose Pizano's, and in detail view, I'll click update button. After that, we should be able to see update component and form field with the description information we are planning to update (Figure 4-20). In the description field, I'll change "Pizza and Pasta" to "Great Place!"

Figure 4-20. *Updating pizzeria's description field with a new record*

After we click submit button and refresh the page, our Pizano's detail view should have a new description (Figure 4-21). Keep in mind we are learning the basics of React and practicing API calls here; later, in a mobile version, we will spend more time on styling.

Figure 4-21. *Updated record*

```
     pizzeriaupdate.js    ×
 1   import React, { Component } from "react";
 2   import axios from "axios";
 3
 4   class PizzaUpdate extends Component {
 5     constructor(props) {
 6       super(props);
 7       this.state = {
 8         obj_to_update: this.props.pizzariaUpdate,
 9         value: this.props.pizzariaUpdate.description,
10       };
11
12       this.handleChange = this.handleChange.bind(this);
13       this.handleSubmit = this.handleSubmit.bind(this);
14     }
15
16     handleChange(event) {
17       this.setState({ value: event.target.value });
18     }
19
20     handleSubmit(event) {
21       event.preventDefault();
22       axios
23         .patch("http://127.0.0.1:8000".concat(this.state.obj_to_update.update), {
24           description: this.state.value,
25         })
26         .then((response) => {
27           console.log(response);
28         })
29         .catch(function (error) {
30           console.log(error);
31         });
32     }
33
34     render() {
35       const { value } = this.state;
36       return (
37         <div style={{ color: "red", border: "1px solid red" }}>
38           <form onSubmit={this.handleSubmit}>
39             <div>
40               <h6>Updating</h6>
41               <input type="text" value={value} onChange={this.handleChange} />
42             </div>
43             <input
44               style={{ backgroundColor: "white" }}
45               type="submit"
46               value="Submit"
47             />
48           </form>
49         </div>
50       );
51     }
52   }
53
54   export default PizzaUpdate;
```

Figure 4-22. *Component PizzaUpdate*

Delete view

Delete is the simplest of all methods, and if you got this far, you should have an understanding of how to do it. We need to add "Delete" button and on click call a method that would send DELETE request to our server.

133

We will start with a custom method field in Serializers. PizzeriaDetailSerializer in serializers.py would be the right place for the delete field. We will define it as SerializerMethodField(). Right after this, we should add "delete" field to a list of fields and construct a method named after that field with a mandatory suffix get. The reverse() function would generate a URL by looking for the right API pointed by the label 'pizzeria_delete' (Figure 4-23).

```
23  class PizzeriaDetailSerializer(serializers.ModelSerializer):
24      update = serializers.SerializerMethodField()
25      delete = serializers.SerializerMethodField()
26
27      class Meta:
28          model = Pizzeria
29          fields = [
30              'id',
31              'pizzeria_name',
32              'street',
33              'city',
34              'state',
35              'zip_code',
36              'website',
37              'phone_number',
38              'description',
39              'logo_image',
40              'email',
41              'active',
42              'update',
43              'delete',
44          ]
45
46      def get_update(self, obj):
47          return reverse('pizzeria_update', args=(obj.pk,))
48
49      def get_delete(self, obj):
50          return reverse('pizzeria_delete', args=(obj.pk,))
51
```

Figure 4-23. *A delete field was added to PizzeriaDetailSerializer in the serializers.py file*

Let's flip back to our front-end project front_pizzavspizza. Let's place the delete function into the PizzaDetail component. We will follow the

134

same steps as we did with Create and Update components. I'll copy my "update" button element and rename it to "delete". Also, onClick handler would invoke deletePizzeria method and pass an object with the attribute "delete".

```
<button
   style={{ backgroundColor: "white" }}
   onClick={() => this.deletePizzeria(obj.delete)}>
   Delete
</button>
```

Maybe it looks a little bit strange that we are using a method that has not been defined yet, but we have walked that road before and have a clear understanding of how it should be designed.

Do not forget to bind the deletePizzeria method to the PizzaDetail component in the constructor method.

```
constructor(props) {
    super(props);
    this.state = {
       showComponent: false,
    };
 this.updatePizzeriaDetails=this.updatePizzeriaDetails.
 bind(this);
this.deletePizzeria=this.deletePizzeria.bind(this);
   }
```

Our deletePizzeria method will contain the Axios delete() method. Make sure you import the Axios library in pizzeriadetail.js on the top of the page. Like this, import axios from "axios". The syntax is very similar to what we have done so far.

```
deletePizzeria(obj){
    console.log(obj);
```

135

```
axios.delete("http://127.0.0.1:8000".concat(obj))
    .then((response) => {
        console.log(response);
      })
    .catch(function (error) {
        console.log(error);
      });
  }
```

We are ready to test our delete feature. My victim is the "My Hometown Pizza" record. By clicking delete button in the detail view, I'll delete that record. Permanently. In the console, you should be able to see the response message fired with status 204, a proof that axios.delete() ran successfully (Figure 4-24). After refreshing our browser, you no longer could find the "My Hometown Pizza" record.

```
▼ Object 🔘
  ▶ config: {url: "http://127.0.0.1:8000/delete/31/", method: "delete", headers: …
    data: ""
  ▶ headers: {content-length: "0"}
  ▶ request: XMLHttpRequest {readyState: 4, timeout: 0, withCredentials: false, u…
    status: 204
    statusText: "No Content"
  ▶   proto  : Object
```

Figure 4-24. *Response message with status 204 after a successful delete request went through*

Please do not pay too much attention to the sequence of my records. I have added and removed a few records as I was testing my code. My advice to you is always run your code and use console.log() to test every step of your program. Do not wait till you finish the whole project.

There's one more thing we could do to make our code cleaner and versatile. In all API calls, we used the http://127.0.0.1:8000 prefix. When you deploy your project on a server, your IP would change. Also, you might want to use a domain name. The beginning of our URL could be set as an environment variable. Environment variables are very convenient. Define variables and they would be available through a global process anywhere within your application. Based on your production circle, you can have a couple of environment files where you would define separate sets of global variables and use them for different development stages. Please do not confuse the React environment variables file with virtual environment in the Django project. In React, .env file plays more like a setting role where you can define APIs, keys, and other project-related variables.

We will create .env file in our main React project folder front_pizzavspizza. In .env file, we would define REACT_APP_URL.

REACT_APP_URL = "http://127.0.0.1:8000"

After we have moved the first part of our URL to .env file, we could access it anywhere in the front-end web app. To put REACT_APP_URL into action, we would need to replace http://127.0.0.1:8000 in all Axios methods with

process.env.REACT_APP_URL

Our PizzaList component in the pizzeriaslist.js file contains two Axios get methods in componentDidMount() and getPizzaDetail(). In the first instance, we need to pass the process.env.REACT_APP_URL variable to get a method like this:

```
componentDidMount() {
  axios
    .get(process.env.REACT_APP_URL)
    .then((response) => {
      this.setState({ pizzeriasData: response.data });
    })
    .catch(function (error) {
      console.log(error);
    });
}
```

The detail URL in getPizzaDetail() comes with an object id and uses concat() method. The environment variable, process.env.REACT_APP_URL, can be appended with the right pizzeria instance using absolute_url attribute.

```
getPizzaDetail(item) {
axios  .get(process.env.REACT_APP_URL.concat(item.absolute_
url))
  .then((response) => {
    this.setState({ pizzeria: response.data });
  })
  .catch(function (error) {
   console.log(error);
  });
  }
```

Following the same logic, you could replace the local server IP http://127.0.0.1:8000 with process.env.REACT_APP_URL environment variable in PizzaDetail, PizzaForm, and PizzaUpdate components. After you are done, restart your server and refresh your browser. Your web app should be running as before.

A couple of thoughts as we are wrapping this chapter. The main intention of this chapter was to show you how to do CRUD with React and practice composing components. As I have mentioned before, React Native is a mobile flavor of React, and it would be a good idea to get a general understanding of its roots and some practical knowledge. By all means, we could have continued with React and add other cool features if our goal was to build a desktop version. I hope now you have a good understanding about components, state, and props. In the next chapters, we would move our application to mobile platforms with the help of React Native. Using native elements of iPhone and Android, we would construct all features of a modern mobile application powered by Python Django.

CHAPTER 5

Introduction to React Native

After we have assembled our application with React, it would be a good time to get familiar with React Native. In this chapter, we will set up general environments for iOS and Android mobile platforms and talk about different simulation and testing options. We will get a feel of React Native and see how it interacts with native mobile elements. By the end of this chapter we will have a core structure for our mobile app.

Setting up the development environment

Before we get to the coding part, we need to choose one of the two methods to launch our mobile project. The first one is React Native CLI (command-line interface), which contains all React Native code and will create the project structure with dedicated folders for iOS and Android components. If you are an experienced mobile developer and familiar with Xcode and Android Studio, then React Native CLI is a good choice for you. The second option, Expo CLI, would better suit beginners and people who want to move faster, spending less time on details. Make no mistake, the Expo CLI framework uses native components too. Expo CLI has a bunch of advantages and is easier to use. With the help of Expo CLI, we will create a great mobile app. Expo CLI is a set of tools built around React Native to help you develop your app faster.[1] In Chapter 8, Expo CLI will compile our code and build stand-alone apps for the App store and Google Play. Without Expo CLI, this process might be too complicated for beginners. If, at any point of the development process, you feel like switching to native components, this would be possible too. At any time, you can eject from Expo CLI to React Native CLI.

To get started with Expo CLI, we need to install it using npm and a variable -g.

```
npm install -g expo-cli
```

After a successful Expo CLI installation, we can create a new React Native project and name it pizzavspizza_app. This would be the home directory for our mobile app.

```
expo init pizzavspizza_app
```

Right after you run the init command, you should see the menu with two main options, Managed workflow and Bare workflow (Figure 5-1). The main difference is that in the Managed workflow template, we would not be allowed to work directly with native components. This is totally OK for unexperienced mobile developers. We will still be able to use native components through React Native components. The Bare workflow, on the other hand, would require more effort and knowledge of iOS and Android native features. TypeScript, a Microsoft programming language, would not work for us, because in this book, we use JavaScript.

For all these reasons, the best choice for us would be the blank template in Managed workflow. Hit blank and wait through the rest of the initialization.

---

[1]https://docs.expo.io

```
(base) programwithus:- programwithus$ expo init pizzavspizza_app
? Choose a template: (Use arrow keys)
 ----- Managed workflow -----
) blank                    a minimal app as clean as an empty canvas
  blank (TypeScript)       same as blank but with TypeScript configuration
  tabs                     several example screens and tabs using react-navigation
 ----- Bare workflow -----
  minimal                  bare and minimal, just the essentials to get you started

  minimal (TypeScript)  same as minimal but with TypeScript configuration
```

Figure 5-1. *Intermediate step in initiating the pizzavspizza_app project; we go with blank template*

Afterward, you should see an invite to change the directory to pizzavspizza_app and the list of commands to launch our application on a variety of mobile platforms (Figure 5-2).

```
(base) programwithus:- programwithus$ expo init pizzavspizza_app
? Choose a template: expo-template-blank

  Using npm to install packages. You can pass --yarn to use Yarn instead.

  Downloaded and extracted project files.
  Installed JavaScript dependencies.

  Your project is ready!

To run your project, navigate to the directory and run one of the following npm commands.

- cd pizzavspizza_app
- npm start # you can open iOS, Android, or web from here, or run them directly with the commands below.
- npm run android
- npm run ios
- npm run web
```

Figure 5-2. *The list of commands to run the application on different platforms*

Using the proposed cd pizzavspizza_app command, get into our home directory. In pizzavspizza_app folder, we can see the React Native project structure (Figure 5-3).

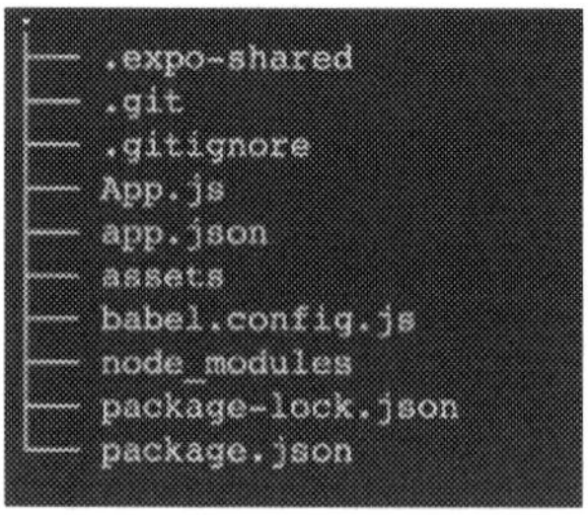

```
├── .expo-shared
├── .git
├── .gitignore
├── App.js
├── app.json
├── assets
├── babel.config.js
├── node_modules
├── package-lock.json
└── package.json
```

Figure 5-3. *React Native project structure*

Most of the folders are already familiar to us. We have discussed them in Chapter 3 of this book. There are a couple of new ones we have not seen before: assets and .expo-shared. The .expo-shared folder contains assets.json file. The purpose of .expo-shared is to share files, and assets. json would keep track of the asset state and make sure that images wouldn't be compressed more than once. An assets directory is a place to store all static files.

To start our React Native project, you can run the start command.

npm start

The npm start command will launch Metro Bundler in your browser running on developer server localhost:19002. No worries if in your case it runs on 19003 or other ports. Metro is a JavaScript bundler. Every time you run it, Expo Metro compiles many JavaScript files into one single file. Also, Metro converts images and other static files into objects. Fast file updating is the main advantage of Metro Bundler.

Our next steps would be to set up iOS simulator and Android emulator and to get them connected to Metro Bundler.

iOS simulator

There are two options for testing your app on iPhone in the development mode. The first one is to install Xcode and simulate any iPhone model that is currently in circulation. Another option is to run your app on an actual iPhone. Expo Client lets you run your app on actual iPhone or Android phone without going through all procedures of the App store or Google Play to see your application in action. We will try this option later in this chapter.

To launch the iPhone simulator, make sure you have Xcode installed on your Mac. If you have not installed it yet, go to Mac App store and search for Xcode. In this book, I use Xcode 11.5 on macOS Catalina 10.15.5.

Immediately upon launching Xcode, you will see the initial menu. You can close it because we are not planning to write any code in Xcode, and there is no need for us to create a new project. Go straight to **Preferences** in Xcode menu, then navigate to **Locations**, and make sure **Command Line Tools** reflects your version of Xcode. In my case, it is Xcode 11.5 (Figure 5-4). If **Command Line Tools** is empty, click it and choose the right version of Xcode you are using. When you are done with Command Line Tools, close **Preferences** menu.

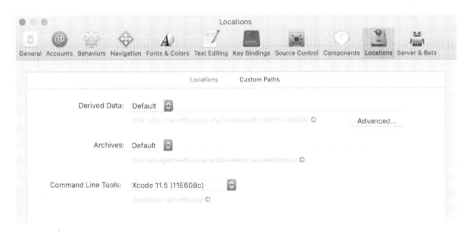

Figure 5-4. *Preferences* ➤ *Locations* ➤ *Command Line Tools: Xcode 11.5*

Go back to **Xcode** menu and choose **Open Developer Tool**; you should see the menu with **Simulator** option. Click **Simulator** and it will launch the interactive iPhone simulator (Figure 5-5).

Figure 5-5. *iPhone simulator*

I'll be using an iPhone 11 model in this book, but you can choose any type of iPhone you prefer. To try another iPhone model, go to **File** menu in the Simulator window, then click **Open Device** and choose **iOS** menu with all the current types of iPhones.

Although you can run two iPhone simulators at the same time, it would not be a good idea because they might clash.

Let's get back to running Metro Bundler and choose **Run on iOS simulator** option (Figure 5-6).

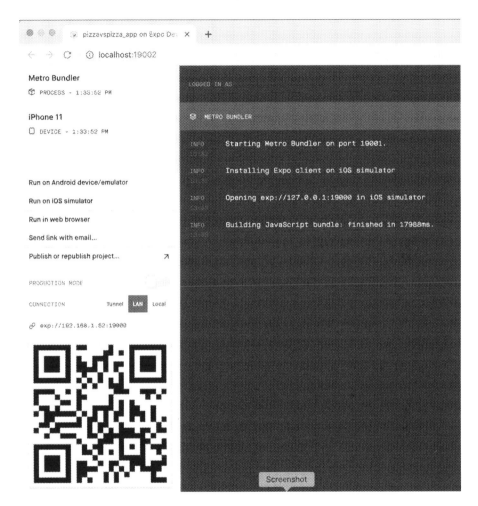

Figure 5-6. *Choose Run on iOS simulator option in Metro Bundler running in the browser*

After you get Metro Bundler connected, your iPhone simulator will ask a permission to connect to Expo and then will show you a friendly message "Hello there, friend!". Please click "Got it" button. On the empty canvas, you should see "Open up App.js to start working on your app!". Following this message, we can open App.js in our React Native pizzavspizza_app and replace this initial message with "Pizza vs. Pizza App" (Figure 5-7).

```
     App.js              ×
1    import React from 'react';
2    import { StyleSheet, Text, View } from 'react-native';
3
4    export default function App() {
5      return (
6        <View style={styles.container}>
7          <Text>Pizza vs. Pizza App</Text>
8        </View>
9      );
10   }
11
12   const styles = StyleSheet.create({
13     container: {
14       flex: 1,
15       backgroundColor: '#fff',
16       alignItems: 'center',
17       justifyContent: 'center',
18     },
19   });
20
```

Figure 5-7. *App component in App.js React Native pizzavspizza_app project*

As soon as you save your changes to App.js, your iPhone simulator should render the new message "Pizza vs. Pizza App" (Figure 5-8). Our iOS simulator has been successfully set up, and now we can get started with the Android emulator.

Figure 5-8. *iPhone simulator with the new message after we made changes in App.js*

Android emulator

If you do not have an Android device, you can install and run your app on an emulator. Our first step would be to download and install Android Studio; you can find it here: `https://developer.android.com/studio`.

Installation is a pretty straightforward process; all you need is to choose **Standard** setup. Keep in mind we will not be writing any code in Android Studio. We will use the emulator feature only.

The whole setup process of Android Studio's tools is very well explained in Expo documentation here: `https://docs.expo.io/workflow/android-studio-emulator/`. I would definitely recommend you to visit this page because some minor things might change with newer Expo versions and Android Studio.

To connect a virtual Android device to Expo, launch Android Studio on your computer. On the bottom of initial menu, look for **Configure** with a gear icon. When you click **Configure**, choose the first option **AVD Manager**. **Android Virtual Device Manager** window will pop up; there, you click **Create Virtual Device** button and choose an Android phone you would like to use as your virtual platform. I will be using Pixel 3a since it is a popular model at the time I am writing this book, and it is in the Google Play store (Figure 5-9). Keep in mind that by the time you get this book, there might be more versions of Pixel and Nexus phones out there on the market.

Figure 5-9. *Create **Virtual Device** button would lead you to **Select Hardware** options*

After you have settled on hardware, proceed with the next button and download the system you would like to run on your Android emulator. I will go with R; it is the latest version of Android system at the moment (Figure 5-10).

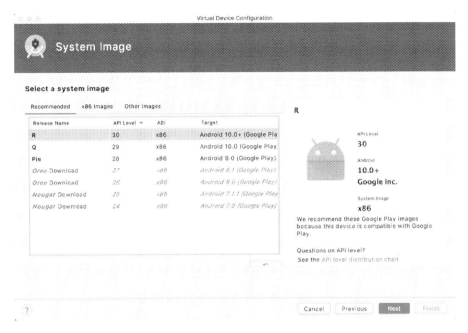

Figure 5-10.   *The next step is to choose a system for your virtual Android phone*

You would be able to confirm your choice after you click the next button in the **Android Virtual Device** window. If everything looks OK and you are happy with the proposed name of your virtual device, click finish button (Figure 5-11).

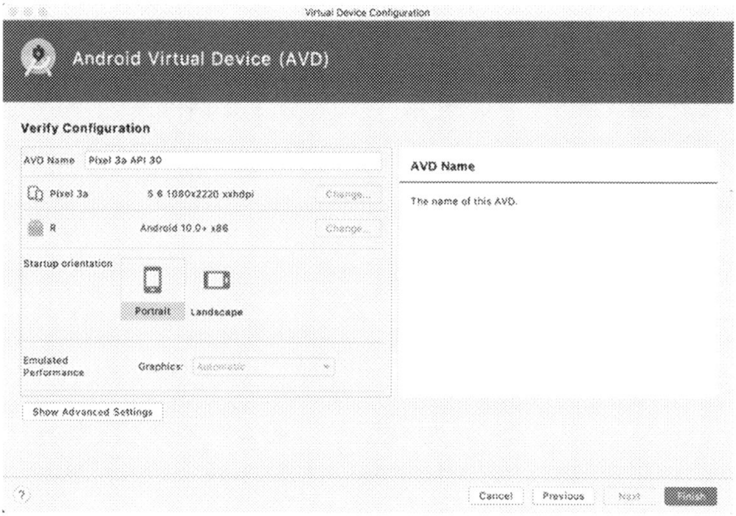

Figure 5-11. *Verify your choice for hardware and system*

Subsequently, you will get to **Android Virtual Device Manager** window that would list all your virtual platforms (Figure 5-12). There, in **Actions**, you will see **play** button to start your device; click it. By the way, you could always get back to AVD Manager window and change the Android emulator settings if you click **Configure** with a gear icon.

Figure 5-12. *Android Virtual Device Manager*

Launch the emulator by pressing play button; this will start your virtual device running on Android system.

The last step would be to get back to **Metro Bundler** and click **Run on Android device/emulator**. At first, your virtual Android phone might ask for a permission, "Permit Drawing Over Other Apps," or would show an empty screen. The Android emulator would need a bit of time to install Expo and upload the project. If it is taking too long and nothing happens, you would need to go back to **Metro Bundler** and click **Run on Android device/emulator** again. Afterward, you should see a familiar Expo greeting "Hello there, friend!". Press "Got it" button, and the "Pizza vs. Pizza" text should appear in the middle of the screen (Figure 5-13).

Figure 5-13. *The React Native project is running on Android emulator and iPhone simulator*

Android Studio comes with ADB (Android Debug Bridge). To use this feature, Mac users would need to add Android SDK location to PATH in the bash_profile file. You can find instructions on how to do that on the same Expo page at `https://docs.expo.io/workflow/android-studio-emulator/` under the section "how to find Android SDK location." This is an optional feature, and I am not going to use it in this book.

Running your project on a physical device

At some point of the development process, you would want to see your app in action on an actual phone. Expo provides an opportunity to try your app without going through the whole nine yards of deploying your project to the App store or Google Play.

To use this option, make sure your iPhone or Android device runs on the same Wi-Fi network as your computer. You would need to download Expo Client app from Apple App store or Google Play (Figure 5-14).

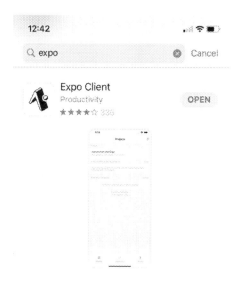

Figure 5-14. *Expo Client in Apple App store*

To connect your Expo Client with Metro Bundler, open the photo camera on your smartphone and point at the QR code on the bottom of Metro Bundler (Figure 5-15). Your device will detect the QR code and will prompt you to open Expo Client app. When Expo Client opens, you should see a familiar greeting "Hello there, friend!" and then your project. If for some reason Expo Client cannot open the project and asks you to try again, make sure that you are connected to the same wireless network and reboot your phone. If, later, you would want to run another app, you might need to reboot your phone again and give Expo Client a minute or two to download the JavaScript code from the development server.

Figure 5-15. *QR code to connect the Expo Client app to your local server*

Publish your project to the Internet

Expo gives us one more option to test your project in the real environment. We can publish our project on Expo's server and share the web address with others. Publishing on Expo's server is not an option for the distribution of your app, but rather a cool feature to share a project with a team of developers working on the same app. Also, if you are working on a demo or a proof of concept and would like to show your killer app to potential investors, this publishing option would give them a chance to try it on their smartphones. Keep in mind that to view your project, they would need to download the Expo Client app from the App store or Google Play on their smartphones.

To run our project online, you would need to find **Publish or republish project...** button on the left side of Metro Bundler and click it. You should see the form where we would specify the name of our app and the URL slug. This information by default comes from the app.json file of our React Native project, but you always can change it in this publishing form. I'll use the pizzavspizza name and the same URL slug with a short description (Figure 5-16).

Figure 5-16. *Publish your project to the Internet form*

One more step is left to publish your project on Expo – registration. After you hit **Publish project** button, flip over to your terminal where Expo is requesting authentication (Figure 5-17).

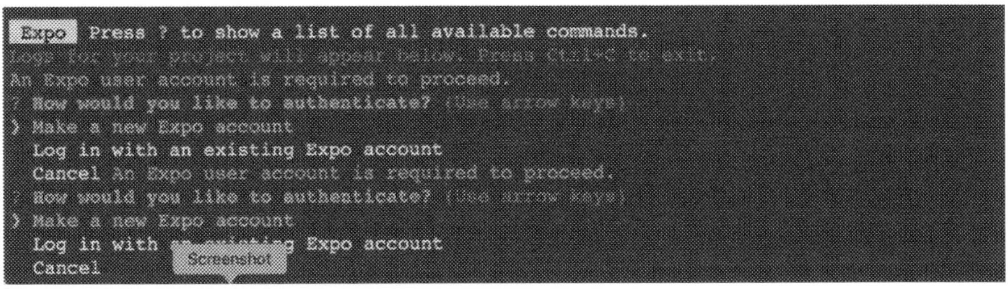

Figure 5-17. *You need to log in before publishing your project*

Using arrow keys, choose **Make a new Expo account** and register. Your username would be used as part of the URL of the project. If everything went successfully, you should see a green message with the newly created

HTTP address to your project. In my case, it is `https://expo.io/` `@programwithus/pizzavspizza`.

Open this address in your browser, and you will see another QR code that you can share with your teammates and potential investors (Figure 5-18). Just navigate your camera on this QR code, and it will offer to open the app in Expo Client. If something goes wrong and your project in Expo Client is not reflecting recent changes you have done, either close and relaunch the Expo Client app or reboot your phone.

Figure 5-18. *You can find your published project on expo.io/@your-user-name/project-name*

Core Components of React Native

React Native and React are conceptually similar. React Native comes with built-in Core Components that are mapped to native iOS and Android elements.[2] It will not be possible to go over all of them in this book. You can find components for your mobile projects and an explanation of them in the official documentation here: `https://reactnative.dev/` `docs/components-and-apis`. In this chapter, I would like to introduce the essential ones. Later, in the next chapter, we will go through more components and use them for our CRUD operations.

---

[2]`https://reactnative.dev/docs/components-and-apis`

View component

Let's flip back to App.js file in our React Native project in the pizzavspizza_ app directory and take a closer look at our main component app.

On the top of the file, we import React because it is the core of React Native project. On the next line, we import built-in components from React Native; they are passed in curly braces.

```
import React from "react";
import { StyleSheet, Text, View } from "react-native";
```

If you are planning to compose a component as a class, you need to import {Component} passed in curly braces as we did in previous chapters. Passing an imported component in curly braces is an efficient way to import elements we would want to use in the file. You do not want to import the whole library; it's too costly for memory. To the default components, StyleSheet, Text, View, we add one more, the Image component.

```
import { StyleSheet, Text, View, Image } from "react-native";
```

The first Core Component you can see in App.js is <View>. View is a container, very similar to <div> in HTML. As a matter of fact, the documentation says that <View> is mapped to <div>[3] if you run the React Native project in a browser. At the same time, <View> is mounted to Android <ViewGroup> and iOS <UIView> component. According to the React Native documentation, <View> is "the most fundamental component"[4] and could be nested with other <View> components.

---

[3]https://reactnative.dev/docs/intro-react-native-components
[4]https://reactnative.dev/docs/view#docsNav

157

StyleSheet component

You have noticed that our View component in App.js file takes props `styles`.

Styles are defined on the bottom of the file as a StyleSheet object. StyleSheet is close to CSS and uses similar attributes for styling, yet these are JavaScript. The main objective of StyleSheet.create() is to validate properties like "backgroundColor" and make sure you will not use CSS "background-color". Keep in mind we work with JSX not HTML and cannot use CSS. The method create() generates a JavaScript object, and we can pass the whole object or separate properties to JSX components.

Very often, people would use style properties

```
style={{backgroundColor: "#fff" }}
```

directly in JSX tag. Although this is possible, you risk that the style would not be applied if you misspelled or used a wrong property name. Besides, having a style set outside of JSX makes code much cleaner. Sometimes, when StyleSheet has a lot of characteristics, experienced developers would move them into a separate file. The React Native documentation has a list of all available properties for StyleSheet; you can look them up here: `https://reactnative.dev/docs/view-style-props`.

Text component

Text is another basic component in React Native. It correlates with the <p> tag in HTML. Text could be nested in <Text> or <View>.

Currently, <Text> Pizza vs. Pizza App</Text> is rendered very small on simulators. We can change the font style, size, and color with style props. In our App.js, I will add a `baseText` property and specify font color, size, and style.

```
const styles = StyleSheet.create({
  container: {
    flex: 1,
    backgroundColor: "#fff",
    alignItems: "center",
    justifyContent: "center",
  },
  baseText: {
    color: "navy",
    fontSize: 30,
    fontStyle: "italic",
  },
})
```

To apply these changes to "Pizza vs. Pizza," we would need to pass the styles object as props to <Text> component.

```
<Text style={styles.baseText}>Pizza vs. Pizza App</Text>
```

You see our simulators get updated as soon as you save the changes to the file (Figure 5-19).

Another way of handling <Text> component would be to define a variable and pass it in the curly braces. For example, we can define a constant mytext in the App function as a string "by ProgramWithUs" and wrap {mytext} with <Text> tags right under the existing text. Like this, const mytext = "by ProgramWithUs". We will brighten this text with a color and add it as props to <Text> component.

```
<Text style={styles.newText}>{mytext}</Text>
```

Now add newText as a new property to the styles object and define color as red.

```
newText:{
    color: "red",
}
```

Right after this, our simulators render two lines of text (Figure 5-19). To save some space in the book, I'll be showing you either iPhone or Pixel phone screens as we implement new features. As you follow along, the iOS simulator and Android emulator should have the same outcomes.

You can see that everything so far is pretty logical. If you want to add a custom style to a component, you need to define a property in Styles and pass it as props directly to the component it was meant to.

Figure 5-19. *Updated version of the App.js file and iOS simulator*

Image component

The Image component can fetch and render images from different sources: static resources, camera roll, and the Web.[5] Our Django Model has image field serving the URL, and we will be using the Image component a lot.

---

[5]https://reactnative.dev/docs/image

Before we get to the part where we would retrieve all our records from our model, we can learn the syntax by adding the image we used in the previous chapters.

Let's add <Image/> tag to our App function in App.js file right above the Text component. Before we proceed, make sure the Image component s imported from React Native on the second line of the App.js file. The structure of this React Native component is similar to the HTML tag <img/>. We need to provide the source of a file within the tag. If the file comes from the Web, we need to include the **uri** key and pass it as an object to source, and it requires extra curly braces. Keep in mind that when you use a photo not from static resources, the Image component demands precise dimensions for the picture. We will add height and width for our pizza image in the styles object as a pizzaImage property. Make sure you add the Image component to the import list of components coming from "react-native".

```
<Image
        style={styles.pizzaImage}
        source={{
          uri: "https://bit.ly/book-pizza",
        }}
/>
```

Define pizzaImage in StyleSheet with height and width as 200 points.

```
pizzaImage: {
    width: 200,
    height: 200,
},
```

After we added the Image component to the App function and saved it, our simulators should render the pizza image (Figure 5-20).

Figure 5-20. *Image component added to App.js file and rendered on Android emulator*

We have experimented with basic React Native components a bit; now it is time to look at navigation.

React Navigation

As we discussed before, an application should be user-friendly and simple to use. Navigation is essential to any mobile app. React Navigation is a very popular platform to build a transition pattern to flip through screens. It does not come by default, and we will need to install it and add dependencies to Expo. If your Metro Bundler is still running, stop it with the Ctrl+C command. Using npm manager, install React Navigation and other libraries for navigation features:

```
npm install @react-navigation/native
npm install @react-navigation/stack
npm install @react-navigation/bottom-tabs
npm install @react-navigation/drawer
```

After successful installation, we would need to add them to Expo:

```
expo install react-native-gesture-handler
expo install react-native-reanimated
expo install react-native-screens
expo install react-native-safe-area-context
expo install @react-native-community/masked-view
```

As always, it would be a good idea to keep an eye on the documentation for updates: `https://reactnavigation.org`.

Here, I will show you how to create a side menu (drawer) and lower tab buttons. Our goal is to link all screens of our app together.

For starters, we need to add more screens to our React Native project. In our main directory pizzavspizza_app, we need to create a new folder `src` where we would keep all our code. In src folder, we will create directory screens, and in it we need one more folder `components` to hold our custom components. In components folder, we would need two JavaScript files – detail_view.js and list_view.js – like in Figure 5-21. If you are using Mac, the Linux command mkdir would help you to create src, screens, and components directories. Files detail_view.js and list_view.js could be launched with the familiar touch command. For Windows, use mkdir and echo, respectively.

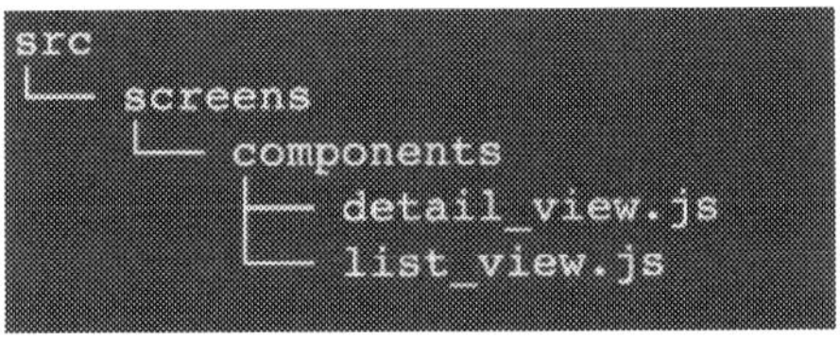

Figure 5-21. *New folder src for our code*

In list_view.js file, we will define our ListView component. In the next chapter, this component would be responsible for retrieving and rendering all our Pizzeria records from the API.

The process of compiling a custom component is similar to what we have done in React. First, you need to import React and basic components from React Native. This time, we will add Button component to our list of imports.

```
import React, { Component } from "react";
import { StyleSheet, View, Text, Button } from "react-native";
```

The component itself structurally looks like any other React component we have done before. In our View tags, we place Text tags with a placeholder "List View" for now and Button tags with "List Item, Click for Details" that on a click would take us to the DetailView component, like this:

```
class ListView extends Component {
  render() {
    return (
      <View style={styles.center}>
        <Text style={styles.title}>List View</Text>
        <Button title="list Item, Click for Details" />
      </View>
    );
  }
}
export default ListView;
```

We add a little bit of style for now to our View and Text tags. With the StyleSheet component, we create object styles and define the center and title like this:

```
const styles = StyleSheet.create({
  center: {
    flex: 1,
    justifyContent: "center",
    alignItems: "center",
  },
  title: {
    fontSize: 36,
    marginBottom: 16,
  },
});
```

The whole list_view.js file should look like the one in Figure 5-22.

```
     list_view.js          ×
1    import React, { Component } from "react";
2    import { StyleSheet, View, Text, Button } from "react-native";
3
4    class ListView extends Component {
5      render() {
6        return (
7          <View style={styles.center}>
8            <Text style={styles.title}>List View</Text>
9            <Button title="list Item, Click for Details" />
10         </View>
11       );
12     }
13   }
14
15   const styles = StyleSheet.create({
16     center: {
17       flex: 1,
18       justifyContent: "center",
19       alignItems: "center",
20     },
21     title: {
22       fontSize: 36,
23       marginBottom: 16,
24     },
25   });
26
27   export default ListView;
28
```

Figure 5-22. *ListView component in the list_view.js file, React Native project*

The next step is to import ListView to App.js file and include it into our return function.

```
import ListView from "./src/screens/components/list_view";
```

<ListView /> tag should be placed inside the App component in the return function under our Text components.

```
export default function App() {
  const mytext = "by ProgramWithUs";
  return (
    <View style={styles.container}>
      <Image
        style={styles.pizzaImage}
        source={{
          uri: "https://bit.ly/book-pizza",
        }}
      />
      <Text style={styles.baseText}>Pizza vs. Pizza App</Text>
      <Text style={styles.newText}>{mytext}</Text>
      <ListView />
    </View>
  );
}
```

When we save these changes, we could see that our original pizza image went up under the notch on iPhone (Figure 5-23). If for some reason your simulator is not being updated and not giving you any error messages, just reboot and rerun your simulator from Metro Bundler.

Figure 5-23. *After we added ListView component to main page, image moved up under the notch*

This does not look pretty, and React Native has a great solution to make sure everything would stay within safe boundaries. There is a SafeAreaView component. Based on a device, it would create a safe padding for our content.

In App.js, we need to replace View with SafeAreaView component in import and in JSX tags.

```
import React from "react";
import { StyleSheet, Text, SafeAreaView, Image } from "react-
native";
import ListView from "./src/screens/components/list_view";

export default function App() {
  const mytext = "by ProgramWithUs";
```

```
  return (
    <SafeAreaView style={styles.container}>
      <Image
        style={styles.pizzaImage}
        source={{
          uri: "https://bit.ly/book-pizza",
        }}
      />
      <Text style={styles.baseText}>Pizza vs. Pizza App</Text>
      <Text style={styles.newText}>{mytext}</Text>
      <ListView />
    </SafeAreaView>
  );
}
```

With SafeAreaView component, our pizza image on the iPhone simulator is placed accurately under the notch. You could see SafeAreaView component in action in Figure 5-25. This is a temporary solution because we are still working on the navigation system. I have pivoted a bit to introduce the SafeAreaView component.

The idea behind ListView component is to render all records and flip over to the detail screen when a user clicks a particular item. DetailView in detail_view.js will be the same as ListView for now. You can copy and paste ListView code into detail_view.js. Make sure you change the component name to DetailView, including export statement on the bottom, and replace the message in <Text> tags to Detail View, like I did here:

```
import React, { Component } from "react";
import { StyleSheet, View, Text } from "react-native";

class DetailView extends Component {
  render() {
    return (
```

```
      <View style={styles.center}>
        <Text style={styles.title}>Detail View</Text>
      </View>
    );
  }
}

const styles = StyleSheet.create({
  center: {
    flex: 1,
    justifyContent: "center",
    alignItems: "center",
  },
  title: {
    fontSize: 36,
    marginBottom: 16,
  },
});
export default DetailView;
```

Next, we clean some space in the App component in App.js and move the code from App function to the ListView component in list_view. js. The incoming code should be placed inside the render() method. Do not forget the style related to text and image. Our updated ListView should look like the one in Figure 5-24. Do not forget to import SafeAreaView to list_view.js file.

```
     list_view.js         ×
1    import React, { Component } from "react";
2    import { StyleSheet, SafeAreaView, Text, Image, Button } from "react-native";
3
4    class ListView extends Component {
5      render() {
6        const mytext = "by ProgramWithUs";
7        return (
8          <SafeAreaView style={styles.center}>
9            <Image
10             style={styles.pizzaImage}
11             source={{
12               uri: "https://bit.ly/book-pizza",
13             }}
14           />
15           <Text style={styles.baseText}>Pizza vs. Pizza App</Text>
16           <Text style={styles.newText}>{mytext}</Text>
17           <Text style={styles.title}>List View</Text>
18           <Button title="list Item, Click for Details" />
19         </SafeAreaView>
20       );
21     }
22   }
23
24   const styles = StyleSheet.create({
25     center: {
26       flex: 1,
27       justifyContent: "center",
28       alignItems: "center",
29     },
30     title: {
31       fontSize: 36,
32       marginBottom: 16,
33     },
34     baseText: {
35       color: "navy",
36       fontSize: 30,
37       fontStyle: "italic",
38     },
39     newText: {
40       color: "red",
41     },
42     pizzaImage: {
43       width: 200,
44       height: 200,
45     },
46   });
47
48   export default ListView;
49
```

Figure 5-24. *Updated ListView component in list_view.js*

The App component will be holding the navigation menu. Based on user's choice, it would render a list screen or a detail screen or any other screen. To set up the navigation for our React Native project, we would need to import components from React Navigation to our main file App.js.

```
import { NavigationContainer } from "@react-navigation/native";
import { createStackNavigator } from "@react-navigation/stack";
```

Speaking of importing, we need to have all our custom components imported too.

```
import ListView from "./src/screens/components/list_view";
import DetailView from "./src/screens/components/detail_view";
```

Since we moved everything from the App component return() function to another file, feel free to remove whatever code is left from the App component. We would no longer be using that code. StyleSheet will be the only component we would need to stay.

NavigationContainer is the main navigation component, and it has to be placed right into the root of the app. Within NavigationContainer, we place other navigation objects like Stack and Drawer. We need to initialize Stack by calling createStackNavigator function. Stack generates routes, referred to as Screens. For each Screen element, we would need to provide a name and our component. The basic structure would look like this:

```
const Stack = createStackNavigator();

export default function App() {
  return (
    <NavigationContainer>
      <Stack.Navigator>
        <Stack.Screen name="Home" component={ListView} />
        <Stack.Screen name="Detail" component={DetailView} />
      </Stack.Navigator>
    </NavigationContainer>
  );
}
```

Screen "Home" would provide a path to ListView component and "Detail" to DetailView. In the final step, we would be passing props on button click, to link the list item and detail screen in ListView component. In list_view.js file, add the function onPress handler with props to navigate to "Detail" Screen.

```
<Button
        title="list Item, Click for Details"
        onPress={() => this.props.navigation.navigate("Detail")}
/>
```

Make sure your code in App.js and list_view.js is similar to mine (Figures 5-25 and 5-26). The button "list Item, Click for Details" on click should take you to the detail screen with our message "Detail View" (Figure 5-26). Please note that on iPhone we have a different native element mapped to <Button> component than in Android, and "list Item, Click for Details" would look different.

Figure 5-25. *App.js file with the navigation and Android emulator*

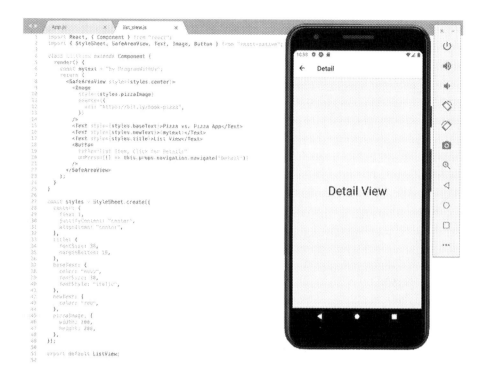

Figure 5-26. *The list_view.js file with added navigation props to Button component and Detail screen on the Android emulator after the "*`list Item, Click for Details`*" button was clicked*

Another very popular navigation component is the Drawer. To make the structure of our project simple and clean, we will create a new directory drawer in `src/screens` and nest it with three components: screenA, screenB, and screenC. For each component, create a file as shown in Figure 5-27.

Figure 5-27. *New directory drawer with screenA, screenB, and*
screenC files

These three files for now would have similar code with components
named after files. We will copy code from detail_view.js and paste it in our
new files. The difference between them would be the component name;
screenA.js would have class screenA extends Component, screenB.js
would have class screenB extends Component, and so on. Also, the text
would be different, reflecting the name of the component. Do not forget to
export each component on the bottom line accordingly. This is an example
for screenA.js. All other components would have the same code. However,
the name of each component would correlate with the hosting file name.
ScreenA component should be in screenA.js, ScreenB in screenB.js, and
ScreenC in screenC.js.

```
import React, { Component } from "react";
import { StyleSheet, View, Text } from "react-native";
class ScreenA extends Component {
  render() {
    return (
      <View style={styles.center}>
        <Text style={styles.title}>Screen A</Text>
      </View>
    );
  }
}
```

```
const styles = StyleSheet.create({
  center: {
    flex: 1,
    justifyContent: "center",
    alignItems: "center",
  },
  title: {
    fontSize: 36,
    marginBottom: 16,
  },
});
export default ScreenA;
```

As a rule of thumb, if you want to use a component, you need to import it. We will import all three components to our App.js file.

```
import ScreenA from "./src/screens/drawer/screenA.js";
import ScreenB from "./src/screens/drawer/screenB.js";
import ScreenC from "./src/screens/drawer/screenC.js";
```

We initialize Drawer object with createDrawerNavigator() function. Make sure you import it first to App.js.

```
import { createDrawerNavigator } from '@react-navigation/drawer';

const Drawer = createDrawerNavigator();
```

We are planning to render one navigator inside a screen of another navigator, and there are certain rules we have to follow.[6] We need to create a separate function renderScreenComponents and place there our Stack.Navigator component with two Stack.Screens "Home" and "Detail". renderScreenComponents should be placed above the App component in the App.js file.

---

[6]https://reactnavigation.org/docs/nesting-navigators/

```
renderScreenComponents = () => (
  <Stack.Navigator>
    <Stack.Screen name="Home" component={ListView} />
    <Stack.Screen name="Detail" component={DetailView} />
  </Stack.Navigator>
);
```

In the return function, we will embed the Drawer object. All React Navigation objects have Navigator and Screen attributes. Our `Drawer.Navigation` structure would look like `Stack.Navigator` with one exception. For "Home" button, we will pass the children keyword instead of the component.

```
export default function App() {
  return (
    <NavigationContainer>
      <Drawer.Navigator>
        <Drawer.Screen name="Home" children={this.
        renderScreenComponents} />
        <Drawer.Screen name="Screen A" component={ScreenA} />
        <Drawer.Screen name="Screen B" component={ScreenB} />
        <Drawer.Screen name="Screen C" component={ScreenC} />
      </Drawer.Navigator>
    </NavigationContainer>
  );
}
```

Our Drawer is connected to the Home screen, and we can pull it from the left side (Figure 5-28). When you push Screen A button in the Drawer, it takes you to ScreenA component, and then you can return to the Home screen by choosing the first option from the same menu. Again, if your simulator/emulator is acting slow, do not hesitate to rebundle the code by clicking Run on iOS simulator or Run on Android device/emulator buttons in Metro Bundler.

Figure 5-28. *App.js file with Stack and Drawer navigation. iPhone simulator with Drawer menu*

Using the same logic, we can add lower tabs to our detail component. On the same level as the drawer folder in src/screens, we need to create new directory tabs. In this tabs folder, we will place two files, tab1.js and tab2.js (Figure 5-29).

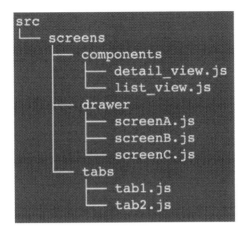

Figure 5-29. *In the src/screens directory, create new folder tabs and place there tab1.js and tab2.js files*

Both files would have similar code. Exactly what we did for drawer files. The only difference would be the component names and text in <Text> tags. The tab1.js file would host TabOne component rendering "Tab One Screen", and tab2.js would have TabTwo component with "Tab Two Screen" text. Make sure you export the right component on the bottom of each file.

Here is an example of the component I would place in tab1.js.

```
import React, { Component } from "react";
import { StyleSheet, View, Text } from "react-native";
class TabOne extends Component {
  render() {
    return (
      <View style={styles.center}>
        <Text style={styles.title}>Tab One Screen</Text>
      </View>
    );
  }
}
```

```
const styles = StyleSheet.create({
  center: {
    flex: 1,
    justifyContent: "center",
    alignItems: "center",
  },
  title: {
    fontSize: 36,
    marginBottom: 16,
  },
});
```

```
export default TabOne;
```

Here, I use TabOne for the component name, and subsequently tab2.js would host the TabTwo component with the text "Tab Two Screen."

In App.js, we would need to import these new components and createBottomTabNavigator from React Native.

```
import { createBottomTabNavigator } from "@react-navigation/
bottom-tabs";
import TabOne from "./src/screens/tabs/tab1.js";
import TabTwo from "./src/screens/tabs/tab2.js";
```

The next step would be to initialize Tab with the createBottomTabNavigator function.

```
const Tab = createBottomTabNavigator();
```

Now we are ready to create a function for the Tab navigation. In the same App.js, we define renderTabComponents, and using the Screen attribute, navigate to TabOne and TabTwo.

```
renderTabComponents = () => (
  <Tab.Navigator>
    <Tab.Screen name="Tab 1" component={TabOne} />
    <Tab.Screen name="Tab 2" component={TabTwo} />
  </Tab.Navigator>
);
```

To make our tabs accessible from the detail screen, we would need to add them as another Screen attribute to the Stack object in renderScreenComponents function and pass renderTabComponents as children props (Figure 5-31).

```
 renderScreenComponents = () => (
  <Stack.Navigator>
    <Stack.Screen name="Home" component={ListView} />
    <Stack.Screen name="Detail" component={DetailView} />
    <Stack.Screen name="Tabs" children={this.
    renderTabComponents} />
  </Stack.Navigator>
);
```

All right, the last step would be to connect Stack object with DetailView. Using the same logic as in ListView, we would need to import Button component into detail_view.js file and add Button to DetailView. This Button component will have the title "Click for Tabs" and onPress handler to navigate to Tabs (Figure 5-30).

```
<Button
title="Click for Tabs"
onPress={() => this.props.navigation.navigate("Tabs")}
/>
```

```
     detail_view.js          ×
1    import React, { Component } from "react";
2    import { StyleSheet, View, Text, Button } from "react-native";
3
4    class DetailView extends Component {
5      render() {
6        return (
7          <View style={styles.center}>
8            <Text style={styles.title}>Detail View</Text>
9            <Button
10             title="Click for Tabs"
11             onPress={() => this.props.navigation.navigate("Tabs")}
12           />
13         </View>
14       );
15     }
16   }
17
18   const styles = StyleSheet.create({
19     center: {
20       flex: 1,
21       justifyContent: "center",
22       alignItems: "center",
23     },
24     title: {
25       fontSize: 36,
26       marginBottom: 16,
27     },
28   });
29
30   export default DetailView;
31
```

Figure 5-30. *Button to invoke tabs in the DetailView component*

Make sure you save all files and run this on a simulator. When you click the "Click for Tabs" button, you should see two tabs on the bottom of your simulator screen (Figure 5-31).

Figure 5-31. *Tab navigation in App.js and Tab1 and Tab2 on the bottom of the iPhone simulator*

I hope you feel more fluent and comfortable moving around with React Native. In the next chapter, we will implement our CRUD functions with the help of the Axios library.

CHAPTER 6

Mobile app

In this chapter, we will assemble our mobile app using all the knowledge we have gained so far. I will try to be logical and extrapolate methods we have used in React, in Chapter 4, to our principal project powered by React Native and applicable to iOS and Android platforms. We will create React Native components and screens correlating to our back-end Django APIs. As we move along, we will take a closer look at styling elements. Also, we will spend a great deal of time working with images. To store more pictures of each pizzeria, we will create a new model and connect it to our Model.

Networking

Our ListView component should be able to fetch all records from our database and serve them using pizzeria_list API. If you do not quite remember the pattern of this API, go to the URL dispatcher in our Django project and look it up by the name. Our APIs should be up and running. Make sure Django's built-in web server is running.

Note Every time before launching Django with the command python manage.py runserver, make sure the virtual environment is engaged.

© Art Yudin 2020
A. Yudin, *Building Versatile Mobile Apps with Python and REST*,
https://doi.org/10.1007/978-1-4842-6333-4_6

Following the same logic we used in Chapter 4, we would need to call the API with a JavaScript library Axios. Install Axios to our latest project pizzavspizza_app. Using npm command, we will install Axios in React Native project.

```
npm install axios --save
```

Due to the fact that accessing the Web is a completely different task than rendering records, it would be a good idea to keep the API's calls isolated from our components in another file and maybe even in a separate directory.

In our React Native project, we need to create a new folder api in src directory right next to screens. Inside api folder, create client.js file (Figure 6-1).

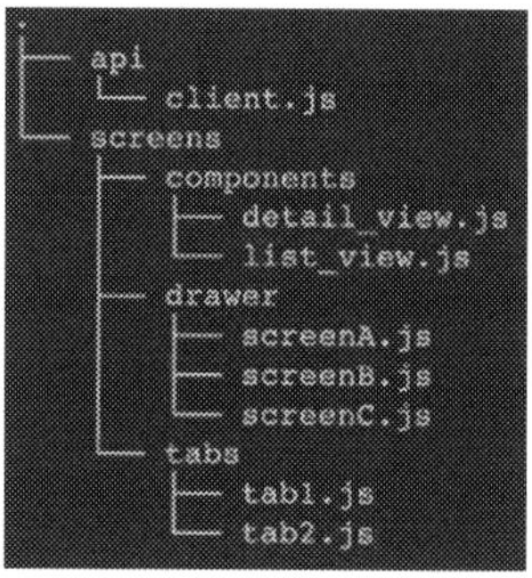

Figure 6-1. *New directory api with client.js file*

client.js will be responsible for all networking communications with the outside world. In this file, we will import Axios and, in create() method, define a baseURL for our back-end server. The create() method would initialize a new Axios instance and set custom defaults for our application. This would be an appropriate place to add headers if you need to call the API with an authentication key or any other arguments.

Note   To establish an instance, create() method must have **baseURL** with uppercase URL at the end. All other spellings would not work. The URL address has no closing "/".

```
import axios from "axios";
export default axios.create({
  baseURL: "http://127.0.0.1:8000",
});
```

Note   In some cases, the Android emulator may not render information coming from a local server. Although we will discuss in detail how to deploy your project to a real server later in Chapter 8, I have our back-end project running on pizzavspizza.com. If your code is correct and the Android emulator still cannot fetch data from your local http://127.0.01:800 server, replace the local URL with the `http://pizzavspizza.com/api` domain in client.js. The Android emulator should reach the Web then. After refreshing the app, you should see the results.

To use the Axios instance in our ListView component, we need to import it to list_view.js file.

```
import client from "./../../api/client";
```

When I was writing this book, I had a dilemma; should I do all components as classes or functions? I know many React Native developers prefer to compile their components as simple JavaScript functions. For starters, it is simpler. Besides, recently, React Native added Hooks to simplify the function compiling process. This new cool feature allows to use componentDidMount features and other lifecycle methods without declaring a class. Since the main idea behind this book is to introduce and explain the logic of Django and React Native, I decided to show you both the class component example and the function component solution. We will start with the class, only because our ListView is already done as a class and we got an idea of how React classes work based on our experience with them from Chapter 4.

Class Component API call

To render a list of items, React Native provides a scrollable built-in solution FlatList. FlatList is specifically designed for list views – logically similar to function map() we have used before. FlatList is scrollable and easy to use. To get started with FlatList basic component, we would need to import it to list_view.js file and append it to the list of elements coming from "react-native".

```
import { StyleSheet, SafeAreaView, Text, Image, Button,
FlatList} from "react-native";
```

Calling an API process would be similar to what we did in Chapter 4. We will go through the same steps. First, fetch an array of records; second, set it as State; and third, render all items in FlatList component as text.

Using Axios instance imported through client.js, we will access our list of records in componentDidMount method. As we discussed before, componentDidMount method would be the best place for an API call. We will request our pizzerias list information through Axios instance in componentDidMount, like this:

```
componentDidMount() {
    client.get("/").then((response) => {
      this.setState({ data: response.data });
    });
  }
```

Next, we need to initialize the constructor and define data as an empty array. Our data would be coming as an array, and we would need to store it in the appropriate structure. To access data in render(), we would need to pass it into the method, const { data } = this.state;.

```
constructor(props) {
    super(props);
    this.state = {
      data: [],
    };
  }
```

Finally, we will insert <FlatList/> element between <Text> and <Button/> elements.

Let's go over the FlatList component for a second. FlatList takes data as an array and iterates through it, rendering each item. Each item must have a unique key passed as a string. Be careful with all attributes and make sure you use correct captions for keyExtractor and renderItem.[1]

```
<FlatList
        data={data}
        keyExtractor={(item) => item.id.toString()}
        renderItem={({ item }) => (
          <Text style={styles.itemText}>
            {item.pizzeria_name}, {item.city}
          </Text>
        )}
      />
```

Every item is wrapped in <Text> tags. Through an item, we can access our pizzeria attributes – item.pizzeria_name and item.city. As I have mentioned before, an id must be a string. Using the JavaScript toString()

---

[1]https://reactnative.dev/docs/flatlist

method, we can convert an integer to an acceptable format. In our case, I have added a style just to distinguish pizzerias from everything else on the screen. No worries, this is just a temporary solution. We will add the appropriate style to components later in this chapter. Insert the new attribute itemText into the styles object on the bottom of the file.

```
itemText: {
  color: "green",
  fontSize: 20,
}
```

If both of your servers, http://127.0.01:800/ and http://localhost:19002/, are running, then you should see the list of our pizzerias rendering on the main "results" screen as you can see in Figure 6-2.

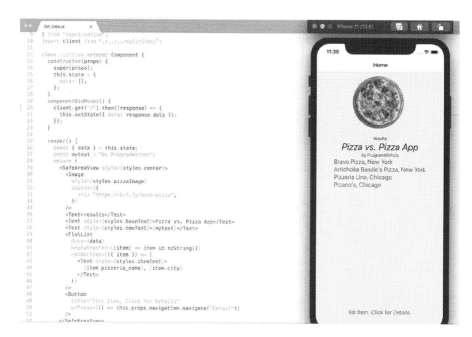

Figure 6-2. *FlatList rendering elements from the Django project*

A very common practice is to use async/await with componentDidMount() method in React Native. The word "async" before the method assures that a promise would be returned by the method. Promises are a built-in solution in JavaScript to support asynchronous programming. The word "await" makes code wait until the promise yields a result. Async/await is just a wrapper around promises. You can learn more about promises at `https://developer.mozilla.org`.[2] Using async/await with API calls is a good practice, and we can implement it with componentDidMount() method in our example.

Since the outcome of the API call might be a failure, it is a good idea to capture an error message. Also, to enhance user experience, professional developers would add some default information or images in case the API call fails. This option would not leave a user with a blank screen and spoil the first impression about the app. In real life, many things could go wrong, not necessarily related to your code – a weak Wi-Fi signal or unreliable third-party API, just to name a few.

Using the "async" keyword before the function name, we can convert componentDidMount() into an asynchronous method.

```
async componentDidMount() {
    try {
      const response = await client.get("/");
      if (!response.ok) {
        this.setState({ data: response.data });
      }
    }catch (error) {
      console.log(error);
    }
}
```

---

[2]`https://developer.mozilla.org/en-US/docs/Web/JavaScript/Reference/Global_Objects/Promise`

The try statement will make an attempt to fetch the information, and if it was successful, it would set the response as data. Otherwise, it would catch an error message. For quicker debugging, many developers would place inside the catch statement a helper function to email them a message with the bug to fix the problem ASAP. We are not going to implement that here.

One last thing we could do here is to get the number of items we have in an array. Data in the constructor holds our incoming information as an array. Using the array attribute length, we can see how long the incoming list is.

Simple message results wrapped in <Text> tags could be released with

```
<Text>{data.length} Pizzerias</Text>
```

I'll place this statement right above the <FlatList> element. You could see the final version of the <ListView> component with the asynchronous componentDidMount method in Figure 6-3.

Figure 6-3. *Final version of ListView defined as a class component in list_view.js*

Note   If your iPhone simulator or Android emulator is acting up, just reboot them. Rebooting should wipe out the memory.

Function Component API call

To illustrate how we can make the same API call with hooks and define a component as a function, I will create a new file function_list_view.js in the components folder (Figure 6-4).

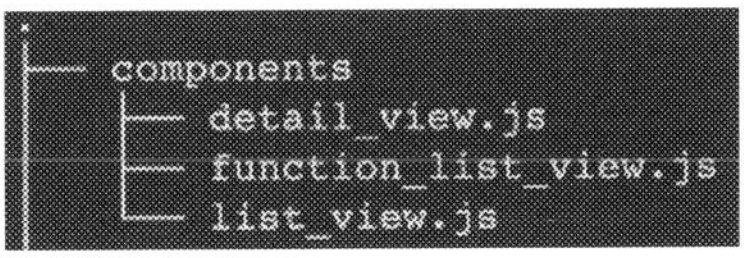

Figure 6-4. function_list_view.js for Function Component in the components directory

On top of the function_list_view.js file, we import useState and useEffect hooks. Please note that we are not importing the **Component** as in the previous example, simply because we will compile everything as a function component.

```
import React, { useState, useEffect } from "react";
```

The first question you would probably ask is "What is a hook?" The formal definition you can find in the React documentation says, "A Hook is a special function that lets you 'hook into' React features."[3] In a nutshell, a useState hook is a substitution of the State attribute in React class. You can achieve the same functionality with hooks in a function component as you would get in the class component with built-in attributes, like State and others. The useEffect hook is a function

---

[3]https://reactjs.org/docs/hooks-state.html

193

equivalent to componentDidMount, componentDidUpdate, and componentWillUnmount methods. You might recall them from React class lifecycle we discussed in Chapter 4, Figure 4-4.

First things first, we need to redirect the ListView component to function_list_view.js file in App.js. Replace ListView import with the following:

```
import ListView from "./src/screens/components/function_list_
view";
```

Many elements of the ListView function in function_list_view.js would be the same as in the previous example. We can just copy the code from the list_view.js file to the new function_list_view.js.

In function_list_view.js file, replace class ListView and constructor with

```
const ListView = () => {
  const [data, setData] = useState([]);}
```

Make sure to check if opening brackets match corresponding closing brackets. Now the ListView component is a functional expression, and the useState hook succeeds the constructor. At the moment, data is defined as an empty array waiting for incoming results. Conceptually, it's similar to what we implemented before with a class constructor.

Inside our ListView component, we will define getList function, very similar to what we did in componentDidMount method. We will use the "async" keyword to make our function asynchronous.

```
const getList = async () => {
    const response = await client.get("/");
    setData(response.data);
  };
```

setData will assign results to the data referred before as a useState hook. If we were writing a class component, we would call an API in componentDidMount method. Since the useEffect hook covers the functionality of componentDidMount, we will invoke our getList function in useEffect. I do not want to place the asynchronous function itself in useEffect Hook, for a simple reason. An asynchronous function always returns a promise. Please note that the useEffect hook uses a second argument, an empty array. This array is used to pass dependencies to useEffect. We do not have any dependencies for this call and leave it empty. If for some reason or by mistake you forget or remove this empty array brackets, the useEffect hook would call the getList function over and over again, consequently hitting an API. In other words, without the second argument, we would end up in an infinite loop. By passing the empty array into useEffect, we execute getList function only once when the component is rendered the first time.

```
useEffect(() => {
    getList();
  }, []);
```

Keep in mind that we no longer need the render() method because it is not a part of a function. A function returns the result, and this is where we keep FlatList component. Also, const { data } = this.state; should be removed. We no longer use State. Everything else following this point would be the same as in the ListView class component before, except props for navigation in <Button> element. We remove <Button> element for now. We will implement it again later in a different manner. Also, we would need to use a return for our item attributes rendered as Text.

```
<FlatList
        data={data}
        keyExtractor={(item) => item.id.toString()}
        renderItem={({ item }) => {
```

195

```
return (
  <Text style={styles.itemText}>
    {item.pizzeria_name}, {item.city}
  </Text>
);
}}
/>
```

Make sure your syntax is correct and you have the same number of closing brackets as the opening ones (Figure 6-5).

Figure 6-5. *ListView component implemented as a function in function_list_view.js*

> **Note**   If you miss console.log() on the debugging console in React
> Native, you can press ⌘ + D in the iPhone simulator and choose the
> Remote JS Debugging option. This will open a new page running in
> the browser on localhost:19001/debugger-ui/. Using Developer Tools,
> you could inspect messages printed with the console.log() function.
> Also, console.log() stuff would be printed in the terminal.

Passing data between screens

Now that we have a list of our pizzeria places, it would be a good idea to fetch all details for a particular place on a click. All we have to do is to call a detail URL and render it on another screen. In Chapter 4, we solved this problem by passing absolute_url attribute of an object as props. In React Native, this operation would be simpler, considering we have a navigation in place.

React Navigation's stack navigator helps us to go from one screen to another by passing props on click. While we are swiping between screens, we might as well pass values.

So far, we have been using button element, but it is bulky and displayed variously on different platforms.

To produce details of a restaurant by a touch, we will need to use TouchableOpacity component. On a press, an element wrapped in TouchableOpacity would fade out and act as a button. We can bind our absolute_url to the navigator and pass it as props.

As always, we would need to import TouchableOpacity into function_list_view.js file.

```
import {
  StyleSheet,
  SafeAreaView,
  Text,
```

```
  Image,
  FlatList,
  TouchableOpacity,
} from "react-native";
```

In the previous example, we got rid of the button element with a navigation. Logically, we would need a navigation at some point, and the best way to define it would be to pass it as an argument in ListView function.

```
const ListView = ({ navigation }) => {
//code
}
```

We can use TouchableOpacity in our FlatList component in return. Each item you want to be clickable should be wrapped in <TouchableOpacity> tags, like this:

```
<FlatList
        data={data}
        keyExtractor={(item) => item.id.toString()}
        renderItem={({ item }) => {
          return (
            <TouchableOpacity
              onPress={() => {
                navigation.navigate("Detail", { objurl:
                item.absolute_url, hey: "Best Pizza" });
              }}
            >
              <Text style={styles.itemText}>
                {item.pizzeria_name}, {item.city}
              </Text>
```

```
        </TouchableOpacity>
    );
  }}
/>
```

TouchableOpacity comes with the event handler onPress. When pressed, it would navigate to a screen name – in this case, it would be "Detail" – and pass additional props to that screen. Props should be passed in the navigate function as a second argument in the form of a dictionary. Just as an example that you can pass anything as props, I would add one more argument – the message "Best Pizza" (Figure 6-6).

Figure 6-6. *ListView component passing props through navigation to DetailView component in function_list_view.js*

To stay consistent, I'll implement DetailView component in detail_view.js file as a function. As in the previous example, we would need to pass the navigation as an argument and add the route. The route will help us to handle parameters passed through the navigation.

```
const DetailView = ({ navigation, route }) => {
        //code
}
```

Let's see if we can grab these params in DetailView component.

To extract params from the navigation, add this code right after the DetailView function header:

```
const { objurl } = route.params;
 const { hey } = route.params;
```

Remove the render method(). Inside the return, replace the <Button> element with

```
<View style={styles.center}>
    <Text style={styles.title}>{ hey }</Text>
    <Text style={styles.title}>{ objurl }</Text>
 </View>
```

After you have done that, you can press any pizzeria name on the main screen, and it should redirect you to the Detail screen with the item id and "Best Pizza" message (Figure 6-7).

Figure 6-7. *DetailView component passing props through the navigation*

Detail view screen

With the URL we have received from the ListView component, we can fetch all details our back-end has to offer about each pizzeria. The process would be similar to what we just did with ListView. We would need useState and useEffect hooks. Let's import them right away.

```
import React, { useState, useEffect } from "react";
```

Speaking of imports, do not forget to import client.js file with an instance of Axios.

```
import client from "./../../api/client";
```

Again, the useState hook would substitute the constructor because ListView is a function component at the present. In the useState hook, we define the detail variable to hold our incoming data and setDetail. The only difference between the current setup and what we did in the previous example would be an empty string as a default value for Detail.

```
const [detail, setDetail] = useState("");
```

We would need a function to make the API call. Create one and name it getDetail. This would be an asynchronous function with an async keyword. Moreover, this function will take an argument, the object URL we passed as props.

```
const getDetail = async (url) => {
   const response = await client.get(url);
   setDetail(response.data);
};
```

It would be a good idea to use try and catch statements again. Maybe the object we are trying to fetch no longer exists. In this case, we would need to catch a 404 error message.

```
const getDetail = async (url) => {
   try {
      const response = await client.get(url);
      if (!response.ok) {
         setDetail(response.data);
      }
   } catch (error) {
      console.log(error);
   }
};
```

The useEffect hook will invoke getDetail function upon rendering DetailView component. Make sure the second argument, an empty array, is in place.

```
useEffect(()=>{ getDetail(objurl); }, [])
```

The moment we get data from our back-end server, we would be able to access all attributes of our object. I will remove the hey props we used for testing purposes and in <View> tags list the main attributes coming from the detail URL. In order to fit all this text on a screen, I'll adjust the font size to 15, like this: title: { fontSize: 15}.

```
<View style={styles.center}>
     <Text style={styles.title}>Pizzeria: {detail.pizzeria_
     name}</Text>
     <Text style={styles.title}>Address: {detail.street}
     </Text>
     <Text style={styles.title}>
       City: {detail.city}, {detail.state},{detail.zip_code}
     </Text>
     <Text style={styles.title}>Web: {detail.website}</Text>
     <Text style={styles.title}>Ph: {detail.phone_number}
     </Text>
     <Text style={styles.title}>Description: {detail.
     description}</Text>
     <Text style={styles.title}>Email: {detail.email}</Text>
   </View>
```

You might ask, "What about the image? A picture is worth a thousand words." Sure thing, we will deal with an image next. Before we get to that part, make sure your ListView component renders details when you press a pizzeria from the list on the main screen (Figure 6-8).

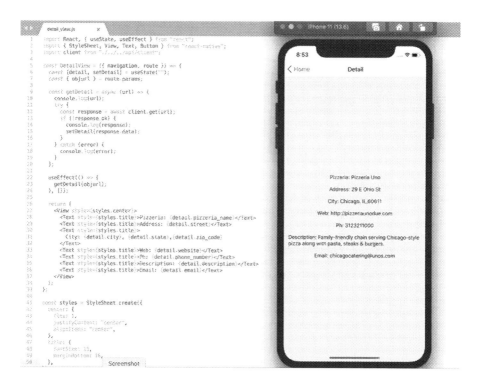

Figure 6-8. *DetailView component, the detail screen rendering information if you press a pizzeria from the list*

Images from HTTP URL

Our DetailView component is working fine, and we can render the image. A picture would require an Image component; we can add it to our imports.

```
import { StyleSheet, View, Text, Image } from "react-native";
```

The Image component must have a source and dimensions for pics coming from the Web. JSX is different from HTML, and we would need to use the "source" verbatim not "src". The source must have an object with a URI key. For dimensions, I'll use width: 200 and height: 200. Our code should be clean and neat, so I will update the StyleSheet with

```
pizzaImage: {
    width: 200,
    height: 200,
    marginBottom: 16,
  }
```

The URI in the source would point to the detail.logo_image URL serving an image. Make sure you have uploaded pictures to your database, or you could use mine, just replace the baseURL: "http://pizzavspizza. com/api" in client.js. Insert <Image> component into <View> tags in the DetailView component.

```
<Image
  style={styles.pizzaImage}
  source={{
    uri: detail.logo_image,
  }}
/>
```

Before you try the image feature, we need to make some adjustments to the global urls.py file in pizzaproject directory in the Django project. We need to add static and media paths for all image files. I will go more into the details about how Django serves static and image files in Chapter 8. We need to import static function and settings into pizzaproject/urls. py like this from django.conf.urls.static import static from django.conf import settings. Also, append the urlpatterns list with the MEDIA_ URL and STATIC_URL paths like this: + static (settings.MEDIA_URL, document_root=settings.MEDIA_ROOT)+ static (settings.STATIC_URL, document_root=settings.STATIC_ROOT). At the end of the day, the detail screen should render the image for a restaurant we have in our database (Figure 6-10).

```
16  from django.conf.urls.static import static
17  from django.conf import settings
18  from django.contrib import admin
19  from django.urls import path, include
20
21  urlpatterns = [
22      path('admin/', admin.site.urls),
23      path('', include('stores.urls')),
24  ]+ static(settings.MEDIA_URL, document_root=settings.MEDIA_ROOT)+ static(settings.STATIC_URL, document_root=settings.STATIC_ROOT)
25
```

Figure 6-9. *Media and Static paths are needed to serve uploaded and static files*

Figure 6-10. *DetailView component, the detail screen rendering an image from db.sqlite3*

Our goal is to have many images of each pizzeria. Users could submit their own images and attach them to a particular restaurant. Sounds like we need a separate table in our database to hold all these images.

If each pizzeria object needs to have a multiple number of images, then we need to define another Model in the Django project models.py file. This Model would be connected to the Pizzeria Model through a foreign key.

Also, this approach could be applied any time you need to bind one Model to another. For example, if later we would want to add comments, or a menu from the restaurant, we could define a new Model for that object and get models connected with a foreign key. This would establish one-to-many relationships. One pizzeria could have many images or many comments or many variations of pizza.

In the Django project models.py, we will add an Image Model with a couple of fields. The Image field would provide a path to the image itself, and we define it as an ImageField instance. Image_title, in case we want to provide a name for an image, would be a string. The most important field would be a ForeignKey instance. We would need it to establish a many-to-one relationship. This field would require the name of the Model it is bound to and an on_delete argument. An on_delete argument is usually set to a CASCADE option, meaning the record would be deleted if the object it was bound to was gone. Also, add a blank argument as True to the ForeignKey field. We would need it in case we want to create a new pizza place and have no photos yet to attach. We might want to add DateTimeField to keep track of most recent uploads. The actual model looks like this:

```
class Image(models.Model):
    pizzeria = models.ForeignKey(Pizzeria, on_delete=models.
    CASCADE,
    related_name='pizzeria_images', blank=True, null=True)
    image = models.ImageField(upload_to='photos')
    image_title = models.CharField(max_length=120, blank=True)
    uploded_at = models.DateTimeField(auto_now_add=True)
```

The inner class Meta in Django is responsible for how the object and its attributes are rendered. It might specify permissions and default ordering. We want to see the recent upload first, and we will set it as metadata under the Image Model.

```
class Meta:
    ordering = ['-uploaded_at']
```

The minus before the field name means that we want to reverse the order and sort it in a descending manner.

Additionally, in our Pizzeria model logo_image field, we would place a default value for an image. If a user wants to create a new pizza place but does not have an image yet, we could provide a default image. You can take any image file and copy it into the /media/pizzariaImages/ folder. If you would like to use my file, you can download it here: https://bit.ly/book-pizzalogo.

Updated logo_image field in Pizzeria would look like this:

```
logo_image = models.ImageField(upload_to='pizzariaImages',
blank=True, default="pizzariaImages/pizzalogo.png")
```

Every time you make changes to models.py, you need to run makemigrations and then migrate. In your pizzaproject directory where the manage.py file is, run the makemigrations command (make sure the virtual environment is activated).

```
python manage.py makemigrations
```

If you got error messages, make sure your fields are correct and the indentation is OK like in Figure 6-11.

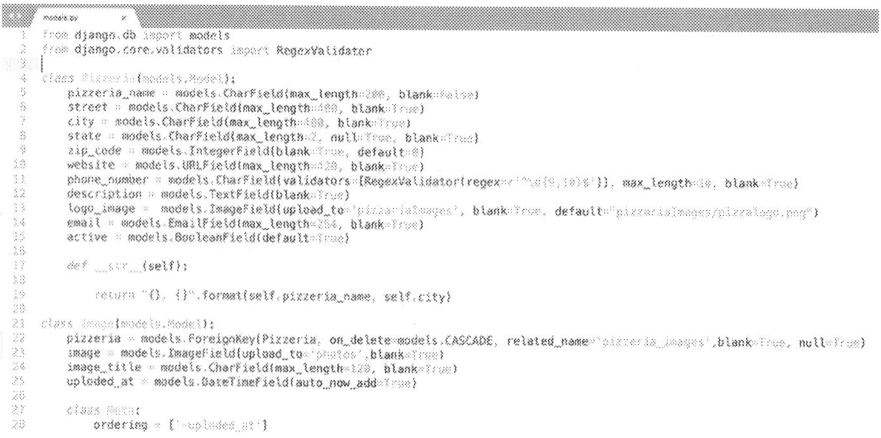

Figure 6-11. *Image model in the Django project models.py file*

The first command, makemigrations, would create a blueprint, and the next command, migrate, would create that table in db.sqlite3 file.

```
python manage.py migrate
```

We need to import the Image model into the admin.py file in the Django project pizzavspizza and register.

```
from .models import Image
admin.site.register(Image)
```

This would give us an option to upload and manage images through the admin menu (Figure 6-12).

```
admin.py              ×
1  from django.contrib import admin
2  from .models import Pizzeria
3  from .models import Image
4
5  admin.site.register(Pizzeria)
6  admin.site.register(Image)
7
```

Figure 6-12. *Register the Image model in the admin.py file*

Django will be serving pizzeria images URLs. We need to include the Image Model in serializers. Import a new Model Image to serializers.py.

```
from .models import Image
```

Using HyperlinkedModelSerializer class to bind one model to another, we define ImageSerializer in serializers.py in the Django project.

```
class ImageSerializer(serializers.HyperlinkedModelSerializer):
    class Meta:
        fields = ['id', 'image', 'image_title', 'uploded_at']
        model = Image
```

We list all fields from the Image Model except the pizzeria field. To nest ImageSerializer in PizzeriaDetailSerializer, we need to define it using related_name we have used in our Image Model "pizzeria_images" (Figure 6-13). We have to use this name as a keyword to connect models together. The argument "many" in ImageSerializer field means that we expect many images, as our relation implies, one to many.

```
pizzeria_images = ImageSerializer(many=True, required=False)
```

Now we can include pizzeria_images field in PizzeriaDetailSerializer fields.

```
class Meta:
        model = Pizzeria
        fields = [
            'id',
            'pizzeria_name',
            'street',
            'city',
            'state',
            'zip_code',
            'website',
            'phone_number',
            'description',
            'email',
            'active',
            'update',
            'delete',
            'pizzeria_images',
        ]
```

Also, I think we should move logo_image field out of PizzeriaDetailSerializer and include it in PizzeriaListSerializer. After all, a logo image should be on the list view. We would need it to make a nice first impression. Finally, our serializers.py should look like the one in Figure 6-13.

Figure 6-13. *PizzeriaDetailSerializer includes ImageSerializer*

Launch a server and add images through the admin menu in your browser.

```
python manage.py runserver
```

I have uploaded my photos, and when I call the Detail View, the Pizzeria object includes fields from a related Image Model under the name "pizzeria_images" (Figure 6-14). Coming up, we will render all these images in the detail screen in React Native app.

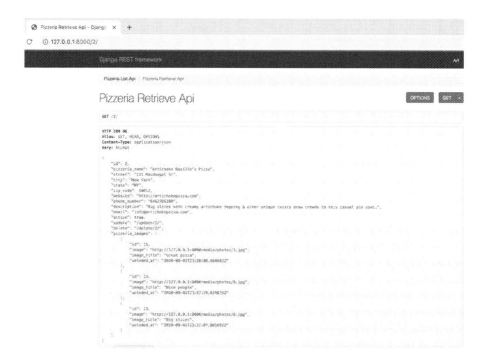

Figure 6-14. *Django REST serving Detail view with a related model Image*

Let's flip back to our React Native project. In Figure 6-14, we can see that images come in an array assigned to the pizzeria_images keyword. If we want to render images one by one, we would need to iterate. Logically, this sounds like a job for a FlatList component.

In detail_view.js file, we append our import list with FlatList component.

```
import { StyleSheet, View, Text, Image, FlatList } from
"react-native";
```

From the previous example with FlatList, we know that it requires an array, id, and some kind of item. To grab each image from pizzeria_images list, we can pass it as a keyword argument data={detail.pizzeria_images} into FlatList. A single image is stored as an object in the Image Model and comes with a primary key or id we can obtain with keyExtractor argument keyExtractor={(item) => item.id.toString()}. The item we want to render would be the image URL. We can simply replace the URI in the Image component source with item.image. Ultimately, FlatList would return the Image component with source={{uri: item.image}}.

```
<FlatList
    data={detail.pizzeria_images}
    keyExtractor={(item) => item.id.toString()}
    renderItem={({ item }) => {
      return (
        <Image
          style={styles.pizzaImage}
          source={{
            uri: item.image,
          }}
        />
      );
    }}
/>
```

The outer curly braces evaluate an expression in JSX, and the inner ones indicate an object. The whole FlatList structure in the DetailView component will replace logo <Image> tags and should look like the one in Figure 6-15.

Figure 6-15. *FlatList element rendering images in the DetailView component*

By default, the FlatList component presents items as a scrollable vertical list. In DetailView, we should probably render images horizontally. In my opinion, that would be more convenient and familiar to users. This is easy to achieve; all we have to do is to add the keyword argument horizontal and set it to true inside the <FlatList/> element, like this:

```
<FlatList
        horizontal={true}
        data={detail.pizzeria_images}
        keyExtractor={(item) => item.id.toString()}
```

```
renderItem={({ item }) => {
  return (
    <Image
      style={styles.photo}
      source={{
        uri: item.image,
      }}
    />
  );
}}
/>
```

Moreover, we can make the detail screen a little bit eye-catching. This would require a lot of code in the StyleSheet, and to make our DetailView cleaner, we should move Styles to another file. Create detail_styles.js file in the components directory. Then copy and paste the Styles object from detail_view.js into new detail_styles.js file. Now that StyleSheet is no longer needed in detail_view.js, let's remove it and import on the top of detail_styles.js.

```
import { StyleSheet } from "react-native";
```

At the same time, we need to bind styles to DetailView component and import it in detail_view.js.

```
import styles from "./detail_styles";
```

After we have bound styles together we can concentrate on styling itself in detail_styles.js. In the Styles object, I want to start with pizzaImage attribute and round up the corners of our squared images. You can find all style props here: https://reactnative.dev/docs/view-style-props. I'll use a couple of essential elements in this book just to give you an idea of how to use them.

For our images, we will use the borderRadius prop and set it to 20 points.

```
pizzaImage: { width: 400, height: 400, borderRadius: 20 }
```

The bigger the value, the rounder your photo would get. I'll increase the width and height of an image to 400 points. The Pizzeria name should be bright and bold. I'll replace the text attribute with a title for a restaurant name and details for everything else. My title would have the fancy font Cochin set to fontFamily prop. I do not think that Android supports Cochin font. If you are designing an app specifically for Android, use any other font of your choice. Font size 40 and bold red color would distinguish it from other text on the screen.

```
title: {
    fontFamily: "Cochin",
    margin: 10,
    marginBottom: 5,
    color: "red",
    fontSize: 40,
    textAlign: "center",
    fontWeight: "bold",
  }
```

The Details text would be much simpler like this:

```
details: {
    margin: 10,
    marginBottom: 5,
    color: "black",
    fontSize: 15,
    textAlign: "center",
    fontWeight: "bold",
  }
```

All old and no longer needed attributes in StyleSheet should be removed. Do not forget to import the styles object after you are done with it and to export default styles, on the bottom of the detail_styles.js file. Also, I'll clean up DetailView component. First, I'll replace style.text with style.title and style.details. Second, I'll remove Pizzeria, Address, and other labels we had on the screen for testing purposes. Probably, leave ph: label; without it, a phone number looks like some sort of a serial number. On your iPhone simulator, you should see pizzeria details like in Figure 6-16 and be able to swipe images from right to left.

Figure 6-16. *Final view of detail screen with detail_view.js and detail_style.js files*

Card list view screen

A card element is a staple of mobile apps. Card is a content container. You can make corners round, title bold, and price and details bright to make your element stand out. The flashier the card style is, the more chances a user would click it. We leave these marketing options to professional designers and implement a simple card element. We will list all our pizzerias as cards on the main screen.

One option would be to add style to FlatList items. This solution would limit the use of our card style in other screens. The main idea of React is to reuse components over and over again; that is why we will implement card as a functional component in a separate file. Moreover, we will place this file into a new folder. I'll name the folder "shared". As the name implies, this would be a folder for all components we might want to use again and share them with among different screens. In the components directory, we will make the new folder "shared" with file card.js (Figure 6-17).

Figure 6-17. *New file card.js in the shared folder inside the components directory*

Our goal is to render each list element in a card container. A React component is like a function; we can pass the main attributes of every pizzeria into a small Card component as props.

In the newly created card.js file, we need to import React and basic components of React Native. The Card component should have an image, title, and some details. Sounds like we need Image and Text. To wrap it all up nicely, we would need the StyleSheet and View components.

```
import React from "react";
import { View, Image, Text, StyleSheet } from "react-native";
```

In the card.js file, we define Card as a functional component and export it on the bottom of the file page.

```
const Card = () => {
  return (
  );
};
export default Card;
```

The barebones of our Card component would be View, Image, and Text elements. We would need an outer <View> container for the logo image and an inner <View> container to hold <Text> items. This structure would be returned by our Card component.

```
<View>
      <Image source={ logo } />
      <View>
        <Text>{ title }</Text>
        <Text>{ details }</Text>
      </View>
 </View>
```

Each container, Image, and Text would require some sort of styling, and we define the Styles object under the Card component. Let's start with the outer container and set layout styling props as the following:

```
container: {
    marginTop: 20,
    backgroundColor: "white",
    overflow: "hidden",
```

219

```
    flex: 1,
    borderRadius: 15,
  }
```

Every card in our list view would have a padding defined with marginTop props. I set it to 20, but you are welcome to play with it and see how it works and what look you would like better. The background would be white to make the pizzeria name and city more visible. Overflow props by default have two options, "visible" and "hidden." Hidden would guarantee that the image would not overshadow our round corners which we set to 15 as borderRadius. Finally, flex would control how our card elements would be placed along the axis.[4]

Image is an important part of the card element, and we want to have 100% width of our container and we set the height to 250 points.

```
logo: {
    width: "100%",
    height: 250,
  }
```

Text elements should be centered with a bit of padding like this:

```
inner: {
    padding: 20,
    flex: 1,
    justifyContent: "center",
    width: "100%",
    height: 100,
}
```

---

[4]https://reactnative.dev/docs/flexbox#flex

Title and details attributes of the card element conceptually would be the same as we had them in the ListView component. However, we can try other colors and fontSize props. Feel free to experiment with colors, sizes, and fonts too.

```
title: {
    fontSize: 28,
    margin: 10,
    fontWeight: "bold",
    color: "black",
    textAlign: "center",
  },
  details: {
    fontSize: 15,
    margin: 10,
    fontWeight: "bold",
    color: "blue",
    textAlign: "center",
  }
```

We would pass {logo}, {title}, and {details} as props to the Card component.

```
const Card = ({ logo, title, details }) => {
//code
}
```

The Image component is very sensitive to dimensions and source, as you may recall from previous examples. The Pizzeria logo would be coming as a URI, and we need to include "uri" into our image source keyword.

```
<Image style={styles.logo} source={{ uri: logo }} />
```

You can see the whole Card component in the cards.js file in Figure 6-18.

Figure 6-18. *Card component in the card.js file*

We import the Card component to function_list_view.js and place it inside our <FlatList> element.

```
import Card from "./shared/card";
```

All pizzeria attributes would be passed as props to the Card component. This Card component will replace <Text> tags in <FlatList> we have used before.

```
<Card
    logo={item.logo_image}
    title={item.pizzeria_name}
    details={item.city}
 />
```

I'll wrap <FlatList> component with <View> tags inside of <SafeAreaView> element. Make sure the View component is imported into the function_list_view.js file. For a new <View> container, we will set the style with padding and gray color like this:

```
container: {
    backgroundColor: "#eeeeee",
    padding: 20,
  }
```

Finally, to clear some space for our cards in the list screen, I'll remove all elements like <Image> for pizza pie and <Text> tags with "Pizza vs. Pizza App". Same goes for style props we no longer use; feel free to remove them. <FlatList> will be the main element of our ListView component as you can see in Figure 6-19.

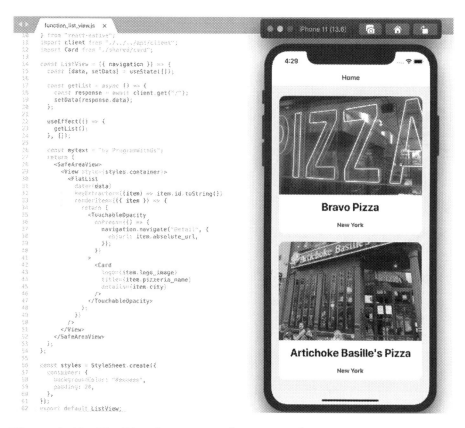

Figure 6-19. *FlatList element rendering Card component*

In this chapter, we have answered the question "how to retrieve data from the Django project and render it on a mobile platform." This chapter is another example that using Django and building a RESTful API structure would give a developer the ability to use any front-end technology. I hope by now you have got the feel of the power and versatility of Django as a back-end. Besides CRUD operations, Django would be a great platform to perform any data analysis, data manipulations, machine learning, and automation utilizing the power of Python.

In the next chapter, we will explore Create operations and see how we can receive data from a user and send it to the back-end.

CHAPTER 7

Assembling versatile mobile application

In the previous chapter, we have implemented the retrieve part of the mobile application. Here, we will learn how to send POST requests and attach images to our records. We will go in baby steps and discuss the whole process from capturing incoming data to forms and other third-party solutions to help us handle and validate information. Creating new records is an essential part of any web app. Along with that, an Image is a vital part of any new record, especially for mobile users. We will break down to the smallest element handling an Image in mobile platforms. Finally, we will take a look at authentication options in Django REST.

Inputting data

Before we use POST request to send the data to the database, I would like to explain to you how to grab a user input on a mobile device. For this task, we would use TextInput, a React Native component. TextInput comes with numerous props. Here, we will discuss the essential ones. If you are planning to build mobile apps for a living, it would be a good idea to get familiar with all of them and read the documentation at `https://reactnative.dev/docs/textinput`.

© Art Yudin 2020
A. Yudin, *Building Versatile Mobile Apps with Python and REST*,
https://doi.org/10.1007/978-1-4842-6333-4_7

As you might recall from Chapter 5, we have the drawer component ScreenA. It is not doing anything at the moment, and we can use it to practice TextInput.

Navigate to screenA.js file and import basic React Native components. Be prepared to update the import list with new components as we move along.

```
import { StyleSheet, Image, SafeAreaView, TextInput, Text }
from "react-native";
```

We rewrite ScreenA class component as a functional expression. Later, we will change the name of this component to reflect the purpose of the code, but for now ScreenA name would work. Inside ScreenA component, we will use SafeAreaView, to make sure all our elements would stay under the iPhone notch. Inside <SafeAreaView> tags, we place the TextInput element like this:

```
const ScreenA = () => {
  return (
    <SafeAreaView>
      <TextInput />
    </SafeAreaView>
  );
};
```

For TextInput component, we will use the simplest styling, just to make it visible on the screen at the moment.

Right under the ScreenA component, we define a styles object and set the following props for the textBox attribute:

```
const styles = StyleSheet.create({
  textBox: {
    marginTop: 200,
    height: 40,
```

```
    borderColor: "gray",
    borderWidth: 1,
    marginRight: 20,
    marginLeft: 20,
  },
});
```

Make sure you bind the style to TextInput in order for styles to apply:

```
<TextInput style={styles.textBox} />
```

If you ran this drawer component on the simulator now, you would see just an empty bordered box in the center of the screen. We need to add a couple of essential props to start with. Our final goal here is to give a user the technical ability to record information on a new pizza place. Prior to building a form with all fields, let's see how the one field input would work. For starters we learn how to grab the name of a place. TextInput comes with built-in features. Let's put these features to use. In TextInput component, we pass placeholder props set to "Pizzeria." autoCapitalize comes with default settings "none," "sentences," "words," and "characters." I think we should capitalize all words in the name. Set autoCapitalize to "words." We will set the autoCorrect feature to false. autoCorrect's job is to check the spelling of an input. You have probably noticed that with names the autocorrect feature acts goofy. Chances are that the pizza place name is not in the dictionary. Not to drive our users nuts over an extraordinary name or brand, we would switch autocorrect off.

```
<TextInput
        style={styles.textBox}
        autoCapitalize="words"
        autoCorrect={false}
        placeholder="Pizzeria"
    />
```

Finally, the iPhone simulator and Android emulator render an empty prompt with the placeholder "Pizzeria" (Figure 7-1).

Figure 7-1. *iPhone and Android render TextInput element*

You can try it and type something in that TextInput element. The question is how we would grab that text so we can use it later. Well, if you want to set some value and use it later, that sounds like State, right? In a functional component, we have to use the useState hook. Go ahead and import it from "react":

```
import React, { useState } from "react";
```

In order for us to use this hook, we need to define an array with two values. First is a variable name we are trying to assign with the value, and the second value should start with "set" to set up the value to the variable. I'll use "pizzeria" as a variable.

```
const [pizzeria, setPizzeria] = useState(" ");
```

The useState hook would have an empty string as a default value. As we start typing something, the text would be set as the value and stored with the "pizzeria" variable. The useState hook would be triggered by onChangeText handler. Add this handler inside <TextInput> tags onChangeText={(text) => setPizzeria(text)}.

If we want to see this in action, we can insert a <Text> element above the input.

```
<Text
      style={{
        marginTop: 100,
        fontSize: 40,
        color: "red",
        textAlign: "center",
      }}
    >
      {pizzeria}
    </Text>
```

I have added a little bit of style to make this output visible. Try it, type something in the prompt box, and you immediately will see this text in red on the screen (Figure 7-2).

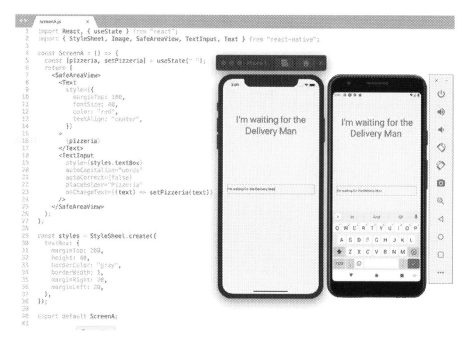

Figure 7-2. *Text entered into TextInput component being rendered on the screen with the help of a useState hook*

This would be the idea behind each field in our form. Use TextInput and define a useState hook. Then we need to validate fields and raise errors if a user inputs data in a wrong format. You might say, this is too much work, there has to be a better way. Yes, there is another way. There are third-party libraries for React forms and field validation. I am talking about Formik and Yup.

Forms with Formik and Yup

Formik is a popular choice of React developers to handle forms. I would definitely recommend you to visit their website: https://formik.org. They have tons of useful information. In the following example we will see how Formic can grab a user's input and then will validate incoming data with Yup. Using the npm command, install Formik and Yup.

```
npm install formik -- save
npm install yup -- save
```

For our form, we would need a submit button. Let's update our imports and add a Button component. Now, we need to import Formik and Yup.

```
import { StyleSheet, SafeAreaView, TextInput, Button, Text }
from "react-native";
import { Formik } from "formik";
import * as Yup from "yup";
```

In ScreenA component, remove the useState hook. Also, remove the useState hook from import. We would no longer need it. Spoiler alert, Formik comes with its own hooks. The text element we have used to see if our TextInput box was working can be removed too. Instead, place the opening and closing <Formik> </Formik> tags into return() right after <SafeAreaView>. For now, I'll use two inputs, pizzeria and city. Not to overwhelm you with many lines of code. You have to understand that in order for Formik to perform its task, it would require at least three ingredients:

1. initialValues (where we initiate input values)

2. onSubmit (what do we want to do with these values)

3. TextInputs with submit button

We are starting with initialValues. This is easy; just list all field values and define them as empty strings and pass as an object.

```
<Formik initialValues={{ pizzeria: "", city: "" }}></Formik>
```

Next, we will define onSubmit as a function that would take values and show them in an alert message.

```
<Formik
        initialValues={{ pizzeria: "", city: "" }}
        onSubmit={(values) => {
          alert(JSON.stringify(values, null, 2));
        }}
 ></Formik>
```

Last but not least, between <Formik> opening and closing tags, we create a function that on submit will handle our incoming values. This function would need JSX with input fields, and they all would have to be wrapped as one element. We might use <View> component, or sometimes people use empty div tags. In this function, we define Formik's handleChange, handleSubmit, and values. Along with event handlers, they would grab and submit values. The TextInput element we already have could be used again. We just need to duplicate it and move them into empty <> tags. I'll leave the necessary props only. Set one for a pizzeria and the other one for city. Logically, we would need to have a submit button under them. As a last touch, I would change the value of marginTop to 50 in styles.

```
{(({ handleChange, handleSubmit, values }) => (
         <>
           <TextInput
             style={styles.textBox}
             value={values.pizzeria}
             type="text"
             placeholder="Enter a new pizza place here"
             onChangeText={handleChange("pizzeria")}
           />
```

```
<TextInput
  style={styles.textBox}
  value={values.city}
  placeholder="City"
  onChangeText={handleChange("city")}
/>
<Button onPress={handleSubmit} title="Submit" />
</>

)}
```

After you enter the pizzeria name and city and then click submit button, the iPhone simulator will render the values as an alert message (Figure 7-3).

Figure 7-3. *Alert message displaying the values we have entered in form fields*

As you remember in the second chapter of this book, we defined the Pizzeria model. We were very specific about the fields. We have set the fields to a specific number of characters we can accept and determined pizzeria_name as a required field. In real life, people always make mistakes and might skip a field accidently. Or, and this happens a lot, enter a value in incorrect format. The bottom line is we need to validate the inputs before we send data to our database. You do not want the POST request to be rejected simply because someone unintentionally missed a field. As I always say, a good developer would guide the user. It is very easy to validate data with Yup library. Yup would be the best option for Formik.

You can use the models.py file in Django project as a reference to implement the same data validation format using Yup methods for the Pizzeria model.

Inside our <Formik> element, we can define validationSchema with the help of Yup.object() function. You can reference all Yup options here: www.npmjs.com/package/yup.

In order for the pizzeria name to be successfully sent to a server, it would have to be a string with a max of 200 characters. Otherwise, we would have to raise an error message: "Must be less than 200 characters." The minimum we can set is three characters with a validation message: "Must be at least 3 characters." According to our Django model, a pizzeria name is a must have. Based on that, we will add the Yup required method to make sure a user has entered the value for a pizzeria name.

```
const validationSchema = Yup.object().shape({
    pizzeria: Yup.string().max(200, 'Must be less than 200
    characters').min(3, 'Must be at least 3 characters').
    required('Required')
  })
```

The city input format would be very close to pizzeria. But according to our Model, it could be left blank and may contain 400 characters. I probably should've checked the world atlas first to see if there was a city with such a long name.

```
city: Yup.string().max(400, 'Must be less than 400
characters').min(3, 'Must be at least 3 characters')
```

Finally, we need to pass this object to <Formik> component.

```
validationSchema={validationSchema}
```

And include <Text> tags with error messages. The errors variable should be added to the list of arguments we use for our TextInput fields. One last thing, let's add color: "red" to styles and pass it as an error attribute.

```
const ScreenA = () => {
  const validationSchema = Yup.object({
    pizzeria: Yup.string().max(200, 'Must be less than 200
    characters').min(3, 'Must be at least 3 characters').
    required('Required'),
    city: Yup.string().max(400, 'Must be less than 400
    characters').min(3, 'Must be at least 3 characters'),
  })
  return (
    <SafeAreaView>
      <Formik
        initialValues={{ pizzeria: "", city: "" }}
        onSubmit={(values) => {
          alert(JSON.stringify(values, null, 2));
        }}
        validationSchema={validationSchema}
      >
        {(({ handleChange, handleSubmit, values, errors }) => (
```

```
            <>

            <TextInput
              style={styles.textBox}
              value={values.pizzeria}
              type="text"
              placeholder="Enter a new pizza place here"
              onChangeText={handleChange("pizzeria")}
            />
            <Text style={styles.error}>{errors.pizzeria}</Text>
            <TextInput
              style={styles.textBox}
              value={values.city}
              placeholder="City"
              onChangeText={handleChange("city")}
            />
            <Text style={styles.error}>{errors.city}</Text>
            <Button onPress={handleSubmit} title="Submit" />
          </>

        )}
      </Formik>
    </SafeAreaView>
  );
};

  error:{
    color: "red"
  }
```

Now, if the user intentionally or by mistake leaves pizzeria field blank, our app would raise a red error message, like the one you can see in Figure 7-4.

Figure 7-4. *Yup raises error messages*

The example we just did perfectly illustrates how Formik and Yup could help us with the form and data validation. Before we get to the POST request, I would like to refactor this code. I will split this file into three modules to make the component cleaner. There will be an actual component, and I think it is about time we rename ScreenA to AddPizzeria. Then there should be a separate file for validationSchema. We need to validate many fields, and it could become messy and confusing. Also, we would need to add a lot of code for styling.

According to our new naming convention, we would need to rename ScreenA to AddPizzeria everywhere, including the name of the file itself. I'll call the file addPizzeria.js.[1] Do not forget to change all instances of

---

[1]Make sure addPizzeria.js starts with a lower case "a" because autocorrect tends to capitalize it.

ScreenA in App.js to AddPizzeria and replace the import with addPizzeria from "./src/screens/drawer/addPizzeria.js";. Right next to the newly renamed addPizzeria.js, create two files for our style, addPizzeria_styles.js (Figure 7-5) and addPizzeria_valid.js.

```
── drawer
    ├── addPizzeria.js
    ├── addPizzeria_styles.js
    ├── addPizzeria_valid.js
    ├── screenB.js
    └── screenC.js
```

Figure 7-5. *We have renamed the screenA.js file to addPizzeria.
js and added addPizzeria_styles.js and addPizzeria_valid.js in the
drawer directory*

Next, import these addPizzeria_styles.js and addPizzeria_valid.js files right above the addPizzeria component.

```
import styles from "./addPizzeria_styles"; import
validationSchema from "./addPizzeria_valid";
```

In addPizzeria_styles.js, import

```
import { StyleSheet } from "react-native";
import validationSchema from "./addPizzeria_valid";
```

and define a structure for the styles object; do not forget to export it on the bottom of the addPizzeria_styles.js file.

```
const styles = StyleSheet.create({
//code
});
export default styles;
```

Here, we would need to define style props for the following attributes: container, image, title, textBox, error, and addButton. By now, you have probably guessed that design is not my strong point, so I invite you to explore fonts, sizes, and colors.

By now, dealing with the Image component should be simple as we have discussed it many times during the course of this book. The Image component requires height and width props.

```
image: {
    width: 200,
    height: 200,
},
```

The error text and input prompt would look like this:

```
error: {
    color: "red",
    fontSize: 18,
    marginBottom: 7,
    fontWeight: "600",
    paddingLeft: 20,
},
textBox: {
    borderColor: "#CCCCCC",
    borderTopWidth: 1,
    borderBottomWidth: 1,
    height: 50,
    fontSize: 25,
    paddingLeft: 20,
    paddingRight: 20,
},
```

Let me remind you that the Button component would be rendered as a button on Android only, so this style would work for Android platforms.

```
addButton: {
    borderWidth: 1,
    borderColor: "#007BFF",
    backgroundColor: "#007BFF",
    padding: 15,
},
```

Finally, we will wrap all our elements with a container View. We will set the color to white, and with the help of width and height, we will make sure that 100% of the screen would be covered.

```
container: {
    justifyContent: "center",
    backgroundColor: "#ffffff",
    width: "100%",
    height: "100%",
},
```

You can see the styles object in Figure 7-6. Make sure you remove the old styles object on the bottom of addPizzeria.js. Otherwise, it would clash with imported styles from addPizzeria_styles.js.

All right, let's move to addPizzeria_valid.js file. On top, we would need to import Yup:

```
import * as Yup from "yup";
```

Move our validationSchema from addPizzeria.js to addPizzeria_valid.js and add all other fields based on our Pizzeria model in models.py. For now, we will skip the logo_image field because for image we will create a special component. Also, we do not need to include an active field; it would be set to True value by default.

Based on what we have done for pizzeria and city fields, you understand the principle behind Yup validation. But how would you validate a phone number or a website address? We could use regex as we did in the Django model. For that, we need to define regex patterns for phone and website.

```
const phone = /^((\\+[1-9]{1,4}[ \\-]*)|(\\([0-9]{2,3}\\)[ \\-
]*)|([0-9]{2,4})[ \\-]*)*?[0-9]{3,4}?[ \\-]*[0-9]{3,4}?$/;
const website = /^((https?):\/\/)?(www.)?[a-z0-9]+(\.[a-z]
{2,}){1,3}(#?\/?[a-zA-Z0-9#]+)*\/?(\?[a-zA-Z0-9-_]+=[a-
zA-Z0-9-%]+&?)?$/;
```

For all fields, we would use string() method, even for zip_code. We would need a string data type to send a POST request. Email is an essential piece of information in any form. Fortunately for us, Yup comes with a special email() validator method, and we will use that for our email field.

```
const validationSchema = Yup.object({
  pizzeria: Yup.string()
    .max(200, "Must be less than 200 characters")
    .min(3, "Must be at least 3 characters")
    .required("Required"),
  street: Yup.string()
    .max(400, "Must be less than 400 characters")
    .min(3, "Must be at least 3 characters"),
  city: Yup.string()
    .max(400, "Must be less than 400 characters")
    .min(3, "Must be at least 3 characters"),
  state: Yup.string()
    .max(2, "Must be exactly 2 characters")
    .min(2, "Must be exactly 2 characters"),
```

```
zip_code: Yup.string()
  .max(5, "Must be exactly 5 numbers")
  .min(5, "Must be exactly 5 numbers"),
website: Yup.string().matches(website, "Enter correct url"),
phone_number: Yup.string().matches(phone, "Phone number is
not valid"),
description: Yup.string().max(500, "Must be less than 400
characters"),
email: Yup.string().email("Not a valid email"),
});
```

Following React guidelines, we need to export validationSchema on the bottom of addPizzeria_valid.js file. You can see the final version of addPizzeria_valid.js in Figure 7-6.

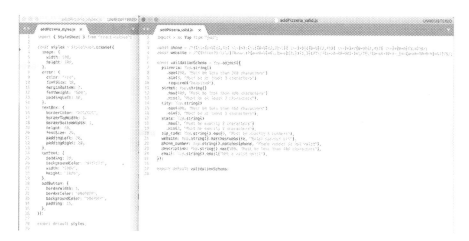

Figure 7-6. *addPizzeria_styles.js and addPizzeria_valid.js in the drawer directory*

After we cleaned the addPizzeria.js file of style and validationSchema, it would be easier for us to concentrate on TextInput fields. We have nine TextInput fields, and down the road we would need to attach an image. To make sure all these fields would fit nicely on the screen of any iPhone or

Android model, we will use the React Native component ScrollView. It is kind of similar to FlatList. A user would be able to scroll through elements. Usually, ScrollView would be applied to a much smaller list, fewer than 100 items. We have less than 100 elements, and ScrollView would be a perfect choice for us. Import the ScrollView component.

```
import {TextInput,
  Button,
  Text,
  Image,
  ScrollView,
  SafeAreaView,
} from "react-native";
```

The barebones of our AddPizzeria component would look like this:

```
const AddPizzeria = () => {
  return (
    <Formik>
      {(({ handleChange, handleSubmit, values, errors }) => (
        <SafeAreaView>
          <ScrollView>
            <Image/>
            <TextInput/>
            <Text ></Text>
            <Button/>
          </ScrollView>
        </SafeAreaView>
      )}
    </Formik>
  )
}
```

<SafeAreaView> will use style={styles.content} from our addPizzeria_
styles.js file. Inside the <Formik opening tag, we will define all initial values
and set them all to strings. In JSON.stringify, replace 2 with 9, the number
of values we are passing.

```
<Formik
    initialValues={{
      pizzeria: "",
      street: "",
      city: "",
      state: "",
      zip_code: "",
      website: "",
      phone_number: "",
      description: "",
      email: "",
    }}
    onSubmit={(values) => {
      alert(JSON.stringify(values, null, 9));
    }}
    validationSchema={validationSchema}
  >
```

As a placeholder, we will use our old image of pizza pie and place it
as a first element inside <ScrollView> tags. It is OK that it is not centered.
We need the default image for now, and later it would be replaced with an
image picker component.

```
<Image
  style={styles.image}
  source={{ uri: "https://bit.ly/book-pizza" }}
/>
```

Each TextInput component would have the same props with different values from our `initialValues` list. We have defined `initialValues` at the beginning of the <Formik>. All TextInputs share the same `style={styles.textBox}`, and under each input, we will place a <Text> element with an error message. You can take this example and use it as a template for all TextInput fields. The final file would look like the ones in Figures 7-7 and 7-8.

```
<TextInput
            style={styles.textBox}
            value={values.street}
            placeholder="Street address"
            onChangeText={handleChange("street")}
        />
<Text style={styles.error}>{errors.street}</Text>
```

Before we implement the POST request with Axios, we need to test our form with an alert message (Figures 7-7 and 7-8). Enter your favorite pizza place name and address to check if your form works correctly. The AddPizzeria component is very concentrated, and the following is the code from addPizzeria.js:

```
import {
        SafeAreaView,
        ScrollView,
        TextInput,
        Button,
        Image,
        Text
} from "react-native";

import { Formik } from "formik";
import styles from "./addPizzeria_styles";
import validationSchema from "./addPizzeria_valid";
```

```
const AddPizzeria = () => {
  return (
    <Formik
      initialValues={{
        pizzeria: "",
        street: "",
        city: "",
        state: "",
        zip_code: "",
        website: "",
        phone_number: "",
        description: "",
        email: "",
      }}
  onSubmit={(values) => {
    alert(JSON.stringify(values, null, 9));
  }}
validationSchema={validationSchema}
>
{(({ handleChange, handleSubmit, values, errors }) => (
<SafeAreaView style={styles.content}>
<ScrollView>
<Image
  style={styles.image}
  source={{ uri: "https://bit.ly/book-pizza" }}
/>
<TextInput
    style={styles.textBox}
    value={values.pizzeria}
    placeholder="Enter a new pizz place here"
    onChangeText={handleChange("pizzeria")}
/>
```

```
<Text style={styles.error}>{errors.pizzeria}</Text>
<TextInput
    style={styles.textBox}
    value={values.street}
    placeholder="Street address"
    onChangeText={handleChange("street")}
/>
<Text style={styles.error}>{errors.street}</Text>
<TextInput
    style={styles.textBox}
    value={values.city}
    placeholder="City"
    onChangeText={handleChange("city")}
/>
<Text style={styles.error}>{errors.city}</Text>
<TextInput
    style={styles.textBox}
    value={values.state}
    placeholder="State"
    onChangeText={handleChange("state")}
/>
<Text style={styles.error}>{errors.state}</Text>
<TextInput
    style={styles.textBox}
    value={values.zip_code}
    placeholder="Zip"
    onChangeText={handleChange("zip_code")}
/>
<Text style={styles.error}>{errors.zip_code}</Text>
<TextInput
    style={styles.textBox}
```

```
    value={values.website}
    placeholder="Website"
    onChangeText={handleChange("website")}
/>
<Text style={styles.error}>{errors.website}</Text>
<TextInput
    style={styles.textBox}
    value={values.phone_number}
    placeholder="Phone number"
    onChangeText={handleChange("phone_number")}
/>
<Text style={styles.error}>{errors.phone_number}</Text>
<TextInput
    style={styles.textBox}
    value={values.description}
    placeholder="Description"
    onChangeText={handleChange("description")}
/>
<Text style={styles.error}>{errors.description}</Text>
<TextInput
    style={styles.textBox}
    value={values.email}
    placeholder="Email"
    onChangeText={handleChange("email")}
/>
<Text style={styles.error}>{errors.email}</Text>
<Button
    style={styles.addButton}
    onPress={handleSubmit}
    title="Submit"
/>
```

```
</ScrollView>
</SafeAreaView>
)}
</Formik>
)}
export default AddPizzeria;
```

Figure 7-7. *First half of the addPizzeria.js file and iPhone simulator rendering an alert message with information I just entered*

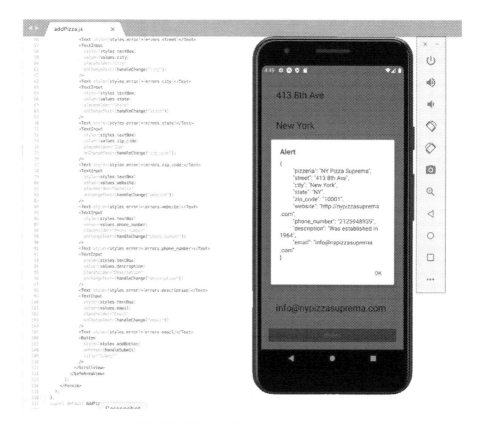

Figure 7-8. *Second half of the addPizzeria.js file and Android emulator rendering an alert message with information I just entered*

Sending data to the API

We have successfully extracted data from the form, and now we can package it and send it to a database. What exactly do I mean by package? I propose to use the FormData object and set the values of inputs to model fields. We will use model fields as keys and compile an object to be sent with a POST request. FormData is commonly used to send forms with attached files. With a FormData object, the Axios post() method would set headers as "content-type":"multipart/form". "Multipart/form" is one of the methods to encode the data that structures the POST request itself.

We would need to use "multipart/form" because later we would attach an image to our form.

To make our POST API call, we will define a new function handleSubmit right above the return method in AddPizzeria component. Inside the handleSubmit function, we will use the Axios instance through `client` and compile the FormData object. The structure of handleSubmit function would look like this:

```
const handleSubmit = (values) =>{
    const data = new FormData();
    client.post(//API call)
}
```

Some developers prefer to create a special file for a layer between the API client and onSubmit handler. We are not going to multiplicate files here, simply to make the process as clear and understandable as it can be.

To compile the FormData object, we would need to define a variable and assign a FormatData() function.

```
const data = new FormData();
```

The FormData function will initialize a new object, and we could append our keys and values to the object.

```
const data = new FormData();
data.append("pizzeria_name", values.pizzeria);
data.append("street", values.street);
data.append("city", values.city);
data.append("state", values.state);
data.append("zip_code", values.zip_code);
data.append("website", values.website);
data.append("phone_number", values.phone_number);
data.append("pizzeria_name", values.pizzeria);
data.append("description", values.description);
data.append("email", values.email);
```

251

We will skip an image field for now. If there is no incoming image, we have a default one in our Django Model.

To make a post() request, we need to pass a URL for the Create View and data. Django URL requires "/create/" extension to set up a new Pizzeria object.

```
client
      .post("/create/", data)
      .then(function (response) {
        console.log(response);
      })
      .catch(function (response) {
        console.log(response);
      });
```

When you finish the handleSubmit function, you need to pass it to onSubmit handler. Replace the alert message and all other code we used before; here is the updated AddPizzeria component:

```
const AddPizzeria = () => {
  const handleSubmit = async (values) =>{
    const data = new FormData();
    data.append("pizzeria_name", values.pizzeria);
    data.append("street", values.street);
    data.append("city", values.city);
    data.append("state", values.state);
    data.append("zip_code", values.zip_code);
    data.append("website", values.website);
    data.append("phone_number", values.phone_number);
    data.append("description", values.description);
    data.append("email", values.email);
```

```
    client
      .post("/create/", data)
      .then(function (response) {
        console.log(response);
      })
      .catch(function (response) {
        console.log(response);
      });
  };
  return (
    <Formik
      initialValues={{
        pizzeria: "",
        street: "",
        city: "",
        state: "",
        zip_code: "",
        website: "",
        phone_number: "",
        description: "",
        email: "",
      }}
      onSubmit={handleSubmit}
      validationSchema={validationSchema}
    >
      {({ handleChange, handleSubmit, values, errors }) => (
        <SafeAreaView style={styles.content}>
          <ScrollView>
            <Image
              style={styles.image}
              source={{ uri: "https://bit.ly/book-pizza" }}
            />
```

```
<TextInput
  style={styles.textBox}
  value={values.pizzeria}
  placeholder="Enter a new pizz place here"
  onChangeText={handleChange("pizzeria")}
/>
<Text style={styles.error}>{errors.pizzeria}</Text>
<TextInput
  style={styles.textBox}
  value={values.street}
  placeholder="Street address"
  onChangeText={handleChange("street")}
/>
<Text style={styles.error}>{errors.street}</Text>
<TextInput
  style={styles.textBox}
  value={values.city}
  placeholder="City"
  onChangeText={handleChange("city")}
/>
<Text style={styles.error}>{errors.city}</Text>
<TextInput
  style={styles.textBox}
  value={values.state}
  placeholder="State"
  onChangeText={handleChange("state")}
/>
<Text style={styles.error}>{errors.state}</Text>
<TextInput
  style={styles.textBox}
```

```
      value={values.zip_code}
      placeholder="Zip"
      onChangeText={handleChange("zip_code")}
  />
  <Text style={styles.error}>{errors.zip_code}</Text>
  <TextInput
      style={styles.textBox}
      value={values.website}
      placeholder="Website"
      onChangeText={handleChange("website")}
  />
  <Text style={styles.error}>{errors.website}</Text>
  <TextInput
      style={styles.textBox}
      value={values.phone_number}
      placeholder="Phone number"
      onChangeText={handleChange("phone_number")}
  />
  <Text style={styles.error}>{errors.phone_number}</Text>
  <TextInput
      style={styles.textBox}
      value={values.description}
      placeholder="Description"
      onChangeText={handleChange("description")}
  />
  <Text style={styles.error}>{errors.description}</Text>
  <TextInput
      style={styles.textBox}
      value={values.email}
```

```
            placeholder="Email"
            onChangeText={handleChange("email")}
          />
          <Text style={styles.error}>{errors.email}</Text>
          <Button
            style={styles.addButton}
            onPress={handleSubmit}
            title="Submit"
          />
        </ScrollView>
      </SafeAreaView>
    )}
  </Formik>
)}
```

We are almost done. However, to successfully acquire our data, the Django REST framework would need to parse it. Django REST comes with four different parsers: JSONParser, FormParser, MultiPartParser, and FileUploadParser.[2] Encoding "multipart/form-data" method we are using in our mobile app would require a MultiPartParser.

To use MultiPartParser in views.py file in the Django project, we would need to import it from `rest_framework.parsers`.

```
from rest_framework.parsers import MultiPartParser
```

And add it to our PizzeriaCreateAPIView as parser_classes.

```
class PizzeriaCreateAPIView(generics.CreateAPIView):
    parser_classes = [MultiPartParser]
    queryset = Pizzeria.objects.all()
    serializer_class = PizzeriaDetailSerializer
```

---

[2] www.django-rest-framework.org/api-guide/parsers/

Make certain that the views.py file was saved and the back-end developer server is running. Enter new information in our AddPizzeria screen and click submit button (Figure 7-9).

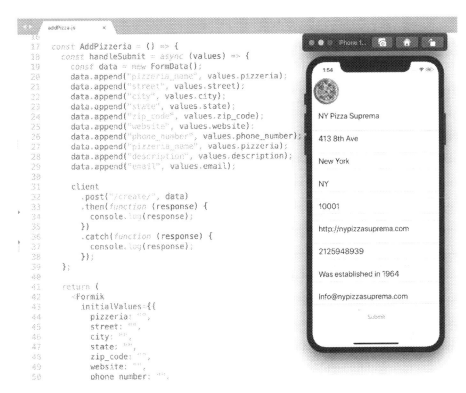

Figure 7-9. *POST request with a FormData object*

To be sure that the object was posted, reload iPhone or Android emulator and retrieve the record in your browser running on 127.0.01:8000 server (Figure 7-10).

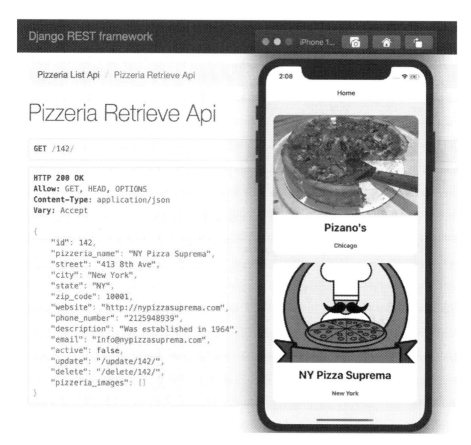

Figure 7-10. *New record was created with the API POST request*

Using images

We can grab an input text and send it over to a server, but what about images? The process of uploading an image to a server would require three steps. First, we need to acquire a permission to get access to photos on a mobile device. Second, we need to select an image from the camera roll where photos are saved. Third, transmit the photo's URI with a POST API call.

The first part sounds like a lot of coding; however, the Expo framework comes with a bunch of useful features like FaceDetector, GoogleSignIn, ImagePicker, and others. In our case, ImagePicker would come in handy to solve the first two steps. ImagePicker is probably one of the most popular Expo features. You should definitely check the documentation (`https://docs.expo.io/versions/v38.0.0/sdk/imagepicker/`). There, you will find a very informative video on how to use ImagePicker.

ImagePicker comes as a separate component, and we need to install it.

```
expo install expo-image-picker
```

In our React Native pizzavspizza_app, we have the component ScreenB that does nothing at the moment. We can use it to practice image picking. Above ScreenB component, import everything from the expo-image-picker package.

```
import * as ImagePicker from "expo-image-picker";
```

ImagePicker comes with methods that would help us to obtain a permission to access camera roll on a phone. To solve this, we would need to use requestCameraRollPermissionAsync() method. This method would return Boolean. If true, then we could have access to a phone's photos folder.[3] Obtaining permission is similar to calling API. We would create a function and invoke it in the useEffect hook. Later, to save a photo's URI, we would need the useState hook. Make sure you have hooks imported.

```
import React, { useEffect, useState } from "react";
```

We can rewrite the ScreenB component as a function expression, to be consistent with other components. Right above return, declare getPermission function. Since requestCameraRollPermissionAsync() is an asynchronous method, our getPermission function should have async/await keywords.

---

[3]`https://docs.expo.io/versions/v38.0.0/sdk/imagepicker/`

```
const ScreenB = () => {
  const getPermission = async () => {};
  return (
    <View style={styles.center}>
      <Text style={styles.title}>Screen B</Text>
    </View>
  );
};
```

Inside getPermission function, we will invoke requestCameraRollPermissionAsync() that would ask a user to grant the permissions. If the user chooses not to grant our app this privilege, then we would raise a fair alert asking for permission.

```
const getPermission = async () => {
    const { status } = await ImagePicker.
    requestCameraRollPermissionsAsync();
    if (status !== "granted") {
      alert("Enable camera roll permissions");
    }
  };
```

The right place to invoke getPermission function would be in the useEffect hook.

```
useEffect(() => {
    getPermission();
  }, []);
```

I might sound like a broken record here, but do not forget to use an empty array as a second argument in the useEffect hook. If you navigate to ScreenB in the drawer, it should raise a permission request to access your photos (Figure 7-11).

```
screenB.js                    ×
1   import React, { useEffect, useState } from "react";
2   import { StyleSheet, View, Text } from "react-native";
3   import * as ImagePicker from "expo-image-picker";
4
5   const ScreenB = () => {
6     const getPermission = async () => {
7       const { status } = await ImagePicker.requestCameraRollPermissionsAsync();
8       if (status !== "granted") {
9         alert("Enable camera roll permissions");
10      }
11    };
12
13    useEffect(() => {
14      getPermission();
15    }, []);
16
17    return (
18      <View style={styles.center}>
19        <Text style={styles.title}>Screen B</Text>
20      </View>
21    );
22  };
23
24  const styles = StyleSheet.create({
25    center: {
26      flex: 1,
27      justifyContent: "center",
28      alignItems: "center",
29    },
30    title: {
31      fontSize: 36,
32      marginBottom: 16,
33    },
34  });
35
36  export default ScreenB;
```

Figure 7-11. *The mobile application is asking for a permission to get access to the camera roll*

Expo would be replaced with the app name in production. Also, this permission was saved, and if later you want to change it, you could do so in settings. If for some reason you decline this request, it would raise "Enable camera roll permissions" alert, and you would need to grant the permission by changing access in the phone's settings.

The next step is to grab an image with ImagePicker. This task could be done with launchImageLibraryAsync() method. launchImageLibraryAsync() returns either {cancelled : true} or {cancelled : false}. {cancelled : true} would be returned if the user did not pick anything. However, if the user picked a photo, then we would receive the image, uri, width, height, exif, and base64. Then we can save the URI with useState hook. Let's start with the hook and use the variable photo to save our object.

```
const [photo, setPhoto] = useState();
```

Now we can define the function to select a photo. Using our previous experience, it would be smart to use a try statement. If the user selects a photo and everything goes smoothly, then we would set the image URI as the photo variable; otherwise, raise an alert message.

```
const selectPhoto = async () => {
    try {
        const result = await ImagePicker.
        launchImageLibraryAsync();
        if (!result.cancelled) setPhoto(result.uri);
    } catch (error) {
        alert("Error, try again");
    }
};
```

We will invoke this function on a press of the button. To see this function in action, we would render the image that was picked. For this, we would need to add Button and Image components to our imports.

```
import { StyleSheet, View, Text, Button } from "react-native";
```

Put these new components to use. I'll replace the old <Text> component with <Button> one. The OnPress handler would call the selectPhoto function.

```
<Button title="Select Image" onPress={selectPhoto} />
```

If we grab the image, then URI would be set as a photo with setPhoto, and we could render it with <Image> component. Make sure the Image component is imported.

```
<Image style={styles.photo} source={{ uri: photo }} />
```

Remember the Image component requires width and height attributes. We would need to add them to the styles object.

```
photo: {
    width: 400,
    height: 400,
  }
```

Try this "Select Image" button. The iPhone simulator comes with preset images, and you can pick one. The Android emulator has no images. We can see that the ImagePicker component works fine on both of them (Figure 7-12). Here, you can see all changes we have made to the ScreenB component and the full solution for ImagePicker.

```
import React, { useEffect, useState } from "react";
import { StyleSheet, View, Image, Button } from "react-native";
import * as ImagePicker from "expo-image-picker";

const ScreenB = () => {
  const [photo, setPhoto] = useState();
  const getPermission = async () => {
    const { status } = await ImagePicker.requestCameraRoll
    PermissionsAsync();
    if (status !== "granted") {
      alert("Enable camera roll permissions");
    }
  };
```

```
  useEffect(() => {
    getPermission();
  }, []);

  const selectPhoto = async () => {
    try {
      const result = await ImagePicker.launchImageLibraryAsync();
      if (!result.cancelled) setPhoto(result.uri);
    } catch (error) {
      alert("Error, try again");
    }
  };

  return (
    <View style={styles.center}>
      <Image style={styles.photo} source={{ uri: photo }} />
      <Button title="Select Image" onPress={selectPhoto} />
    </View>
  );
};

const styles = StyleSheet.create({
  center:{
    flex:1,
    justifyContent:"center",
    alignItems:"center"
  },
  title:{
    fontSize:36,
    marginBottom:16,
  },
```

```
photo: {
    width: 400,
    height: 400,
  },
})
```

```
export default ScreenB;
```

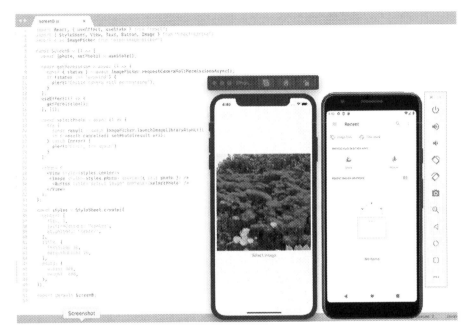

Figure 7-12. *The ImagePicker component picks an image from the camera roll*

The first two steps of our initial plan to get permissions and grab an image are completed. The final step, uploading an image to a server, could be split into two parts: build a reusable component and use that component in the AddPizzeria form or any other place in the app.

We can refactor our existing code in screenB.js file and save it as a reusable component. In the shared folder where we keep reusable and shareable components, create a new file photo.js (Figure 7-13).

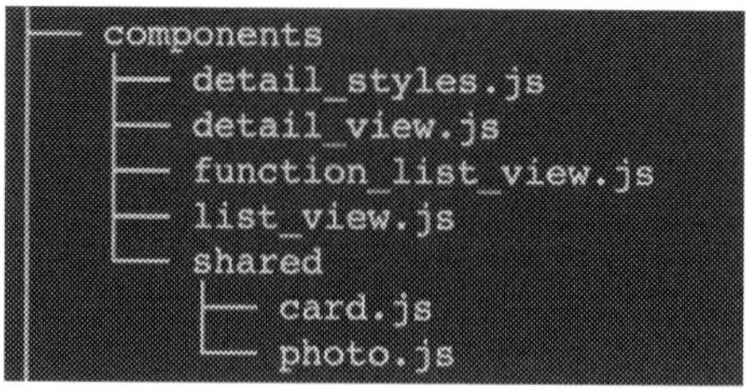

Figure 7-13. *New photo.js file in the shared directory to store a reusable PhotoPicker component*

In photo.js file, I'll declare a new component PhotoPicker. The name PhotoPicker suggests that this is a wrapper for Expo ImagePicker component. On the top of the file, we need to import the essential stuff. It's very similar to what we used in screenB.js file, except for the useState hook. We will need this hook in AddPizzeria component.

```
import React, { useEffect } from "react";
import { View, StyleSheet, Image } from "react-native";
import * as ImagePicker from "expo-image-picker";
const PhotoPicker = () => {
  return;
};
export default PhotoPicker;
```

Following the logic in the previous example, we would need to obtain a permission to get access to camera roll and select a photo. I'll just copy getPermission function from screenB.js file and call it in the useEffect hook.

```
const getPermission = async () => {
    const { status } = await ImagePicker.
requestCameraRollPermissionsAsync();
```

```
  if (status !== "granted") {
    alert("Enable camera roll permissions");
  }
};
useEffect(() => {
  getPermission();
}, []);
```

Right after this, we can copy and paste selectPhoto function to photo.js from screenB.js file.

```
const selectPhoto = async () => {
    try {
      const result = await ImagePicker.
launchImageLibraryAsync();
      if (!result.cancelled) setPhoto(result.uri);
    } catch (error) {
      alert("Error, try again");
    }
  };
```

For this component, we would need to set up a simple style object. Using StyleSheet component, we will create this object with two attributes, container and img. Container will provide the color and position the element in the center. The img attribute will provide dimensions and round the corners of an incoming photo.

So far, everything is similar to what we have done before. PhotoPicker is a reusable component and will take an image URL as props. We can define it as a photo. This photo would be returned or rendered by our component. But what if there is no image selected yet? How would we mark that field? We can place a temporary placeholder as before. This time, we could use an icon from Expo. Font Awesome icons are available through @expo/vector-icons library, and it is included in Expo. Here, you can find the list of all icons: `https://icons.expo.fyi`.

Here, I'll use a simple picture icon. We need to import the icon family on top of the file, and then we can use an icon component.

```
import { SimpleLineIcons } from "@expo/vector-icons";
```

Using conditional rendering, we can return the following statements wrapped in <View> tags, because a React component can return only one container.

```
return (
    <View style={styles.container}>
      {photo == "" ? (
        <SimpleLineIcons name="picture" size={100}
        color="black" />
      ) : (
        <Image style={styles.img} source={{ uri: photo }} />
      )}
    </View>
  );
```

With the help of React conditional rendering, we can create if and else scenarios and show a component based on some conditions. If you want to learn the rules and syntax, visit the React documentation: `https://reactjs.org/docs/conditional-rendering.html`. There, you can find and practice numerous examples.

If there is no photo, URI comes as an empty string and then returns a picture icon with size and color props. Otherwise, it renders the selected image, and the variable photo would pass the URI. This is my code for the PhotoPicker component:

```
import React, { useEffect } from "react";
import { View, StyleSheet, Image } from "react-native";
```

```javascript
import * as ImagePicker from "expo-image-picker";
import { SimpleLineIcons } from "@expo/vector-icons";

const PhotoPicker = ({photo}) => {
  const getPermission = async () => {
    const { status } = await ImagePicker.
      requestCameraRollPermissionsAsync();
    if (status !== "granted") {
      alert("Enable camera roll permissions");
    }
  };
  useEffect(() => {
    getPermission();
  }, []);

  const selectPhoto = async () => {
    try {
      const result = await ImagePicker.launchImageLibraryAsync();
      if (!result.cancelled) setPhoto(result.uri);
    } catch (error) {
      alert("Error, try again");
    }
  };

  return (
    <View style={styles.container}>
      {photo == "" ? (
        <SimpleLineIcons name="picture" size={100} color="black" />
      ) : (
        <Image style={styles.img} source={{ uri: photo }} />
      )}
    </View>
  );
};
```

```
const styles = StyleSheet.create({
  container: {
    alignItems:"center",
    backgroundColor: "white"
  },
  img:{
    width: 100,
    height: 100,
    marginTop: 20,
    marginBottom: 20,
    overflow: "hidden",
    borderRadius:10,
  },
})
```

```
export default PhotoPicker;
```

If you want to test it, we would need to import PhotoPicker component into addPizzeria.js file.

```
import PhotoPicker from "../components/shared/photo.js";
```

And replace <Image> element with the <PhotoPicker photo={" "}/> component with an empty string passed as props. You can see our default icon right above the form fields, replacing the old pizza image (Figure 7-14).

Figure 7-14. *PhotoPicker component rendering the default picture icon*

Our job is to click that picture icon and select a photo from camera roll. When we pick the right photo, we would save it in useState hook and append URI to the data object.

To make our icon clickable, we would use React Native TouchableWithoutFeedback component. The documentation assures that it is an "extensive and future-proof way to handle touch-based input"[4] – exactly what we need here.

Import it in photo.js file.

```
import { View, StyleSheet, Image, TouchableWithoutFeedback }
from "react-native";
```

_____

[4]https://reactnative.dev/docs/touchablewithoutfeedback

We will wrap <View> container with <TouchableWithoutFeedback> tags and use event handler onPress. The OnPress handler will invoke onPress function that we would need yet to define.

```
return (
    <TouchableWithoutFeedback onPress={onPress}>
      <View style={styles.container}>
        {photo == "" ? (
          <SimpleLineIcons name="picture" size={100}
          color="black" />
        ) : (
          <Image style={styles.img} source={{ uri: photo }} />
        )}
      </View>
    </TouchableWithoutFeedback>
  );
```

What about the function onPress? What should happen on a press? As a part of our plan, we would need to invoke a selectPhoto function. However, the user might change his or her mind; then we would need to give the user another chance to pick a photo again.

Before, we have used a simple JavaScript alert function to see how inputs worked. This time, we would need to use a React Native Alert Core Component. How is that different from the alert function? Well, for starters, it comes with buttons and you could make a choice. Also, since it is a native component, it would be the most efficient choice for a React project.

Add Alert to the list of our imports.

```
import {
  View,
  StyleSheet,
  Image,
```

```
TouchableWithoutFeedback,
Alert,
} from "react-native";
```

Our onPress function would have two options: if there is no photo selected yet, you could choose one with the help of selectPhoto(), or if there was a photo, Alert would ask you if you want to replace it with another photo. A positive answer would trigger the selectPhoto function again.

```
const onPress = () => {
    if (photo == "") selectPhoto();
    else
      Alert.alert("Photo", "Would you like to use another
      photo? ", [
        { text: "Yes", onPress: () => selectPhoto() },
        { text: "No, keep it!" },
      ]);
  };
```

Before we put it to test, we need to replace setPhoto in the selectPhoto function. We used setPhoto as a part of the useState hook, and we do not use it here. We will replace setPhoto with a function onPressPhoto.

```
const selectPhoto = async () => {
    try {
      const result = await ImagePicker.
      launchImageLibraryAsync();
      if (!result.cancelled) onPressPhoto(result.uri);
    } catch (error) {
      alert("Error, try again");
    }
  };
```

OnPressPhoto would help us to set URI as a useState hook in the AddPizzeria component, and we would use it as props in the PhotoPicker component.

```
const PhotoPicker = ({ photo, onPressPhoto }) => {
            //code
}
```

Here, you can see the fully updated and ready for work PhotoPicker component.

```
import React, { useEffect } from "react";
import { View, StyleSheet, Image, TouchableWithoutFeedback,
Alert } from "react-native";
import * as ImagePicker from "expo-image-picker";
import { SimpleLineIcons } from "@expo/vector-icons";

const PhotoPicker = ({ photo, onPressPhoto }) => {
    const getPermission = async () => {
        const { status } = await ImagePicker.
          requestCameraRollPermissionsAsync();
        if (status !== "granted") {
          alert("Enable camera roll permissions");
        }
    };
    useEffect(() => {
      getPermission();
    }, []);

    const selectPhoto = async () => {
      try {
        const result = await ImagePicker.launchImageLibraryAsync();
        if (!result.cancelled) onPressPhoto(result.uri);
```

```
    } catch (error) {
      alert("Error, try again");
    }
  };
  const onPress = () => {
    if (photo == "") selectPhoto();
    else
      Alert.alert("Photo", "Would you like to use another
        photo? ", [
        { text: "Yes", onPress: () => selectPhoto() },
        { text: "No, keep it!" },
      ]);
  };
  return (
    <TouchableWithoutFeedback onPress={onPress}>
      <View style={styles.container}>
        {photo == "" ? (
          <SimpleLineIcons name="picture" size={100}
            color="black" />
        ) : (
          <Image style={styles.img} source={{ uri: photo }} />
        )}
      </View>
    </TouchableWithoutFeedback>
  );
};

const styles = StyleSheet.create({
    container: {
        alignItems:"center",
        backgroundColor: "white"
    },
```

```
    img:{
        width: 100,
        height: 100,
        marginTop: 20,
        marginBottom: 20,
        overflow: "hidden",
        borderRadius:10,
    },
})
export default PhotoPicker;
```

In order to pass onPressPhoto, we would need to flip over to AddPizzeria.js file and import useState hook.

Then, define the useState hook in the AddPizzeria component, or you can copy and paste it from screenB.js file.

```
const [photo, setPhoto] = useState("");
```

Update <PhotoPicker> component with onPressPhoto props (Figure 7-16).

```
<PhotoPicker photo={photo} onPressPhoto={(uri) =>
setPhoto(uri)} />
```

The iPhone simulator picks a photo if you press that picture icon on the AddPizzeria screen (Figure 7-15). If you press it again, you can replace the image with another photo from camera roll.

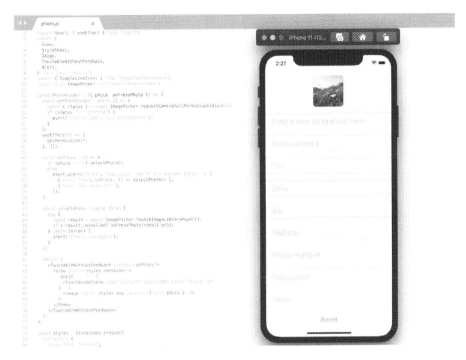

Figure 7-15. *You can choose a photo from the camera roll in AddPizzeria form*

The final step of our plan is to send the photo's URI with the data object to a server. The handleSubmit function in AddPizzeria component calls `http://127.0.0.1:800/create/` URL, and that invokes PizzeriaCreateAPIView in the Django project views.py file. Accordingly, PizzeriaCreateAPIView serves PizzeriaDetailSerializer from serializers. py. Apparently, PizzeriaDetailSerializer lacks `logo_image` field which we would like to use to upload our photo as a logo for the new pizza place. Let's fix that and insert `logo_image` into PizzeriaDetailSerializer fields.

```
class PizzeriaDetailSerializer(serializers.ModelSerializer):
    update = serializers.SerializerMethodField()
    delete = serializers.SerializerMethodField()
    pizzeria_images = ImageSerializer(many=True,
    required=False)
```

```python
    class Meta:
        model = Pizzeria
        fields = [
            'id',
            'pizzeria_name',
            'street',
            'city',
            'state',
            'zip_code',
            'website',
            'phone_number',
            'description',
            'email',
            'logo_image',
            'active',
            'update',
            'delete',
            'pizzeria_images',
        ]

    def get_update(self, obj):
        return reverse('pizzeria_update', args=(obj.pk,))

    def get_delete(self, obj):
        return reverse('pizzeria_delete', args=(obj.pk,))
```

Now, flip back to AddPizzeria.js file, and in handleSubmit function, append this field with values to the data object.

```javascript
data.append("logo_image", {
    uri: photo,
    name: "filename.jpg",
    type: "image/jpg",
});
```

Besides the URI itself, I have provided the name and type of the file. Also, I'll wrap our API call in try and except statements. Using the photo with nice flowers from camera roll, I'll try to add my favorite Giordano's place to our list (Figure 7-16).

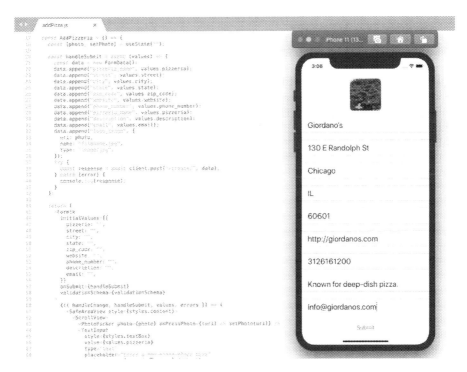

Figure 7-16. *Uploading a photo with the AddPizzeria form*

It looks like we've done it! But how would the user know that the record was created successfully? To inform the user, we will use an Alert component.

To reload the app from inside, we need to use the NativeModule. Update the list of imported components in addPizzeria.js.

```
import { SafeAreaView, ScrollView, TextInput, Button,
NativeModules,Text, Alert } from "react-native";
```

With the Alert component, we will inform the user that the record has been successfully created and on press will reload the app and redirect to the home screen. We will store this code as a separate function, because if we decide to alter the message down the road, we would not want to mess with handleSubmit function. I'll call this function postedAlert.

```
const postedAlert = () => {
    Alert.alert("Success!", "Thank you! ", [
      {
        text: "Go to main screen",
        onPress: () => NativeModules.DevSettings.reload();

      },
    ]);
  };
```

And we will invoke the function postedAlert in a try statement if the record was successfully sent (Figure 7-17). Here, you can see the final version of the addPizzeria.js file:

```
import React, { useState } from "react";
import {
  SafeAreaView,
  ScrollView,
  TextInput,
  Button,
  NativeModules,
  Text,
  View,
  Image,
  Alert,
} from "react-native";
import { Formik } from "formik";
```

```
import client from "./../../api/client";
import styles from "./addPizzeria_styles";
import validationSchema from "./addPizzeria_valid";
import PhotoPicker from "../components/shared/photo.js";

const AddPizzeria = ({ navigation }) => {
  const [photo, setPhoto] = useState("");
  const postedAlert = () => {
    Alert.alert("Success!", "Thank you! ", [
      {
        text: "Go to main screen",
        onPress: () => NativeModules.DevSettings.reload(),
      },
    ]);
  };

  const handleSubmit = async (values) => {
    const data = new FormData();
    data.append("pizzeria_name", values.pizzeria);
    data.append("street", values.street);
    data.append("city", values.city);
    data.append("state", values.state);
    data.append("zip_code", values.zip_code);
    data.append("website", values.website);
    data.append("phone_number", values.phone_number);
    data.append("description", values.description);
    data.append("email", values.email);
    data.append("logo_image", {
      uri: photo,
      name: "filename.jpg",
      type: "image/jpg",
    });
```

```
  try {
    const response = await client.post("/create/", data);
    postedAlert();
  } catch (error) {
    console.log(error);
  }
};
return (
  <Formik
    initialValues={{
      pizzeria: "",
      street: "",
      city: "",
      state: "",
      zip_code: "",
      website: "",
      phone_number: "",
      description: "",
      email: "",
    }}
    onSubmit={handleSubmit}
    validationSchema={validationSchema}
  >
    {(({ handleChange, handleSubmit, values, errors }) => (
      <SafeAreaView style={styles.content}>
        <ScrollView>
          <PhotoPicker photo={photo} onPressPhoto={(uri) =>
          setPhoto(uri)} />
          <TextInput
            style={styles.textBox}
            value={values.pizzeria}
            type="text"
```

```
    placeholder="Enter a new pizza place here"
    onChangeText={handleChange("pizzeria")}
  />
  <Text style={styles.error}>{errors.pizzeria}</Text>
  <TextInput
    style={styles.textBox}
    value={values.street}
    placeholder="Street address"
    onChangeText={handleChange("street")}
  />
  <Text style={styles.error}>{errors.street}</Text>
  <TextInput
    style={styles.textBox}
    value={values.city}
    placeholder="City"
    onChangeText={handleChange("city")}
  />
  <Text style={styles.error}>{errors.city}</Text>
  <TextInput
    style={styles.textBox}
    value={values.state}
    placeholder="State"
    onChangeText={handleChange("state")}
  />
  <Text style={styles.error}>{errors.state}</Text>
  <TextInput
    style={styles.textBox}
    value={values.zip_cide}
    placeholder="Zip"
    onChangeText={handleChange("zip_code")}
  />
```

```
<Text style={styles.error}>{errors.zip_code}</Text>
<TextInput
  style={styles.textBox}
  value={values.website}
  placeholder="Website"
  onChangeText={handleChange("website")}
/>
<Text style={styles.error}>{errors.website}</Text>
<TextInput
  style={styles.textBox}
  value={values.phone_number}
  placeholder="Phone number"
  onChangeText={handleChange("phone_number")}
/>
<Text style={styles.error}>{errors.phone_number}</
Text>
<TextInput
  style={styles.textBox}
  value={values.description}
  placeholder="Description"
  onChangeText={handleChange("description")}
/>
<Text style={styles.error}>{errors.description}</
Text>
<TextInput
  style={styles.textBox}
  value={values.email}
  placeholder="Email"
  onChangeText={handleChange("email")}
/>
```

```
            <Text style={styles.error}>{errors.email}</Text>
            <Button
              style={styles.addButton}
              onPress={handleSubmit}
              title="Submit"
            />
          </ScrollView>
        </SafeAreaView>
      )}
    </Formik>
  );
};
export default AddPizzeria;).
```

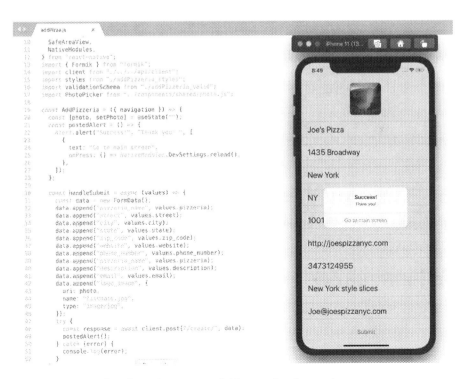

Figure 7-17. *The function postedAlert raised an alert message*

You have to understand that the possibilities of what to do after the user has created a record are endless, and reload is the simplest one. Another obvious option would be to redirect to the "home" screen and update the useEffect hook to return the updated list of pizzerias. Or maybe redirect with no alert message. I'll leave it up to you. On press, the alert message will reload our app, and we will see our newly created records (Figure 7-18).

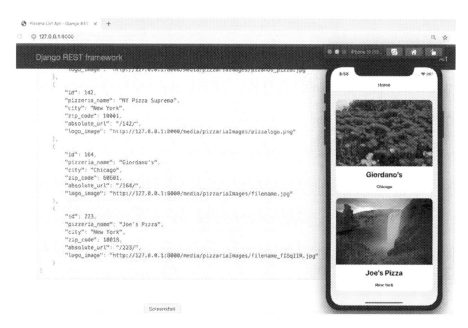

Figure 7-18. *Django renders the list of Pizzerias, and we see the same record on the "Home" screen of our app*

Authentication

One of the reasons why we use Django and not anything else is that Django comes with a modern authentication tool. You do not have to use third-party solutions or pay for authentication services. The Django

REST framework comes with token-based HTTP authentication.[5] Using this tool, you can set permissions for Views and actions. For example, only authorized users could have access to PizzeriaCreateAPIView or see information like a personal account.

Authtoken is very easy to install and use. First, we would need to add "rest_framework.authtoken" to the installed apps list in settings.py in the Django project.

```
INSTALLED_APPS = [
    'django.contrib.admin',
    'django.contrib.auth',
    'django.contrib.contenttypes',
    'django.contrib.sessions',
    'django.contrib.messages',
    'django.contrib.staticfiles',
    'corsheaders',
    'rest_framework',
    'rest_framework.authtoken',
    'stores',
]
```

The Authtoken app comes with Models, and we need to run migrate command.

```
python manage.py migrate
```

After Models were migrated, you can restart your developer server. As a last step of the installation process, we need to add the URL pattern to the main URL dispatcher in pizzaproject/urls.py.

Import views from the Authtoken app and provide the URL pattern (Figure 7-19).

---

[5]www.django-rest-framework.org/api-guide/authentication/

```
from rest_framework.authtoken import views
path('api-token-auth/', views.obtain_auth_token)
```

```
from django.conf.urls.static import static
from django.conf import settings
from django.contrib import admin
from django.urls import path, include
from rest_framework.authtoken import views


urlpatterns = [
    path('admin/', admin.site.urls),
    path('', include('stores.urls')),
    url(r'^api-token-auth/', views.obtain_auth_token)
]
```

Figure 7-19. *URL dispatcher pizzaproject/urls.py*

It is time to generate a token! Navigate to 127.0.01:8000/admin/. It might ask you to log in. On the administration page, you should see the Auth Token App and Tokens model. Click Tokens, and in the upper-right corner, press the Add Token button. Then choose a user you would like to generate a token and click save. My database currently has just one superuser, me, so I'll add myself a token. In Figure 7-20, you can see the generated token in the Tokens model.

Figure 7-20. *Django Administration Authtoken has generated a token*

The only way to see the token and the Authtoken app in action is to send a POST request. Before we build a front-end solution for that, we can use the Postman app (www.postman.com). Postman is a very popular platform for testing APIs. It is free and I have it running on my computer. If you do not want to install this app, that is OK; just take a look at Figure 7-21. On a second thought, I would recommend you to install this free app on your computer for your future RESTful projects.

Figure 7-21. *Postman app returns a token if you send a POST request with a username and password*

In the Postman app, we would need to provide a URL we would like to hit. In our case, it is http://127.0.0.1:8000. I will change the settings in Postman to a raw JSON input.

Our auth API requires two arguments, username and password. In raw format, I'll pass them as a JSON dictionary {"username": "art", "password":"programwithus123". You should use your credentials to obtain a token. After Authtoken receives correct credentials, it would return the token, as you can see at the bottom of Figure 7-21.

This token would work as a key. If you decide to lock some views and allow authenticated users only to call that API, then a token should be added to the headers of an HTTP request.

Let's build a logging form in our React Native app and obtain a token based on a username and password. ScreenC component is vacant, and we can use it for the login form. Technically, this api-token-auth API call would be no different than any other POST request.

Since we just went through the whole process of creating a record, I'll go a little bit faster and copy our AddPizzeria form to screenC file.

We will name this component LoginForm. Copy the Formik form we have used before or create one from scratch. We need two fields, username and password. For our login screen, we need a title. Using Text tags, I'll create a title like this:

```
<Text>Login to your account</Text>
```

and place <Text> and the form in <View></View> tags.

```
<Formik
      initialValues={{
         username: "",
         password: "",
      }}
      onSubmit={handleSubmit}
      validationSchema={validationSchema}
   >
      {({ handleChange, handleSubmit, values, errors }) => (
         <SafeAreaView style={styles.content}>
            <View style={styles.container}>
               <Text style={styles.title}>Login to your account
               </Text>
```

```
<TextInput
  style={styles.textBox}
  value={values.username}
  type="text"
  placeholder="Username"
  onChangeText={handleChange("username")}
/>
<Text style={styles.error}>{errors.username}</Text>
<TextInput
  style={styles.textBox}
  value={values.password}
  placeholder="Password"
  onChangeText={handleChange("password")}
/>
<Text style={styles.error}>{errors.password}</Text>
<Button
  style={styles.addButton}
  onPress={handleSubmit}
  title="Submit"
/>
      </View>
    </SafeAreaView>
  )}
</Formik>
```

To stay consistent with the name of the component, we can rename the file itself to loginForm.js. Do not forget to replace old ScreenC imports everywhere in App.js with LoginForm component.

```
import LoginForm from "./src/screens/drawer/loginForm.js";
```

and

```
<Drawer.Screen name="Login" component={LoginForm} />
```

Also, validationSchema and styles would be very similar to what we used before, yet we need to change something. To speed up the process you can copy and rename addPizzeria_styles.js and addPizzeria_valid.js to loginForm_styles.js and loginForm_valid.js (Figure 7-22).

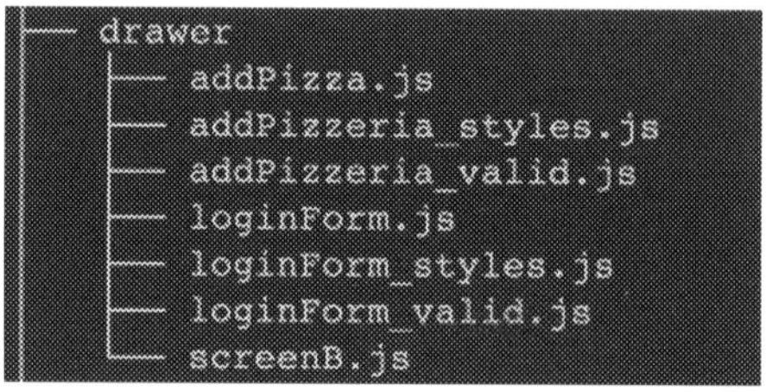

```
— drawer
  ├── addPizza.js
  ├── addPizzeria_styles.js
  ├── addPizzeria_valid.js
  ├── loginForm.js
  ├── loginForm_styles.js
  ├── loginForm_valid.js
  └── screenB.js
```

Figure 7-22. loginForm.js (former screenC) loginForm_styles.js and loginForm_valid.js in the drawer directory

loginForm_valid.js would have a validationSchema but much shorter than we used to have. We need to validate the username and password only. I'll add required() method to the password field.

```
import * as Yup from "yup";

const validationSchema = Yup.object({
  username: Yup.string()
    .max(200, "Must be less than 200 characters")
    .min(3, "Must be at least 3 characters")
    .required("Required"),
  password: Yup.string()
    .max(400, "Must be less than 400 characters")
    .min(3, "Must be at least 3 characters")
    .required("Required"),
});
export default validationSchema;
```

loginForm_styles.js file succeeds the majority of style attributes, except image. I will add two more attributes: container and title. The title would be used for the <Text> element and the container for <View>. Again, do not be afraid to experiment with style on your own.

```
import { StyleSheet } from "react-native";

const styles = StyleSheet.create({
  error: {
    color: "red",
    fontSize: 18,
    marginBottom: 7,
    fontWeight: "600",
    paddingLeft: 20,
  },
  textBox: {
    borderColor: "#CCCCCC",
    borderTopWidth: 1,
    borderBottomWidth: 1,
    height: 50,
    fontSize: 25,
    paddingLeft: 20,
    paddingRight: 20,
  },
  content: {
    padding: 20,
    backgroundColor: "#ffffff",
    width: "100%",
    height: "100%",
  },
  addButton: {
    borderWidth: 1,
    borderColor: "#007BFF",
```

```
    backgroundColor: "#007BFF",
    padding: 15,
  },
  container: {
    paddingTop: 200,
  },
  title: {
    fontSize: 30,
    color: "black",
    textAlign: "center",
    paddingBottom: 50,
  },
});
export default styles;
```

Based on the changes we just made, we would need to adjust our imports in loginForm.js file.

```
import React from "react";
import { TextInput, Button, Text, View, SafeAreaView } from
"react-native";
import { Formik } from "formik";
import client from "./../../api/client";
import styles from "./loginForm_styles";
import validationSchema from "./loginForm_valid";
```

We need to alter the handleSubmit function accordingly to a new form and call "/api-token-auth/" API. To see if we get back any token from the POST request, we will use a simple JavaScript alert() function.

```
const handleSubmit = async (values) => {
    const data = new FormData();
    data.append("username", values.username);
    data.append("password", values.password);
```

```
    try {
      console.log(data);
      const response = await client.post("/api-token-auth/", data);
      alert(response.data.token);
    } catch (error) {
      console.log(error);
    }
  };
```

Here, you can see the code from loginForm.js:

```
import React from "react";
import { TextInput, Button, Text, View, SafeAreaView } from
"react-native";
import { Formik } from "formik";
import client from "./../../api/client";
import styles from "./loginForm_styles";
import validationSchema from "./loginForm_valid";

const LoginForm = () => {
  const handleSubmit = async (values) => {
    const data = new FormData();
    data.append("username", values.username);
    data.append("password", values.password);
    try {
      console.log(data);
      const response = await client.post("/api-token-auth/", data);
      alert(response.data.token);
    } catch (error) {
      console.log(error);
    }
  };
```

```
return (
  <View>
  <Text>Login to your account</Text>
  <Formik
    initialValues={{
      username: "",
      password: "",
    }}
    onSubmit={handleSubmit}
    validationSchema={validationSchema}
  >
    {({ handleChange, handleSubmit, values, errors }) => (
      <SafeAreaView style={styles.content}>
        <View style={styles.container}>
          <Text style={styles.title}>Login to your account
              </Text>
          <TextInput
            style={styles.textBox}
            value={values.username}
            type="text"
            placeholder="Username"
            onChangeText={handleChange("username")}
          />
          <Text style={styles.error}>{errors.username}</Text>
          <TextInput
            style={styles.textBox}
            value={values.password}
            placeholder="Password"
            onChangeText={handleChange("password")}
          />
          <Text style={styles.error}>{errors.password}</Text>
```

```
      <Button
        style={styles.addButton}
        onPress={handleSubmit}
        title="Submit"
      />
    </View>
  </SafeAreaView>
  )}
</Formik>
</View>
)}

export default LoginForm;
```

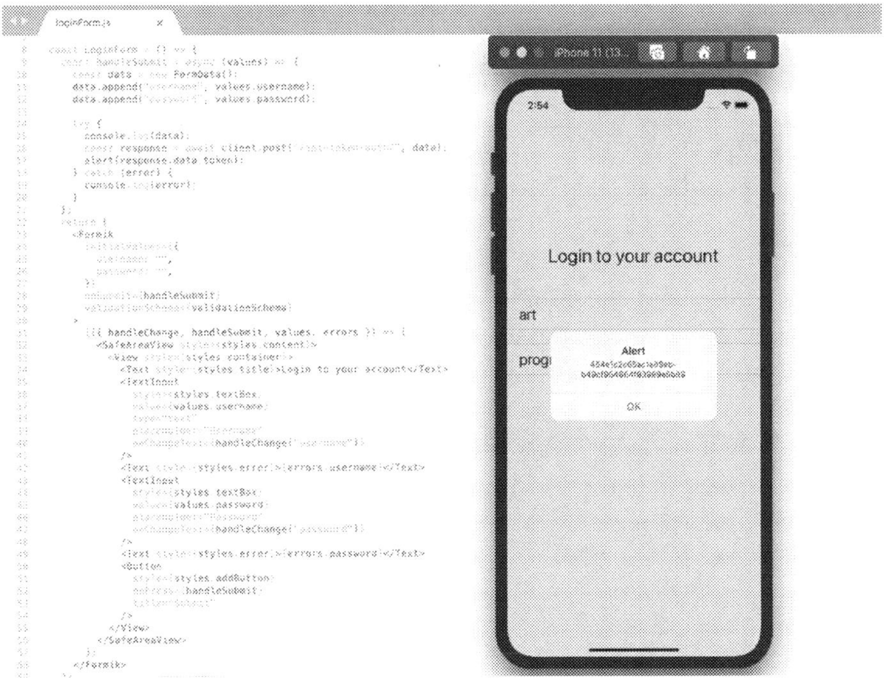

Figure 7-23. *Django returns an authentication token based on the username and password*

Let's test our LoginForm component. If I enter my username and password on the login screen, Django returns my token. This is the same token we have seen before in the Postman app (Figure 7-23). Login information is very sensitive; make sure you get it right.

If you are wondering how a user could get registered in the first place, the answer would be to follow all the steps we implemented for PizzeriaCreateAPIView. Step one, in the Django project, create a View and Serializer as a form. In the URL dispatcher, add a new API end to invoke the View. Step two, in the React Native app, write a new component with a form and use Axios to handle a POST request.

Let's start with a new View in views.py. We can name this view UserCreateView. For UserCreateView, we would need access to Django's default User model. We can get that access through get_user_model method. To show you how to use permissions in Django REST, we would import permissions from rest_framework and allow anyone to use UserCreateView View.

```
from django.contrib.auth import get_user_model
from rest_framework import permissions
```

UserCreateView would require a Serializer. We do not have one yet. Later, we would need to create UserSerializer. Add UserSerializer to the Serializers import.

```
from .serializers import (
    PizzeriaListSerializer,
    PizzeriaDetailSerializer,
    UserSerializer
)
```

Now define UserCreateView. First of all, it will inherit from generics. CreateAPIView. We have talked about generic Views earlier in this book.

For Model, we would use the default User model. Django comes with a simple built-in User model. If you need to add more attributes to the User model, you could extend it with a one-to-one relation later. We need to specify the type of data parser as MultiPartParser. This time, we add permission_classes and set it as AllowAny. Finally, we would use UserSerializer to accept and validate incoming data.

```
class UserCreateView(generics.CreateAPIView):
    model = get_user_model()
    parser_classes = [MultiPartParser]
    permission_classes = [permissions.AllowAny]
    serializer_class = UserSerializer
```

Following our steps, now would be the time to define UserSerializer in serializers.py.

In serializers, we would also need to get access to the User model; import get_user_model.

```
from django.contrib.auth import get_user_model
```

The get_user_model method would smooth the communication with the User model. We would need to use it twice so we can save it with the variable UserModel.

```
UserModel = get_user_model()
```

UserSerializer will inherit from ModelSerializer. As a safety measure, we will make the password as a write_only field. To validate data and create an instance of User, Django REST recommends using create() and save() methods. In UserSerializer, we will make sure that username and password fields are validated and saved. The create method would return a User instance if it was created successfully. The ModelSerializer serializer requires a Model, and we will provide UserModel.

```
class UserSerializer(serializers.ModelSerializer):
    password = serializers.CharField(write_only=True)
    def create(self, validated_data):
```

```
user = UserModel.objects.create(
    username=validated_data['username']
)
user.set_password(validated_data['password'])
user.save()
return user

class Meta:
    model = get_user_model()
    fields = [ "username", "password"]
```

You can see UserCreateView and UserSerializer in Figure 7-24.

Figure 7-24. *UserCreateView in views.py and UserSerializer in serializers.py*

The final step, as you know by now, is to add a URL pattern to the URL dispatcher. The process is pretty logical. Define a View; create the URL to invoke that View. The API endpoint for UserCreateView would be in the same global pizzaproject/urls.py file where we defined the URL for Authtoken. UserCreateView is defined in stores/views.py, and we would need to import it in urls.py.

```
from stores.views import UserCreateView
```

You can use any pattern for your views. I think patterns should be simple and Search Engine Optimization–friendly. For UserCreateView, we will use "/register/".

```
path('register/', UserCreateView.as_view(), name="create_user")
```

The final version of pizzaproject/urls.py should look like the one in Figure 7-25.

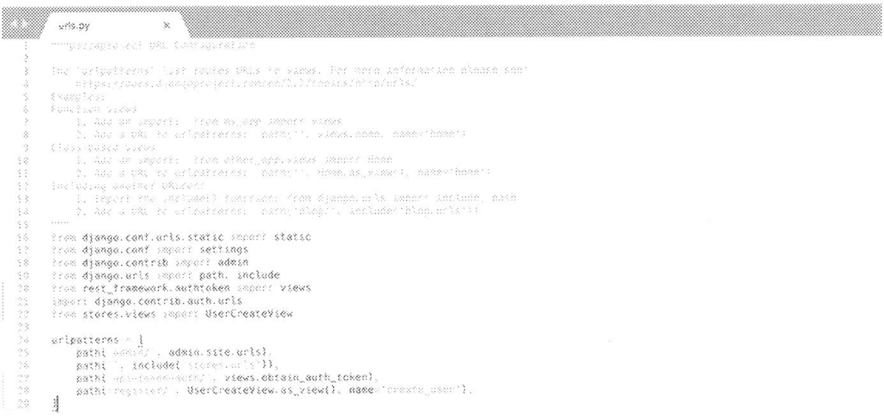

Figure 7-25. *URL pattern to create a new user in the urls.py file*

Our back-end part is ready, and we can start with a front-end part. We still have screenB.js file with ScreenB component that we do not need any more. We can rename screenB.js to regForm.js (Figure 7-26).

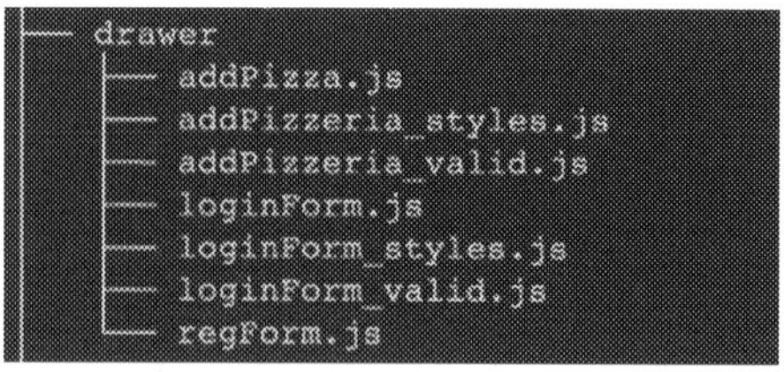

```
   drawer
   ├── addPizza.js
   ├── addPizzeria_styles.js
   ├── addPizzeria_valid.js
   ├── loginForm.js
   ├── loginForm_styles.js
   ├── loginForm_valid.js
   └── regForm.js
```

Figure 7-26. *regForm.js (former screenB.js) in the drawer directory*

RegForm component would be very similar to LoginForm component. We will copy everything from loginForm.js and paste the code in regForm.js.

Let's replace LoginForm with RegForm component. Do not forget to import regForm.js and replace ScreenB component with RegForm in App. js file. We can use the same style and validation schema for the RegForm component. I'll just change the text in <Text> tags to "Registration".

Only one major thing would be different, a URL pattern in post() method. Later, you can refactor this code and create a shareable component for the login and registration forms. Let's replace the URL in handleSubmit function.

```
const handleSubmit = async (values) => {
    const data = new FormData();
    data.append("username", values.username);
    data.append("password", values.password);

    try {
      console.log(data);
      const response = await client.post("/register/", data);
    } catch (error) {
      console.log(error);
    }
  };
```

Make sure your RegForm component looks like my code in regForm.js.

```
import React from "react";
import { TextInput, Button, Text, View, SafeAreaView } from
"react-native";
import { Formik } from "formik";
import client from "./../../api/client";
import styles from "./loginForm_styles";
import validationSchema from "./loginForm_valid";

const RegForm = () => {
  const handleSubmit = async (values) => {
    const data = new FormData();
    data.append("username", values.username);
    data.append("password", values.password);
    try {
      console.log(data);
      const response = await client.post("/register/", data);
    } catch (error) {
      console.log(error);
    }
  };

  return (
    <View>
    <Text>Login to your account</Text>
    <Formik
      initialValues={{
        username: "",
        password: "",
      }}
      onSubmit={handleSubmit}
      validationSchema={validationSchema}
    >
```

```
    {({ handleChange, handleSubmit, values, errors }) => (
      <SafeAreaView style={styles.content}>
        <View style={styles.container}>
          <Text style={styles.title}>Login to your account
              </Text>
          <TextInput
            style={styles.textBox}
            value={values.username}
            type="text"
            placeholder="Username"
            onChangeText={handleChange("username")}
          />
          <Text style={styles.error}>{errors.username}</Text>
          <TextInput
            style={styles.textBox}
            value={values.password}
            placeholder="Password"
            onChangeText={handleChange("password")}
          />
          <Text style={styles.error}>{errors.password}</Text>
          <Button
            style={styles.addButton}
            onPress={handleSubmit}
            title="Submit"
          />
        </View>
      </SafeAreaView>
    )}
  </Formik>
  </View>
  )}

export default RegForm;
```

We can try our RegForm component and enter a username and password on the Registration screen. I have used the name Tim, my good friend, as a username. Programwithus456 is the password. If we open Django admin in the browser and navigate to the Users model, we could see that a new user was created (Figure 7-27).

Figure 7-27. *A new user has been added through the RegForm component*

To close the circle and automate generating token process in Django REST, we can assign a token to any user upon registration. In the create method of UserSerializer, we will add another create method for the Token model.

Python runs in sequence, and we have to generate a token after a User instance was created.

```
class UserSerializer(serializers.ModelSerializer):
    password = serializers.CharField(write_only=True)
    def create(self, validated_data):
        user = UserModel.objects.create(
            username=validated_data['username']
        )
```

```
user.set_password(validated_data['password'])
user.save()
new_token = Token.objects.create(user=user)
return user
```

```
class Meta:
    model = get_user_model()
    fields = [ "username", "password"]
```

We use the Token model in UserSerializer, and we need to import it into serializers.py.

```
from rest_framework.authtoken.models import Token
```

To test my code, I'll register my friend Tommy, and you can see the system has automatically generated the token (Figure 7-28).

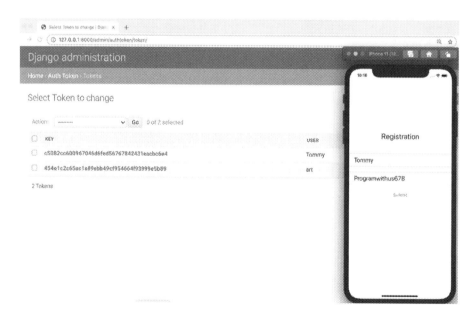

Figure 7-28. *A new token was generated for a new user*

We have implemented all the major web app operations in this book. Everything else would be a variation of what we have covered here. To get fluent with these technologies, you should keep working on this project or maybe start a new project to implement new features and style it to perfection.

In the next chapter, I will show you how you can deploy our code on a live server and make it accessible to everyone. Also, we will create two stand-alone mobile apps – one for Apple App store and the other one for Google Play store.

CHAPTER 8

Production

To make our back-end accessible, we need to deploy it to a server. Also we will generate an iOS app and Android app for Apple App store and Google Play store. We will start with Django deployment. There are numerous options on the market to host Django-powered apps: AWS, Heroku, and A2 Hosting, just to name a few. For my projects, I use DigitalOcean. I am not going into pricing analysis here or deep comparison of pros and cons. I use DigitalOcean for a simple reason: they are located in New York. I would like to support the local community. Besides, DigitalOcean provides $100 credit for new users, which is more than enough for our project. You would need to register using this link to claim this offer: `https://m.do.co/c/7b96bd81f2d1`.

If you are planning to host a large scalable project, you should do a deeper research. The deployment concepts I am about to use here would be transferrable to any other Linux platform. After we deploy our back-end application, we will build two stand-alone apps. One would be an iOS app for Apple App store and the other one Android for Google Play store.

Note DigitalOcean provides a $100 60-day credit for new users if you register using this link: `https://m.do.co/c/7b96bd81f2d1`.

© Art Yudin 2020
A. Yudin, *Building Versatile Mobile Apps with Python and REST*,
https://doi.org/10.1007/978-1-4842-6333-4_8

Django project deployment

Note   To deploy a Django project, I'll be using Git and GitHub. If you are not familiar with Git, go over the Git Basics at `https://git-scm.com/doc`, and make sure it is installed on your computer. Git comes as a standard feature with Xcode.

Before we start the process, we need to prepare our Django project for deployment. First, I want to add /api/ to all URLs in Django's local Stores app. As we discussed before, the main advantages of using Django as a back-end are versatility and the option to have more than one front-end. By grouping all our APIs for Store URLs with /api/ prefix, we would show that these endpoints would serve API endpoints. At the same time, we would have more options open to create URLs for HTML templates if needed in the future. For example, later, we might want to use a blank URL pattern for the lending page. Insert /api/ path in urlpatterns for stores.url in the main URL dispatcher pizzaproject/urls.py.

```
path('api/', include('stores.urls'))
```

If, later, you want to create new apps in your Django project, you can have a custom URL prefix for each app.

Second, Django will be serving Images, JavaScript, and CSS files as static files. Usually, you have two sets of settings, one for the development server, what we have been using so far, and the other one for production. Go to settings.py file in our Django project, there on the bottom of the file, you can find the link to the documentation, `https://docs.djangoproject.com/en/3.1/howto/static-files/`.

To help the server get access to static files, we need to provide static and media paths. In the main urls.py file, we need to import settings and the static function.

```
from django.conf.urls.static import static
from django.conf import settings
```

For a static function to do its job, we need to add paths to static files and media files (Figure 8-1).

```
+ static(settings.MEDIA_URL, document_root=settings.MEDIA_ROOT)
+static(settings.STATIC_URL, document_root=settings.STATIC_ROOT)
```

Figure 8-1. *Add static and media paths to urlpatterns*

Flip back to settings.py file in pizzaproject directory. We went over many settings in Chapter 1, and you probably remember that in production mode, DEBUG should be set to False.

```
DEBUG = False
```

The ALLOWED_HOSTS list should contain all domains and IP addresses for this project. Since we do not have any yet, we can use '*'; it means that the project could be hosted on any domain or IP. This is not a good option for security reasons, and you should replace it with a domain or IP address as soon as you get one.

```
ALLOWED_HOSTS = [ '*' ]
```

On the bottom of the settings.py file, we need to provide settings where Django should look for static files. Before, we were serving static files from a personal computer; now, we are about to deploy our project on a remote server, so the path for static files would be different. Usually, I have two options for development and production modes and use DEBUG to toggle between them. When I want to update my project, I run it on the local development server on my machine. For faster debugging, I keep the DEBUG variable set to True, and static files are served from my Mac. When I push my code to the server, I switch DEBUG to False for a security purpose. DEBUG set to False would provide different paths for static and media files.

```
if DEBUG is True:
    STATIC_URL = '/static/'
    STATICFILES_DIRS = [
        Path(BASE_DIR, "/static/")
    ]
    MEDIA_URL = '/media/'
    MEDIA_ROOT = Path(BASE_DIR, 'media')
else:
    STATIC_ROOT = '/var/www/static/'

    STATICFILES_DIRS = [
        Path(BASE_DIR, '/var/www/static/')
    ]
    MEDIA_URL = '/media/'
    MEDIA_ROOT = Path(BASE_DIR, '/var/www/ /media/')
```

We do not have an exact path for static files on the server yet; that is why, for the time being, I use STATIC_ROOT = '/var/www/static/'.

A SECRET_KEY is a very important element of your project, and you should not have it accessible to anyone except your team. You can save it in a separate file and then just import it.

The classic way to deploy a project is to use Git. Git is a version control and a standard tool to keep track of all the changes you have done to your code. If you use Git on a regular basis, you would never lose a snippet of your code. Also, it might be a good idea to keep your code in a remote repository to share it with your team. For this, you can use either GitHub or Bitbucket. For this project, I have created a GitHub repository: `https://github.com/programwithus/BookProject`.

You can find my code there, and I'll use it to deploy my back-end project on a server. If I add something else down the road, like a landing page, you could also find it there. If you don't have a GitHub or Bitbucket account, open one. It is free. Make a new repository. If you want to follow my code precisely, then you should name your repo BookProject. If you are not sure how to create a new repo, explore GitHub or Bitbucket; they have tons of tutorials on how to get started with their services and Git in general.

There is one little thing I like about GitHub. When you create a new repository, they would offer you a `.gitignore` file. An essential bit to keep a local virtual environment and a database out of a remote repo. If for some reason you did not get it with a repo, create it yourself. Just form a new file and name it `.gitignore`. Make sure you have that dot at the beginning. Virtual environment files, databases, and files with sensitive information should not be taken to a remote repository. We do not need them on the server either. We will initialize a virtual environment and new database right there on the server. In `.gitignore` file, you list all the files that you do not want to be tracked by Git and taken to a remote repository. At the very least, place these files in your .gitignore file.

```
venv/
db.sqlite3
__pycache__/
```

Now let's get back to our Django project; open it in the terminal or CMD. Make sure requirements.txt file has all installed dependencies.

```
pip freeze > requirements.txt
```

Also, check if you have a `.gitignore` file. The dot in front makes this file invisible when you run `ls` command on Mac or `dir` on Windows. You need to use

```
ls -a
```

on Mac to see all hidden files or run

```
dir /ah
```

in MS-DOS and the Command Prompt on Windows.

Initialize Git in the main folder pizzavspizza with the command

```
git init
```

First, add `.gitignore` file and commit changes.

```
git add .gitignore
git commit -m "gitignore"
```

Then repeat these two steps for all other files.

```
git add *
git commit -m "initial commit"
```

Now that all files are saved locally, we can add a remote address; provide your repo URL from GitHub or Bitbucket as your_remote_repo_url.

```
git remote add origin your_remote_repo_url
```

Make sure it was added.

```
git remote -v
```

After this command, you should see your remote origin for fetch and push operations.

The last step would be to send your code to the remote repo.

```
git push origin master
```

After this command, the code should be on GitHub, and you can see it in your repo.

Now it is time to configure a droplet on DigitalOcean. Please make sure you are registered and can log in to `www.digitalocean.com`.

If you logged in, then, on the top of the page, you can see a create button; click it and choose droplets. The "Create Droplets" menu offers a bunch of server configuration options. We will use Ubuntu for Linux, basic cheapest plan and closest to home datacenter. In my case, it would be New York (Figure 8-2). Obviously, if you are in Europe or Asia, you would pick the closest datacenter to potential users of your app.

Figure 8-2. *Droplet configuration on DigitalOcean, part 1*

315

Choose a strong password for your server and a simple hostname. I will use the name "`pizza`" for my droplet, simple enough not to deal with typos later. One thing I learned the hard way is always back up your apps. I'll markup the Enable backups option, but for you that would be optional (Figure 8-3). Click Create Droplet, and in a minute or two, you should have a working server with a unique IP address (Figure 8-4).

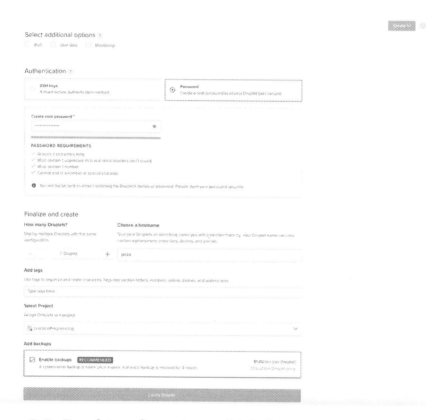

Figure 8-3. *Droplet configuration on DigitalOcean, part 2*

Figure 8-4. *Droplet Pizza with a unique IP address on DigitalOcean*

With an IP address, you can access your droplet through command line. Open your terminal for Mac or CMD if you use Windows.

To get connected to the droplet, we will use the SSH protocol and your unique IP (you can find it on DigitalOcean admin page, Figure 8-4).

```
ssh root@your_IP_adress
```

The system will ask you if you want to get connected to a server; type yes. This will prompt you to enter the password you have created when we were configuring the droplet.

Before we install Apache2 server, Python, and Django, we need to update Ubuntu. In your command line, after `root@pizza:~#` type the following commands:

```
sudo apt-get update
sudo apt-get upgrade
```

The sudo command will give you superuser rights to install packages on Linux, and apt-get will smooth the installation process. During installation, the system might ask you if you want to proceed; choose "Y" for yes. Updating might take some time; make sure you wait till you see empty command line starting with `root@pizza:~#`.

We need to install Git.

```
sudo apt-get install git
```

Now we need to install Apache HTTP Server platform.

```
sudo apt-get install apache2
```

And of course, we need to install Python and the virtual environment.

```
sudo apt-get install python-pip python-virtualenv
```

To smooth out communications between Django and Apache2, we would need to install a couple of Python libraries. Some of them might ask if you want to continue; just choose "Y" option.

```
sudo apt-get install python-setuptools python-dev build-
essential
```

```
sudo apt-get install libapache-mod-wsgi-py3
sudo apt-get build-dep python-imaging
sudo apt-get install python3-pip apache2 libapache2-mod-wsgi-py3
```

Django requires a virtual environment, and for that we need to create a special directory. Keep in mind that Apache has built an infrastructure, and we need to seed our project into the www folder.

```
cd /var/www
mkdir venv && cd venv
```

In the venv folder, we will initialize and activate the virtual environment with Python3.

```
virtualenv -p python3 .
source  bin/activate
```

The dot after the python3 command is not a typo. It means initialize the virtual environment within the folder venv. If your virtual environment is activated, you can check the Python version.

```
python - -version
```

No worries if the Python version was lower than the most recent one out there; all we need is Python 3, no matter what number comes after the period. Currently, mine shows Python 3.6.9.

We can clone our code from a remote repository to a server. But before that, we can update our settings.py file for static and media paths. Now we know them. The paths would look like this:

```
/var/www/venv/your_remote_repo_name/pizzaproject/static/
```

/var/www/venv is what we already have.

your_remote_repo_name should match your remote repo name on GitHub or Bitbucket.

pizzaproject is the home directory of our project. In future projects, this should match the home project directory.

Static and media directories should be placed in the home project directory on the server. We do not have them yet, but we are about to create them.

With these updates, my settings.py would look like this:

```
if DEBUG is True:
    STATIC_URL = '/static/'
    STATIC_ROOT = '/static/'
    STATICFILES_DIRS = [
    Path(BASE_DIR, "static")
    ]
    MEDIA_URL = '/media/'
    MEDIA_ROOT = Path(BASE_DIR, 'media')
else:
    STATIC_URL = '/static/'
    STATIC_ROOT = '/var/www/venv/BookProject/pizzaproject/
    static/'
    MEDIA_URL = '/media/'
    MEDIA_ROOT = Path(BASE_DIR, '/var/www/venv/BookProject/
    pizzaproject/media/')
```

Due to changes, we need to update our remote repository. Run git status command, and you will see all modified files in red.

```
git status
```

After git status you should see pizzaproject/pizzaproject/settings.py printed in red color.

Then you need to add either all files that have been changed by using "*" for all files or a specific file, for example, settings.py.

```
git add *
```

If you run the git status again, you will see that the color of `pizzaproject/pizzaproject/settings.py` has changed to green. Green color means that it was added and now Git tracks the file. The next command should "commit" our changes.

```
git commit -m "updates to settings.py"
```

In general, the message following commit command should reflect the changes you are committing. Later, if you want to reset the repository, the message would help you identify the commit you are looking for.

The last step on your computer would be to send changes to a remote repo.

```
git push origin master
```

After we have updated our remote repo, we can clone it to the server. In the activated virtual environment venv folder, clone your remote repo.

```
git clone you_remote_git_repo
```

If you want to use my code, then you should run

```
git clone https://github.com/programwithus/BookProject.git
```

Get into your project folder; in my case, it is

```
cd BookProject
```

Install all dependencies from requirements.txt.

```
pip install -r requirements.txt
```

For our static and media files, we need to create special folders in pizzaproject directory.

```
cd pizzaproject
mkdir static staticfiles media
```

The Linux pwd command can get you an exact path to a file or a folder. Windows command cd prints the current directory.

```
/var/www/venv/BookProject/pizzaproject
```

Make sure this path – or if you use a different naming convention, your path – matches what we have in the settings.py file (Figure 8-5).

```
127  if DEBUG is True:
128      STATIC_URL = '/static/'
129      STATIC_ROOT = '/static/'
130      STATICFILES_DIRS = [
131      Path(BASE_DIR, "static")
132      ]
133      MEDIA_URL = '/media/'
134      MEDIA_ROOT = Path(BASE_DIR, 'media')
135  else:
136      STATIC_URL = '/static/'
137      STATIC_ROOT = '/var/www/venv/BookProject/pizzaproject/static/'
138      MEDIA_URL = '/media/'
139      MEDIA_ROOT = Path(BASE_DIR, '/var/www/venv/BookProject/pizzaproject/media/')
```

Figure 8-5. *Final settings for static files in settings.py*

Now we need to create a database and a superuser.

```
cd pizzaproject
python manage.py migrate
python manage.py createsuperuser
```

This routine is no different from what we did in Chapter 1, when we were launching the Django project.

Note   Every time you make changes to your project and you would
want to update the code on the server, you need to follow these
steps:

1. `git add files-you-want-to-add` (in your local git
    repository on your machine)

2. `git commit -m "message"`

3. `git push origin master`

4. Log in to the server with `ssh root@your-ip`

5. `cd /var/www/venv` (get into the venv directory and activate
    the virtual environment)

6. `git pull origin master` (to fetch updates from a remote
    repo, run this command in your project directory on a server)

7. `python manage.py collectstatic` (if you need to update
    static files on a server, make sure you run this command from
    your Django project on a server)

8. `service apache2 restart`

After we have cloned the Django project to the server, we would need
to connect Apache with WSGI. By default, Apache has a virtual host file
000-default.conf. We need to change configurations and point Apache
to wsgi.py in the pizzaproject directory. It is really difficult to edit files in
Nano or Vim text editors on a server. My advice is compile a file in Sublime,
Atom, or Visual Studio and just replace the default code in 000-default.conf
with your configurations. In 000-default.conf, we need to provide paths
and grant rights to access static and media files. Specify the version and
path to Python. Finally, point Apache to wsgi.py file.

```
<VirtualHost *:80>
  ServerName localhost
  ServerAdmin webmaster@localhost

Alias /static /var/www/venv/BookProject/pizzaproject/static
<Directory /var/www/venv/BookProject/pizzaproject/static>
   Require all granted
 </Directory>

Alias /media /var/www/venv/BookProject/pizzaproject/media
<Directory /var/www/venv/BookProject/pizzaproject/media>
   Require all granted
</Directory>
<Directory /var/www/venv/BookProject/pizzaproject/pizzaproject>
    <Files wsgi.py>
        Require all granted
    </Files>
</Directory>

WSGIDaemonProcess home python-path=/var/www/venv/BookProject/
pizzaproject/:/var/www/venv/lib/python3.6/site-packages
WSGIProcessGroup home
WSGIScriptAlias / /var/www/venv/BookProject/pizzaproject/
pizzaproject/wsgi.py

 ErrorLog ${APACHE_LOG_DIR}/error.log
 CustomLog ${APACHE_LOG_DIR}/access.log combined
</VirtualHost>
```

Line /var/www/venv/BookProject/pizzaproject/pizzaproject/wsgi.py
has pizzaproject twice; this is no mistake but the correct path to wsgi.py file.

Copy this code, make sure paths match what you have on your server, and using the Nano editor, open 000-default.conf file on the server with this command:

```
sudo nano /etc/apache2/sites-available/000-default.conf
```

Now replace default configurations with our settings; make sure you save changes with "Y".

We are almost there. The last step would be to provide permissions to write to the database. sudo chown is a command to change the ownership of a file or a folder. Chown stands for change file owner. The sudo chmod 755 command would allow everyone to read and execute the files. sudo chmod 777 means making the file readable, writable, and executable by everyone. Security specialists might argue that we would need to limit permissions to specific users, and I would agree with them. However, here, we would use the 777 code simply because Linux settings are out of the scope of this book, and we are just learning how to deploy a Django project on a server. Follow these commands to provide permissions to write and read to a database.

```
sudo adduser $USER www-data
sudo chown www-data:www-data /var/www/venv/BookProject/pizzaproject
sudo chown www-data:www-data /var/www/venv/BookProject/
pizzaproject/db.sqlite3
sudo chmod -R 775 /var/www/venv/BookProject/pizzaproject
```

According to our model, all pizzeria images should be stored in the pizzariaImages folder in the media directory; create pizzariaImages.

```
cd media
mkdir pizzariaImages
```

Then give permission to add images.

```
sudo chmod 777 /var/www/venv/BookProject/pizzaproject/media/
pizzeriaImages
```

We need to gather all HTML, JavaScript, and image files in the static directory. Make sure you are in the pizzaproject directory where the manage.py file is and run the collectstatic command.

```
python manage.py collectstatic
```

The last step would be to restart Apache for our changes to take effect.

```
service apache2 restart
```

After deployment, you should be able to open your project in the browser with an IP address. The 500 Error message would most of the times mean something is wrong in 000-default.conf file. Go back to 000-default.conf file and make sure you have provided correct paths. Another option to find where the error is coming from is to run command python manage.py check.

At the moment, our app is not rendering much because we have created a brand-new database. All our records stayed in the local database. You can log in and create a couple of records, the same way we did in Chapter 2.

```
http://your-ip-address/admin/
```

If later you would want to replace the IP address with a domain name, get one, and using instructions they provide, point your domain name to the IP address. Also, you can find "add domain" option right next to your droplet (Figure 8-4) in DigitalOcean dashboard.

As I have mentioned before, you can find my Django app at http://pizzavspizza.com/api/ (Figure 8-6).

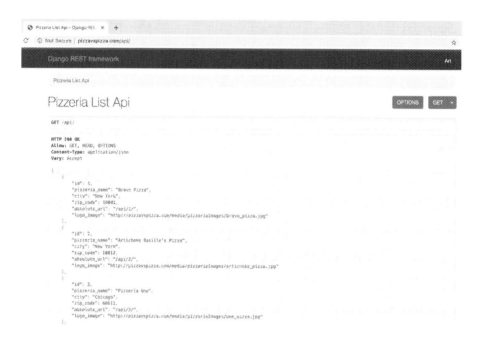

Figure 8-6. *Django project deployed on a server*

Stand-alone apps

Here, we will convert our front-end project to iOS and Android apps. Our back-end is running on the server, and to make API calls, we would need to provide either a new IP address (from a hosting provider, Figure 8-4) or a domain name if you got one. I'll be using `http://pizzavspizza.com/api/` for back-end APIs.

We can simply replace our local server with a domain name in client.js file. However, it would be better to set up the domain or IP of the back-end as an environment variable, similar to what we did at the end of Chapter 4. To implement environment variables in our React Native app, we would need to install react-native-dotenv library.

```
npm install react-native-dotenv
```

Navigate to babel.config.js file, right next to App.js. Add react-native-dotenv to module.exports function in babel.config.js file like this:

```
module.exports = function (api) {
  api.cache(true);
  return {
    presets: ["babel-preset-expo", "module:react-native-dotenv"],
  };
};
```

The react-native-dotenv module lets you import environment variables from .env file. Create .env and .babelrc files right next to .gitignore file (you can use the ls -a command to see all invisible files) (Figure 8-7). If in your future projects you use a private key as an environment variable, add .env file to .gitignore file. This would keep sensitive data from a remote repo. .babelrc file is used to run plugins and libraries that we don't want to be transformed by babel.[1]

```
.                          .git                  node_modules
..                         .gitignore            package-lock.json
.DS_Store                  .vscode               package.json
.babelrc                   App.js                src
.env                       app.json              web-build
.expo                      assets
.expo-shared               babel.config.js
```

Figure 8-7. *New .env and .babelrc files. To see all files, use the ls -a command*

In .env file, we will define the API_URL.

```
API_URL=http://pizzavspizza.com
```

Make sure there is no closing "/".

---

[1]https://babeljs.io/docs/en/config-files#project-wide-configuration

In .babelrc file, add "module:react-native-dotenv" as plugin.[2]

```
{
  "plugins": [
["module:react-native-dotenv"]
  ]
}
```

Also, you might consider setting multiple environments for development, staging, and production. Then, you just create more files, `.env.development`, `.env.staging`, and `.env.production`. In this book, we will use just `.env` file.

Our old IP address in the client.js file can be replaced with the import from .env.

```
import axios from "axios";
import { API_URL } from "@env";

export default axios.create({
  baseURL: API_URL,
});
```

Since we have a new prefix "api" for all our URLs, we need to update our ListView and AddPizzeria components, specifically the Axios client where we call APIs.

Let's update the ListView component in function_list_view.js, and in the getList function, pass "/api" in the get method.

```
const getList = async () => {
    console.log(client);
    const response = await client.get("/api");
    setData(response.data);
  };
```

---

[2]www.npmjs.com/package/react-native-dotenv

Now we can move to the AddPizzeria component and add "api" to the post method. Also, all other components where you call API should be updated with the /api/ prefix.

```
try {
    const response = await client.post("/api/create/", data);
    postedAlert();
} catch (error) {
    console.log(error);
}
```

Before publishing your app as a stand-alone iOS or Android app, it would be a good idea to give it a test drive and publish it on Expo. We have covered the process in Chapter 5, running your project on a physical device.

Note   Before publishing your app, consider replacing installed dependencies with npm modules from CDN (content delivery network); this would drastically reduce the size of your app.

If your app is running on Expo and there are no errors,[3] then we can start setting up our app for the building process. We will be using Expo to build iOS and Android apps. The whole process is very well described here: `https://docs.expo.io/distribution/building-standalone-apps/`.

---

[3]Expo might give you yellow warnings; you can dismiss them.

I'll start with the settings for iOS and Android in App.js. Add information for "ios".

```
"ios": {
    "supportsTablet": true,
    "bundleIdentifier": "com.programwithus.pizzavspizza",
    "buildNumber": "1.0.0"
  }
```

bundleIdentifier is supposed to use a reverse domain name convention to uniquely identify our app in the App store. programwithus. com is my domain. You should use your own unique name. It is totally fine if you do not have a domain name; you can use any unique name. buildNumber is a version of our upload. Every time you upload a newer version, you should increase this number.

For "android" we need to provide similar information. Package also uses a reverse domain name convention, and versionCode works as an app version. If for some reason you skipped running your app in Expo in the Internet part, make sure you have values for "name" and "slug" in app. json file (Figure 8-8).

```
"android": {
    "package": "com.programwithus.pizzavspizza",
    "versionCode": 1
  }
```

Figure 8-8. *Final configurations in the app.json file*

Last but not least is the app icon. There are strict guidelines on that. An icon should be a png file with 1024px by 1024px dimensions. We are using Expo and it takes care of every aspect of our app. You can just place your png file with correct dimensions into assets folder of our React Native app. Make sure you named it icon.png. We might need icons for App store and Google Play store. You can generate icons on App Icon Generator resource (https://appicon.co) for free. App Icon Generator would make sure that your image would be cropped and saved based on the current iOS and Android standards.

Note   Before publishing your app to the App store or Play store, make sure it is running with no bugs on Expo when you publish your project to the Internet and running it in the Expo app on a phone.

---

iOS app and App store

To build a stand-alone iOS app, you would need to be enrolled to the Apple Developer Program (`https://developer.apple.com`) and purchase an annual membership for $99. The whole process of registration might take a couple of days. Also, they might ask you to submit your id to verify your identity. The registration process is straightforward, and when your enrollment is approved, you can start building an iOS app with Expo.

In the React Native directory, run Expo build command.

```
expo build:ios
```

Expo will ask you if you want to use the `archive` option for App store or the `simulator` to run your app on the iOS simulator. Since I am planning to deploy my app to Apple App store, I'll choose `archive`. Next, it would ask you if you have access to Apple App store. Yes, I have enrolled into the Apple Developer Program. Then you'll need to provide your Apple id and password. After all the information is verified, Expo would offer you to generate an Apple Distribution Certificate. I'll choose this option. After that, Expo would generate an Apple Push Notifications Service Key, unless you want to upload your own file. I'll let Expo generate a new key. Same would be true for Apple Provision profile. At the end of this process, Expo would place our app in a queue (Figure 8-12). You can follow the process if you open the Expo dashboard by opening the URL you can see in the terminal or log in to Expo.io (Figure 8-9). If you are in a hurry, you can always switch from a free community plan to priority builds if you upgrade your account for $29 a month. You can find this option in Expo account settings.

Figure 8-9. *You can monitor the status of your iOS app build on Expo.io*

After the build process is finished, you can download your iOS app as a file (Figure 8-9). The process we have started a couple of chapters before is complete, and the result is the iOS app.

To share your iOS app with the world, submit it to Apple App store. In the Apple Developer, you will find the link to App Store Connect. Click My Apps button, and click the plus sign to add a new app. New App window in App Store Connect would require an initial information for your app. SKU and Bundle id sound confusing at first. For SKU, you should provide the value for `"bundleIdentifier"`: `"com.programwithus.pizzavspizza"` (Figure 8-10).

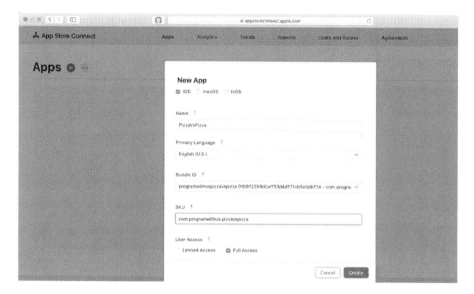

Figure 8-10. *Uploading the iOS app via App Store Connect*

With the help of Expo, Bundle id would be there; you'll have to choose it from the drop-down list. The process of submitting an app to Apple App store is relatively easy, and App Store Connect would guide you from here.

Android app and Google Play store

If you have set all the necessary settings in the app.json file for Android (Figure 8-8), then we can move to building the stand-alone Android app part. After we built the Android app, we could download it as a file and submit it to Google Play store. In the main folder of our React Native app, run the command

```
expo build:android
```

After this command, Expo would give you two options: apk and app-bundle. If you are heading for production, then you should choose app-bundle; however, if you just want to see how your app would work on an Android device, then select apk. I'll choose app-bundle. The next question from Expo would be about a Keystore. A Keystore is a system for cryptographic keys. You would need a Keystore to update your app in the future. You can generate keys yourself or let Expo do it. I'll let Expo generate my keys. This process might get you an error message. Expo would ask you to install JDK. JDK stands for Java SE Development Kit, and you can download it for free on the Oracle website (`www.oracle.com/java/technologies/javase-jdk11-downloads.html`).

After Expo generates your keys, the Android app build is just a matter of time. Expo will put your request in a queue, and you can see the progress if you open your Expo dashboard (Figure 8-11) by either logging in to Expo.io or using the URL you would find in your terminal. At the moment, there are 69 Android apps before me in the queue (Figure 8-12). If you are in a hurry, you can always switch from a free community plan to priority builds if you upgrade your account for $29 a month. You can find this option in Expo account settings.

Figure 8-11. *You can monitor the status of your Android app build on Expo.io*

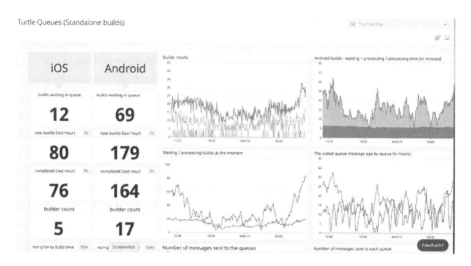

Figure 8-12. Expo.io provides information on how many Android and iOS apps for build are before you in a queue

After Expo finished building your stand-alone Android app, you can download it as a file from Expo Build Details. Use the same URL from the terminal as before to open Expo Build Details or log in to Expo.io. The process we have started a couple of chapters before is complete, and the result is the Android app.

To upload and update your Android app to Google Play store, you need to use keys. The Keystore Expo has generated for us. To see them, run the command in the main React Native app directory.

```
expo fetch:android:keystore
```

This command will get your secret key and password for your Android app. Also, you can find the same key and password in .jks (yourAppName. jks) file in the home directory; by default, it will be added to .gitignore file. Make sure you save them someplace safe.

Technically, we are done here; the last step is to upload Android app
file to Google Play store. You can open a new developer account here:
`https://play.google.com/apps/publish/signup/`. Google Play would
require a registration fee of $25. After a successful registration (Figure 8-13),
you would be able to upload your Android app to Google Play store. That
app icon we have created with the help of App Icon Generator would come
in handy here.

Figure 8-13. *Google Play Console where you can upload your*
Android app

We have come to the end of this book, and now it is the time to sum
up what we have learned during this journey. First of all, I would like to
take a look at the big picture. We have developed a mobile app powered by
Django.

We have covered all the main components of Django. Using RESTful
architecture, we created back-end web applications. I hope by now you
have a solid understanding of how to launch your next Django project.

With the help of React and React Native, we have designed three different UIs. The first UI would work as a desktop web app. iOS and Android would be two stand-alone apps people could use on their smartphones.

The intention of this book is to give you a push to develop more cool apps using the modern technologies we have learned here. Obviously, Django and React would ship more updates in the future with extra features. That is why I think my role here was to explain the main concepts behind these technologies and teach you how to build cool and versatile apps on your own. Do not be afraid to experiment, and keep an eye on the official documentation we have discussed here to build more sophisticated web apps.

Index

A

absolute_url attribute, 138, 197

AddPizza component, 274

AddPizzeria component, 243, 251, 266, 277, 329

addPizzeria.js file, 249, 250

addPizzeria_styles.js, 242

addPizzeria_valid.js, 242

Admin app, 18

Administration Authtoken, 288

admin.site.register command, 43

Alert component, 279, 280

Alert message, 232, 233, 245

Allowed hosts, 20, 211, 311

Android app, 334–338

Android emulator, 147–152

Android Virtual Device Manager, 147, 149, 150

App.js, 77, 78

App.js React Native, 146

App store, 332–334

ASGI modules, 23

as_view() method, 50

Asynchronous function, 195, 202

Async keyword, 191, 194, 202

Auth app, 18, 35

Authentication

create() and save() methods, 299

Formik form, 290

get_user_model method, 299

handleSubmit function, 302

JavaScript alert() function, 294

LoginForm, 290, 294

loginForm_styles.js, 292, 293

loginForm_valid.js, 292

regForm.js, 302

required() method, 292

rest_framework.authtoken, 287

token, 297, 306

URL dispatcher pizzaproject/ urls.py, 288

URL pattern, 301

UserCreateView, 301

UserCreateView and UserSerializer, 300

validationSchema and styles, 292

Auth Password Validators, 22

Authtoken app, 288, 289

axios.delete(), 136

Axios get method, 106, 137

axios.patch() method, 128, 129

axios.post() method, 112, 114, 116, 122

© Art Yudin 2020
A. Yudin, *Building Versatile Mobile Apps with Python and REST*,
https://doi.org/10.1007/978-1-4842-6333-4

Printed in the United States
By Bookmasters